BEHOLD!

Other books by Bethsheba Ashe

The Genesis Wheel & other Hermeneutical Essays
The Hermeneutics of Aleister Crowley
Five: Adventure on Islay Island (fiction)
Chariot
Aleister Crowley's Secret Temple
Two Sun Sunday (Screenplay)

BEHOLD!

The Art and Practice of Gematria

Bethsheba Ashe

AEON

First published in 2023 by
Aeon Books

Copyright © 2023 Bethsheba Ashe

British Library Cataloguing in Publication Data

A C.I.P. for this book is available from the British Library

ISBN-13: 978-1-80152-067-6

Typeset by Medlar Publishing Solutions Pvt Ltd, India

www.aeonbooks.co.uk

The author has provided a free online gematria calculator webpage to accompany this book. Please go to:
The Shematria Gematria Calculator https://www.shematria.com

We encourage students of the formal system of rhetoric math in the Bible to share their findings by submitting their results to our database. Please see our submission page:
https://www.shematria.com/subm

In memory of Chan Alectrum,
(14/3/1962–4/3/2021).
May he achieve the
accomplishment of his will.

For Andres Pedraza, with love and appreciation.

*It is the glory of God to conceal a word
and the glory of kings to reveal a word.*

Proverbs of Solomon.

CONTENTS

PREFACE

> To learn for learning's sake, not because it's going to get you some-
> thing, necessarily, but because you have faith that the things that
> interest you will help you become who you need to be.
>
> Austin Kleon

This Aeon edition of *Behold* was rewritten and expanded following the
release of details concerning the Mt. Ebal curse tablet. This tiny tablet,
dated to the late Bronze age (circa 1440 BCE), employs mathematics in
the construction of the curse text, which is evidence that gematria is a
truly ancient practice.

The discovery makes the need for a handbook on formal gematria
even more urgent, so that epigraphers, both amateur and professional,
have the tools they need to decipher mathematical texts, both in the
Bible and from archeological digs.

This newly emerging subset in the field of epigraphy needs its amateur researchers, because the amount of deliberately written calculations in the Bible is immense, and still needs to be deciphered. The only
way I see this happening is in the sort of crowd-sourced enterprise akin

to one that mapped the human genome, which is why I've written this book, and why I'm asking for your participation in the project.

What you'll get out of it is the pleasure of being able to better interpret the text of the Bible for yourself, and come to your own conclusions about what you read, once you have all the facts.

ויאמרו אליו איה שרה אשתך ויאמר הנה באהל

Genesis 18:9

And they said to him:
"Where is Sarah your wife (111)?"
And he said:
"Behold! In the tent (111)!"

A Biblical Joke.

CHAPTER 1

Lost in translations

The concept of progress acts as a protective mechanism to shield us from the terrors of the future.

From Collected Sayings of Muad'Dib, by Princess Irulan
Frank Herbert (*Dune*)

I have learned a deep distrust of translations, though I'd rather have them than not. Languages evolve to express the cultural norms, mores, and world-religious views of the people who use them. Translations that are made centuries or millennia after their initial composition can miss a great deal of context, simply because the daily lives of the writers are so very different.

The words of the Bible carry within them a patina of that which was every day and familiar in the lives of the ancients. To understand these writers, we have to go through a process of mental adjustment in our thinking. We have to strip ourselves down, divesting ourselves mentally of all our modern knowledge of science and technology. We must set aside what we know of physics and astronomy, and put away our twenty-first century beliefs and convictions, so that we can come to appreciate the perspectives of Biblical writers.

1

This is not to say that ancient ideas are not at the roots of modern thinking when it comes to philosophical concepts such as the zero, or the idea that numbers are an inherent quality to our universe. Surely, human beings have always asked the big questions and sought answers to these, but modern answers are conceptualized by modern systems, and systems are particular beasts, usually self-serving and self-referencing, dissimilar from one another in their efforts to frame a particular question from a particular perspective and knowledge base.

For the mystic, systems are used to inspire transcendental states of being through philosophical reductions that unite all things with their opposites, but while we can reconcile any number of opposites within our own consciousness to cause transformative states of being that may bring us closer to God-consciousness, I think it is asking too much for ancient and modern systems to bear anything but a basic correspondence or passing relationship to one another. To understand the ancient worldview, knowledge of string theory and the big bang probably aren't going to be of any good to us.

Even if Hebrew is your first language, the lives of the ancient Hebrews were qualitatively different from the lives of modern Jews. There are things that modern people take for granted that weren't part of the ancient world, and there were things that ancient people took for granted that aren't part of the modern world.

The practice of rhetoric math (math without notation) was one of those things that didn't survive the march of progress, and knowledge of it almost passed out of human memory. Not everything is known of the lives of the ancients, though archaeologists and historians try their best to present a coherent picture of the past. Not everything was written down. The ancients left no records showing how people were taught to read and write, and there are no records showing how the ancients thought people should do mathematics. We may be used to manuals and guidebooks, and such things are pervasive in our information-rich society, but knowledge of these things were not taught in books. Writing a book, or even a chapter for a book, was a much more time-intensive task for a man or woman working with parchment and quill, frequently by candlelight. We just type our words into a device and think nothing of it. If you really want to develop some empathy for an ancient scribe, try writing everything that you'd usually type in a day with a pen for a week, and then see how you begin to prioritize what you write. Keep a pen and ink diary of your week, too, and record your results. Then reflect upon the fact that ancient writers were not only composing prose but were embedding it with calculations too. Personally, I can only stand in awe of their accomplishments.

It's largely thanks to the fact translations of the Bible are available that I've been able to write this book. I certainly couldn't have gotten along without translations. I'm not Jewish and Hebrew is not my first language. I'm a cryptographer, and though rhetoric mathematics isn't a code, it did need to be deciphered before it could be read. Because the oral tradition had been hidden or lost, the principles upon which guided the practice had to be carefully reconstructed by analyzing the function of each word and charting the common areas of classification.

> ... the work of creation is a deep mystery, not understandable from the verses, and it cannot be known except through the received tradition going back to Moses our teacher who received it from the mouth of the Almighty, and those who know it are required to hide it.
>
> Therefore Rabbi Isaac said that the Torah didn't need to begin with "In the beginning God created" and the story of what was created on the first day, and what was done on the second day and the remaining days, and the lengthy telling of the creation of Adam and Eve, and their sin and punishment, and the story of the Garden of Eden and Adam's exile from it, for all this cannot be understood with full understanding from the verses.
>
> The Rambam on Genesis 1

I'm going to teach you how to read rhetoric mathematics. You won't need to learn Biblical Hebrew for this, but you will need to know the basics about the language so that you are not completely dependent upon translations.

Professional translators say that any translation is only as good as the ability of the translator to contextualize the meaning of the text. They wrestle with the disconnect between modern life and ancient living everyday.

Alfred Korzybski famously said, "A map is not the territory it represents, but if correct, it has a similar structure to the territory, which accounts for its usefulness." We can carry the metaphor forward to say translation is like a map that is laid over another map and the points of intersection are made useful. Yet each one who walks the perimeter of these maps will experience the territory differently, according to their own lights and experiences.

There's a noticeable delay in the translations of mystical Jewish writings. Almost 300 years passed after the books of the *Zohar* were written before they received their first (partial) translation in 1887,[1] and the first-ever complete translation of this seminal work of Jewish mysticism[2] was not available until 2018.[3]

In antiquity, translations of the Hebrew Bible were initially banned, and the Sages (*Tannaim*, teachers) prohibited any discussion of the Merkabah, the texts of Genesis 1–2, and Ezekiel. The ban on translations and the judgement set against discussions of Genesis, Ezekiel and the Merkabah were later rescinded:

> GEMARA: The Gemara poses a question: You said in the first clause of the mishna: Nor may one expound the Design of the Divine Chariot by oneself, which indicates that the topic may not be learned at all, and yet you subsequently said: Unless he is wise and understands most things on his own, which indicates that an individual is permitted to study the Design of the Divine Chariot. The Gemara explains: This is what the mishna is saying: One may not expound the topic of forbidden sexual relations before three students, nor the act of Creation before two, nor may one teach the Divine Chariot to one, unless that student was wise and understands on his own.
>
> Chagigah 11b:8–9, The William Davidson Talmud

It really is something that you're supposed to hit upon in the course of your studies by yourself, according to your own ingenium, through the hints, as it were, and by reading between the lines.

I believe it is the fear of mistranslation in such a crucial area as the inspired knowledge of God that leads to a cultural reluctance among Jewish people to translate their works of mysticism. The more sacred a text is, the more secret it becomes, and secrecy is imagined like regal clothing which adorns the otherwise naked brilliance of God.

We just have to look at translations of the Tanakh (Hebrew Bible) to see why their caution is fully justified. Even the most modern and up to date Bibles include mistranslated words, and these mistranslations have shaped our modern common understanding of the text in some fairly crucial ways. For instance, there is the word וממנו (*mmnv, minimu*) which is a linchpin to understanding creation and the Garden of Eden story. In the Bible it is translated into English variously as "from", "at", or even "of us", but it actually means quite literally "from his number" or "from his portion". For instance:

> And said YHVH Elohim 'Behold, the Adam has become like one
> from his number, to know good and evil knowledge'
>
> Genesis 3:22

It's not just in translation that this verse is misunderstood. *Mmnv* is a direct reference to the scribal practice of rhetoric mathematics and would have been understood as such by the writer's audience, who would have looked up the gematria value of the calculation in the verse, and then worked out the Reversal Cipher for טוב ורע "good and evil", and to see that it read לסר סבה.

לסר could be conjugated as "to the one who turns", or "to the one who is sad" and סבה may mean "reason/cause", or "a turn" (of events). It makes a profound philosophical point in this context, that the knowledge of good and evil leads to a sad turn, and could be said to be the cause of sadness. סר is sometimes used in the sense of turning away from God. It's interesting to compare this statement with the first two of the four noble truths of the Buddha, "life is suffering" and "suffering is caused by desire", because the desire of Adam and Eve was for knowledge. Adam was like a blind man without the knowledge of good and evil, and only after he had satisfied his desire and illuminated himself by eating the fruit of the tree were his eyes (ע) opened. It's due to the gematria of the verse that we see this fruit is "light".

To be really thorough about our reflections upon this verse we ought to think upon the ways that the word "knowledge" was used in ancient times. Besides being an intellectual pursuit, knowledge could also signify intimate and sexual knowledge, i.e. "And so Adam 'knew' his wife". Knowledge could be something you did as well as something for which you had a mental construct for.

The mistranslations of the word ממנו, *mmnv* ("from his number") distort the intent and the logic of the verses they appear in, and this word appears 1223 times in the Hebrew Bible, mostly being translated as "at". It's a major oversight in translation. I only noticed it because only the leading prefix of the word (the mem) is being translated and I got curious about the rest of the word.

I recently noticed that the word בְּצַלְמֵנוּ in Genesis 1:26 has the ending of מֵנוּ. It's usually translated as "in Our Image". In 1:27 the word is בְּצַלְמֹו which lacks the letter nun, so the reading of "in Our Image" is justified, but I think the translator has made an assumption that מֶנוּ in 1:26 is just a suffix rather than a portmanteau (a word made by blending two or more words). If we consider the ending in context of the word's position in the verses, it is followed by כִּדְמוּתֵנוּ, "like our resemblance", which is merely a vague qualification of "in our Image". The word can be read with equal justification from a technical perspective:

> And said Elohim, Let us make man in the reflection of his number,
> like our resemblance, and let them rule …

Given the importance that ancient scribes gave to the letters and values of the Holy Name, I think this is a better translation which is more in keeping with the tradition.

It's one of the reasons why I'll be teaching you about the Hebrew prefixes and suffixes as part of this course of instruction. I want my readers to be sharp and confident when they look at a Hebrew text; to see the logic of the verse, and be able to appreciate how the translation fits (or diverges) from the original texts, even if they don't read or speak the Hebrew language.

As for this last, if you work with an interlinear (word to word translation) Bible to practice the art of gematria everyday, you will naturally develop a vocabulary of Biblical Hebrew words over time, and after a few years you'll be able to read Biblical Hebrew for yourself. It's a major side-benefit, and a strategic way to trick your brain into learning Biblical Hebrew.

Prior to taking up gematria, I'd wanted to be able to read Biblical Hebrew, but when I thought of doing a course on it, my mind shuddered away. For one, I couldn't justify the expense, and for two, I do better in student-led learning environments. Autodidactic learning is tremendously empowering and all it costs you is your time. Plus, there are things that formal institutions don't teach, but which are still highly valuable to know.

The major component to learning Biblical Hebrew is simply acquiring the vocabulary, and that can be done while having fun with gematria and gaining moral and philosophical instruction at the same time. Your brain will be doing its usual pattern recognition thing as you work with the text, and slowly, surely, eventually you'll find that you can read Biblical Hebrew.

Professional translators will tell you that we should always be wary of considering any translation to be "authoritative" in a final sense. When it comes down to it, how well people from different lands, different cultures, and different times understand one another is always a work in progress, but the encouraging thing is that there *is* progress and there *is* an increase in genuine transmission, reception and understanding.

In my experience, people don't really take on board the concept of ancient rhetoric math until they've slept on it. That may be because the brain has several separate areas for numbers and calculations, and to understand ancient math we have to create new synaptic links between letters and numbers. Because we generally don't have these synaptic links, the spheres of writing and math are separate in our minds. It has thrown math into a purely abstract dimension—becoming all map and no territory, and if you haven't made these connections, you'll find it impossible to conceptualize an ancient worldview with that modern divorce between writing and calculation.

When you go into any esoteric course of study you have to have a little bit of faith in the material to do its work on you. You are reading the text, but in doing so, it is also writing itself within you, and when you sleep it will change associations in your brain—nudging, modifying your mental map of reality.

To read the Bible in an informed manner you have to imagine an ancient time where writing and math were complementary and done at the same time to convey a holistic meaning to the reader. It is a qualitatively different way of thinking, and it means you approach the text in a receptive manner, open to information that may be conveyed to you by the writer in other ways than a simple linguistic record.

There's plenty of evidence that people who could write and include math in their writings were highly respected in ancient times. We see that their writings were copied and shared by other scribes who saw the value of them. It is more common than not to find gematria in the books of the Bible and it may be that the inclusion of gematria was one of the criteria by which the Sopherim (biblical scribes) measured a book when it came to establishing the Tanakh. It seems that even in books that are largely *not* written with gematria tend to have the first or last verse include a calculation.

The Sopherim were scribes, copyists, editors, and teachers working between 5th C. BCE and 200 BCE. They interpreted the Tanakh and taught biblical law and ethics. The biblical word ספר, *sapher*, meant "count", and ספר *sepher*, meant "book". ספר, *sapher*, also meant "scribe". The *im* on the end of *sepher* or *sapher* makes the words plural, like an *s* on the end of an English noun.

The Sopherim were respected people, and leaders of Jewish religious communities. They were known for their learning in writing and mathematics and celebrated for having initiated rabbinic studies. They are occasionally referenced in the Tanakh itself:

> Your heart will meditate on terror. Where is the scribe? Where is he who weighs? Where is he who counts the towers?
>
> Isaiah 33:18

In the Book of Chronicles, there are a class of people who are called "*Chashab*", which means (according to Strong's concordance) "make account of, conceive, consider, count, cunning man, work, workman, devise." These *Chashab* were people who could make an account of a matter, quite literally. It's the way the word is used to refer to knowledge of both writing and math that displays the synthesis in the ancient worldview of the matter.

The first issue people face when getting to grips with ancient rhetoric math is that we moderns use separate Arabic numerals. The second issue is that we use notation for functions like addition (+), subtraction (−), multiplication (×) and division (÷). We learn that this is how math is done when we are children, and as adults it seems so entirely natural to do it this way that we don't consider there is any other way to do it. Many people need to first challenge that assumption before they go any further in the practice of ancient rhetoric math.

Our modern way of doing math began in the early middle ages. In the year 999, Pope Sylvester II introduced a new model of abacus, which adopted tokens representing Hindu–Arabic numerals from one to nine. Leonardo Fibonacci brought this system to Europe with his *Liber Abaci* (1202).

When Europe adopted Arabic numerals (0123456789), we see a division begin between Jewish Philosophy and Kabbalah, and it's a disconnect that remains even to this day. When communication is divided into separate dualistic spheres of writing and math, then logic, rationality and science are made enemies of mysticism. Though the ancients employ logic and math in the service of mysticism, it's a modern reaction to reject that such a thing could really ever have happened because it lies outside of the experiences of people who live in our time.

Yet historically, the ancient practice of math emerged substantially earlier than the art of writing. I asked Professor Karenleigh A. Overmann[4] about this and she told me:

Because number systems precede writing systems, they can be very old indeed; we just don't know how old (though the answer most likely lies somewhere in the Palaeolithic). By the time there is linguistic insight into Semitic languages (proto-Semitic in the 4th millennium BCE), the counting system contains a term for 10,000, which indicates that the number system was well elaborated, socially useful, and much older than the 4th millennium BCE.

She said that the early period of Mesopotamian writing was based on accounting, and the earliest written records are akin to grocery lists, receipts, or spreadsheets.

The issues that surround translation and the essential mindset of the reader are far from being the only barriers to the exegesis (a critical explanation or interpretation of a text) of the Bible and other Hebrew mystical texts. There are passages in the Tanakh and the works of Kabbalah that are impossible to understand without sight of a diagram called variously "the Seven Palaces" and the "Merkabah" (Chariot).

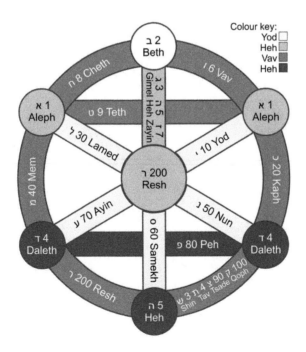

The Seven Palaces, or Merkabah.

It is written in the Tosifta on Megillah that "many have expounded upon the Merkabah without ever seeing it."

The difference between biblical mystics and kabbalists appears to be that in ancient times, mystics sought to understand God's creation, and they used the alphabet to categorise all things that were universal in the experiences of human beings. They arranged this into the chart of the Merkabah and supposed that all these things existed in a primordial

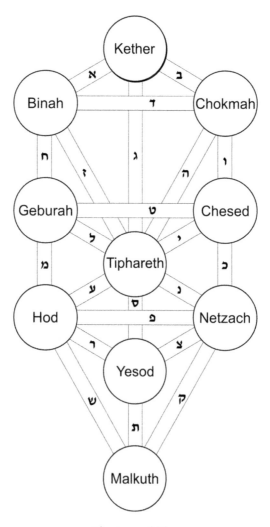

The tree of life.

fashion, reminiscent of Plato's later idea of the world of Forms in his allegory of the Cave. However, while they carefully charted out creation in this world of formation (Yetzirah), they left the world of Motion (Assiah) largely untouched. This changed with the publication of the *Sepher Yetizrah*, which inspired the Kabbalists to make a microcosmic complement to the Chariot, reflecting the creative potency of the letters down into the world of Assiah. They called it the Zeir Anpin (Tree of Life).

From the Seven Palaces were made ten sephiroth. From the Seventh Palace (at the top), which is the House of God, descended the three supernal sephiroth of Kether, Chokmah, and Binah, and from the First Palace (at the bottom), which is the Palace of the Heh, descended the two lower sephiroth of Yesod and Malkuth. The letters on the Palaces were redistributed to the extra paths these extra divisions created.

What this means is that it is as impossible to fully understand the references of biblical writers to their system of categories for creation

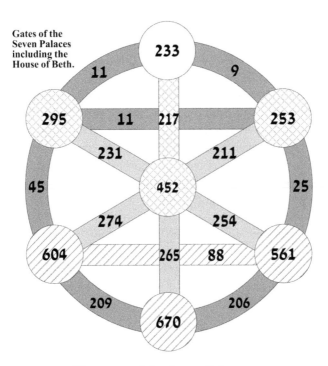

The gates of the Seven Palaces.

without sight of the Merkabah, as it is to understand the Zohar without sight of both the Tree of Life, and the Merkabah.

In the Zohar's book of Vayechi 96, Rabbi Aba says the measurement of the span of the Holy One from Heaven to earth was the secret of 670 years. To calculate the gates of the Seven Palaces is to see how these 670 years accumulate in the Palace of the Heh, and thus to the Sephiroth of Malkuth in the world below.

What Rabbi Aba doesn't explain is the reason why it is 670 years and not some other span of time. Rabbi Aba had sight of the Seven Palaces and his comment about 670 years is only meaningful to someone who had already calculated the Gates of the Seven Palaces (a process of adding together sequences of letters from the diagram). The Gate of 670 belongs to the First Palace, where all the blessings from heaven arrive on the earth.

Most information and study that goes on in occult and Kabbalistic circles is focused almost exclusively on the study of Etz Chaim (the Tree of Life). The Tree has come to represent both the macrocosm and the microcosm, and all four worlds, mostly thanks to the influence of Lurianic Kabbalah, but to understand earlier Kabbalah and the mindset of biblical authors we have to factor in the Seven Palaces. When we do, we see that there is a definite spatial and mathematical reference for the number 670 which is the sum of all the stages of creation resulting in life on earth—of day & night (א), the sky (ג), fire which dries the land (ש), the doors (ד) between heaven and earth (by which vegetation came to earth), time (ת), light from the stars coming to earth (ה), birds and fish (ו), beast and insect (ז), the form of man (ח), food and sustenance for all living (ט), work & rest (י), mist & fertility (כ), the *neshamah* & *nephesh* (ל), pregnancy (מ), death (and the afterlife) (נ), the branching river (ס), the temptation of the eye to light and life (ע), courtship and mating (פ), childbirth (צ), woman (ק), and marriage and the solar journey through life (ר). All these things were part of the Name of God, YHVH, and each letter of the name denotes a section of the Seven Palaces. These were all that were "good", and the Kabbalists sought to find their reflection in themselves in order to come closer to El through his Name.

The gate value of 670 is also referred to in calculation in Genesis 1:10, after Elohim commands the dry land to appear:

טוב ויקרא אלהים ליבשה ארץ ולמקוה המים קרא ימים וירא אלהים כי ("And called Elohim to dry earth and the collection [of] the waters called seas, and saw Elohim it was good.")

ימים + המים + המים + ארץ + ש + אלהים = 670.

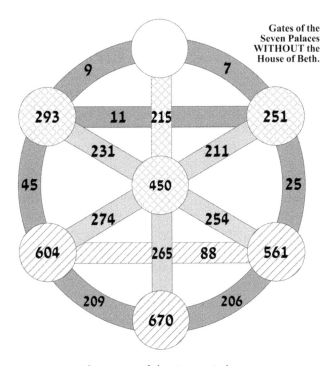

**Gates of the
Seven Palaces
WITHOUT the
House of Beth.**

The gates of the Seven Palaces.

The correspondence of 670 to the Gate of the First palace is a deliberate one. In the minds of the scribe and his audience, they can visualize the process of creation emerging step by step through a mathematical weaving of the letters together, because they have seen the diagram.

It is not possible to discover these things when the Merkabah (Seven Palaces) is hidden from sight and clothed in secrecy, and yet even when the Merkabah is not hidden, it guards its secrets, for its true worth is only gained after we make use of it to meditate upon our true place in the world and our relationship with all that is divine.

Essentially, the Merkabah was viewed as a blueprint of creation, and is told in a literary format in Genesis 1–2. Each of the verses is associated with a letter of the alphabet. The design of the first Temple also reflected this blueprint in its architectural symbolism.[5]

Merkabah mysticism employed this blueprint (or chart/design) to ascend to God, but note that it only flourishes once the second Temple has been destroyed. A priest walking around the Temple had no need of talismans, because the various sections and chambers of the Temple provided an architectural symbolism to focus on, by which they sought to become closer to God.

Most of the gematria or rhetoric math of the Bible appears to me to be basic arithmetic rather than calculus, with the exception being in the internal mathematics of the Seven Palaces, which might be classified as a "set" these days.[6] But on the other hand, I'm not a mathematician so perhaps it is merely that I fail to recognize more complex mathematics in the Bible through unfamiliarity, and I shall be proven incorrect on this point.

From antiquity, there seems to have been a continuous lineage of those who knew the Merkabah. The Sages Rabbi Yochanan Ben Zakkai (d. circa 80 CE) and, later, Rabbi Akiva (d. 135 CE) were deeply involved in Merkabah exegesis. New life was injected into the tradition with the rise of Kabbalah. However, in the Christian community, knowledge of the Merkabah and the biblical ciphers appears to have been lost quite quickly after the early period (100 CE). If the Roman Catholic Church retained any knowledge of it at the higher levels of the clergy is unknown, but it's probable that knowledge of it was lost during the persecutions of the Gnostics, who also used rhetoric math in their compositions. My theory is that Christian teachers stopped teaching biblical gematria for fear they would be identified with Gnostic Christians. It is a pity, because it has meant the more profound metaphysical ideas held by Christian scribes have been overlooked, and some of the details about the life of Jesus remain unappreciated or as points of contention that are bounced around between scholars.

The Talmud says that the ancient Sages likened Torah study to honey that drips from the honeycomb and gematria to the sweet desserts of wisdom. Of course, a dessert is not the main meal, but what is a full meal without the looked-for sweetness of the dessert? It is the sweetness of the dessert that signals to the stomach the meal is at an end and one can walk away from the table satisfied. So it is with the Bible, which is stuffed with these numerical sweetmeats with which the scribes would underline a point, or clarify something in the verse(s). Sometimes, they would even make jokes with it.

I think perhaps that is the most telling sign of a good biblical scholar— whether they get the jokes or not.

ראובן שמעון לוי ויהודה:
יששכר זבולן ובנימן:
דן ונפתלי גד ואשר:
ויהי כל נפש יצאי ירך יעקב שבעים נפש ויוסף היה במצרים:

Reuben Simeon Levi and Judah Issachar Zebulun and Benjamin Dan and Naphtali Gad and Asher and were all the souls who were descendants of Jacob seventy souls for Joseph was in Egypt. – Exodus 1:2-5.

ראובן שמעון לוי ויהודה +
יששכר זבולן ובנימן +
דן ונפתלי גד ואשר +
נפש + יעקב + ע + נפש + ויוסף +מ = 2170
2170 / 70 = 31.

CHAPTER 2

Studying the bible

When I find a gematria calculation in a text, I take a moment of pure pleasure in the finding of it, and I also spare some time to wonder what the reaction of the writer's immediate audience would have been?

I'm hunting for the best exegete of that text. The rule is that this should flow from using the same methodologies that were employed by the writer. It's only when we accept this principle that we truly become a part of that writer's audience—the people they were really writing for. You're effectively taking a seat at the table and it's time for dessert.

The gematria of the Hebrew Bible doesn't support the view that the Bible is the "infallible Word of God" as some Christians see it. Biblical authors may have been inspired by God, but they weren't some type of puppet possessed by God to write a book. It's entirely reasonable to accept that the relationship of those ancient scribes to God was a little more complicated and interactive than that, involving free will as well as service.

It's probably true that ancient scribal authors were sometimes divinely inspired to practice the art of gematria, and they believed they could come closer to God by its practice. They charted all the many ways that they thought God was manifest in the world and within consciousness. For them to say they knew God's name was not to say that they knew God (אל), for who can know God? But they could see the light (א) and the dark (א), the sky (ג) and the sun and the moon. They could feel the breath (ד) of the wind on the nape of the neck, and observe the passage of time (ח). It was accepted by the ancient nation of Israel that for everything that is manifest by God in creation there was a letter for it, and the Name of YHVH represented them all.

This name of God ("El") has form and encompasses everything. We cannot turn around and look at anything (any part of the Name) without recognizing that El is there too, beyond our perception.

Joseph Gikatilla (1248–after 1305) said of the Holy Name:

> It includes in it all the other holy names, even the Torah, there are no names, of all the other holy names that are not included in the name Hashem. After we have told you this you should understand how much you should meditate and be careful when you pronounce God's name, you should know, when you pronounce God's name you are pronouncing all the names of God, is it if you are now with your mouth wearing the spiritual weight on your tongue; the name of God, all his holy names and the entire world. If you understand that you should not take the name of God in vain.[7]

Whatever state of mind in which ancient scribes sat down to write, their thoughts were mediated through their arts of composition. Their writings took real work and application to produce drafts and calculations and elements of word play that were all compiled in their final manuscript. They were alive to God's presence in the world—God was without, within, and everywhere.

To learn to practice biblical hermeneutics like an ancient scribe, it's necessary to know the difference between Hebrew verbs, nouns, prepositions, and adjectives, because they comprise different elements of the formal system. There are online references that define these and they are mostly correct. Where they are not reflects the difference between how modern people think of concepts such as "time" as either a noun or a verb when used in a sentence.

One modern misconception about gematria which I'll clear up immediately is that it was copied from the Greeks. In actual fact, the earliest evidence of Hebrew gematria is found in the text of the Mt. Ebal curse tablet, discovered by the team of Scott Stripling in 2019. The tablet dates to the late Bronze age (circa 1440). When we compare the main Hebrew cipher to the Greek cipher used in the Christian canon then we see there has been a transposition of the cipher from Hebrew to Greek. We'll return to this subject later.

When I practice gematria with the Bible, I try and put myself in the shoes of ancient biblical authors. I try to peer across time with my mind's eye to understand the author's life, and grok their headspace as best I can. I wonder how they would have thought of the world around them, and what feelings might they have harbored? What attitudes? What was important to them? What would have made them laugh, cry, or thrown them into a rage? I want the whole picture; the whole movie, with commentary from the editor. I want to know how the author's message relates to the beliefs and worldview of their readers at the time.

On a practical level, once you've gotten outside of yourself and you're actually doing the work of calculation, then you have to be prepared to pay very close attention to the construction of words and their relationships to one another. There's a certain pacing and music to biblical calculations that you grow familiar with over time.

It also pays to know the meaning of the Hebrew prefixes and suffixes, and to be able to bring your own judgment to bear upon what would have been thought to have been a noun or a verb by ancient Hebrews.

You should try and school yourself to follow the semantic logic of a sentence, and you need to pay special attention to the relationship of one word with the next word and prior word. As you build the calculation, it's normal to make errors in syntax, and so it's usually preferable to check the calculation is properly formed before computing its result, and then checking again afterwards that the calculation matches the logic of the verse.

I sometimes tell people that they have to approach the matter as if it's half a logic problem, and half a cryptic crossword question that has mated with a line of Sudoku. I joke, but some calculations are extremely long, and a scribe like Ezekiel (for instance) delighted in making use of all the mnemonic and calculating words available to him. He was a great artist, and no doubt he probably had a following in Jerusalem at that time that delighted in trying to solve the calculations of this master, but I'd advise you to put off studying Ezekiel in any detail until you've gotten really good at the practice. He can bamboozle a newbie.

Uncovering and reconstructing the scribal practice of rhetoric math has been in many ways like learning a new language. The discovery process has been a lengthy and time consuming one spanning most of my recent years. But in organizing, refining and setting down what I understand of the art, I hope to shorten the amount of time it takes my readers to acquire the ability. It is the difference between learning to read hieroglyphs now, and learning to read hieroglyphs before Jean-François Champollion had deciphered them from the Rosetta stone.

My Rosetta stone was a cipher, and the classification of words into their constructs was an important part of the deciphering process. There are flag-words in the bible that signal where important gematria is. There are words that are reserved to hold set values ("mnemonic words"), and these are usually representative of a value of a letter of the alephbet. And there are verbs and prepositions set aside ("calculating words") that represent types of calculations to be done in a sum (rhetoric math). To establish any word as a "flagword", "mnemonic word", or "calculating word", every instance of it had to be checked and scored. Considerations to be weighted were whether the scribe typically uses gematria; whether the scribe is employing gematria in that particular verse; the style of the scribe; the length and difficulty of the calculation; and the presence of other flagwords, mnemonic words and potential mnemonic words in each calculation. It is only after extensive investigation that a word can be placed in any one of the three categories.

When practicing gematria, it is only after a verse is calculated that can it be considered with the rest of the levels of exegesis.

In the Talmud, these different levels of Torah exegesis are called the PaRDeS, which is an acronym of Peshat, Remez, Derash, and Sod. Peshat is a plain reading of the text, Remez is an allegorical approach, the Derash is a comparative method, and the Sod is secret and sacred hermeneutical knowledge that knits together all the rest.

This doesn't just have an application to Jewish texts. It's a good way of approaching an exegete of Christian texts and those of the Holy Books of Thelema too.

Gematria didn't become my special interest overnight. It emerged from my studies in Hermetic Qabalah.[8] I studied the works of Aleister Crowley in particular, which is peppered with references to gematria, and there are parts of *Liber AL vel Legis* that require the reader to have a working knowledge of biblical ciphers, and of the Seven Palaces; such as the famous riddle of AL II:76.

Before 2014, I had been using Standard Gematria/Isopsephy ciphers. I had seen, as many students of the occult do, that gematria had "something to it", but I was puzzled by the weight and importance that Aleister Crowley placed upon the practice. When viewed through a severely skeptical monocle it can look like occult number-wang. At that time, gematria appeared to me to be little more than a form of numerology. I thought it could be useful for working with the subconscious by providing a means for ideas to surface through free-association. But I was open to the idea that it could have originally been something else.

Gematria is still viewed primarily as a free-association tool by most occultists who are blissfully unaware of its true origins. Gematria ciphers can, of course, be put to the purposes of numerology but that's not why they were made or how they were used in ancient times.

With gematria, key pieces of information are hidden that make holistic good sense with the narrative. We are not left guessing at what the author meant, and the text is properly read by you, and has a chance to work its magic upon your psyche.

Knowing the gematria of biblical texts can make a difference in how you receive the essential message that is woven into the story. It can be the difference between, for example, whether you think of God in the Garden of Eden story as a kind and loving God that laments the loss of Adam and Eve from Eden due to their own foolishness, or a harsh and punishing overlord out to curse Adam and Eve for their disobedience. You can see an entire extra dimension to the narrative that is hidden away in the gematria. It's just as if you had become an initiate of the ancient first Temple at Jerusalem, and were learning the secrets that were forbidden to be known outside of the priestly cult.

To be able to decipher these texts, a person needs to be in possession of the precise ciphers that were used in Biblical times. The cipher key must fit the lock, and be capable of conveying a hidden calculation exactly as the scribe composed it.

These cryptographic pre-conditions are not present and not necessary in the practice of numerology. Almost any number system will (and does) do. This is not a slight on practitioners of numerology, nor any other method that is designed to facilitate the access of the conscious mind to the subconscious or collective unconscious. It's simply that gematria and numerology are apples and oranges to each other, rather like the differences between astronomy and astrology.

Before I discovered the true ciphers for the Bible, I looked at the matter with a cryptograph's eye. I knew of a couple of Professors that had opined that it was not only possible, but that it was even likely for there to be gematria in the Bible, though they suggested that the practice was kept in closed circles and was sacred/secret. Certainly, the Sages never published the biblical ciphers in the Talmud nor the Mishnah, and as the biblical ciphers were a part of the knowledge of the Merkabah, this is entirely consistent with their prohibition on discussing it. So I knew that I was not out on a wild goose chase, but had a chance to find something significant if I pursued the matter with all due diligence. My opinion was that the gematria of *The Book of the Law*[9] and the Bible was missing because the ciphers needed to decode them were not yet public knowledge. It was a big mystery to me at the time, and I love a good mystery, so while I studied you could say I was on the alert for clues, though the topic seemed opaque and hermetically sealed.

I was still looking for answers when, after twenty years of studying Hermetic Qabalah, I decided to turn my attention to the traditional Jewish Kabbalah at its origin. The learning curve was steep and I dove into Mather's (Golden Dawn) copy of *The Kabbalah Unveiled*. I knew the Hebrew alphabet and a handful of Hebrew words, and *Kabbalah Unveiled* was the only readily available partial translation of the Zohar that was available at the time. It was also on the recommended reading list of Aleister Crowley's Order of the A.'.A.'. The "partial" nature of this work is often critiqued, but as it turns out, the included works were chosen with great care. Translated to Latin by Christian Knorr von Rosenroth, one of its texts, the *Sepher Dtzeniouthia* ("Book of Concealed Mystery") proved itself to be named with exquisite accuracy, for it contained a riddle that allowed the reverse engineering of the Tree of Life into the Seven Palaces.

Unlike the public version of the Seven Palaces that was published by Dion Fortune, this diagram had paths between the palaces and letter attributions to both. Once I could see the letters arranged in this fashion, I developed an appreciation of the numerical properties of the diagram. It has been deliberately fashioned so that each section is represented by a letter from the name of God, YHVH. Each letter represents a quality of the macrocosm as the ancients conceived of it. It was the macrocosmic counterpart to the Tree of Life, and pertained to the world of Yetzirah rather than Assiah.

The Seven Palaces is central to the esoteric literary tradition of the Merkabah mystics (100 BCE–1000 CE), but its origins are attested in the literature of ancient Ugarit (up to 1050 BCE[10]) and Sumeria. It was a core part of the esoteric doctrines of ancient Israel, and knowledge of it has echoed down the highway of history.

The bottom three Palaces spell out the name of the God Hadad, who was the son of El in the Baal texts of Ugaritic Literature. They state that Hadad lived in the Seven Palaces of his Father so the legend supports the ancient provenance of the diagram.

If the Canaanites of Ugarit assigned numbers and letters to their conception of the Seven Palaces, then it stands to reason that it was done prior to the destruction of the city of Ugarit in 1050 BCE, and we could hypothesize a probable date for the practice of rhetoric math to that period. We need not rely on the Canaanite legends for that however, because just recently we have discovered that the Mt. Ebal curse tablet contains gematria, and that has been dated to 1440 BCE, thus placing the practice of gematria to the Late Bronze age and earlier if we allow a certain passage of time for the practice of Hebrew rhetoric math to develop into a system and adopt conventions.

The Mt. Ebal curse tablet is the hottest discovery in the archaeological world right now, and distinguished Professor Gershon Galil[11] has called it "the most ancient and the most important Hebrew inscription ever found."

It was written in the first true alphabetic script (the Proto-Consonantal Script) and includes the three lettered name of God; יהו YHV. One reason why it is so fascinating to Bible scholars is that the Bible relates how Israel was commanded by God to make blessings upon Mt. Gezer and curses upon Mt. Ebal. The reason why it is particularly relevant to our practice is because of the convention in biblical rhetoric math which made a blessing, ברך, a multiplication by two, and a curse, ארור, a division by two. The inscription says:

אתה ארור לאל יהו ארור תמת ארור ארור מת תמת ארור אתה ליהו ארור

> AThH ARVR LAL IHV ARVR ThMTh ARVR ARVR MTh ThMTh
> ARVR AThH LIHV ARVR
>
> You are cursed by God YHV, cursed to die, cursed, cursed, to die death, cursed, cursed you are by YHV, cursed.

The calculation in the tablet's text requires that you replace אתה with ישראל, "Israel", because the curse is against Israel. There are established conventions for using the אתה in this fashion in Biblical texts. The resulting sum is split into two segments of seven words:

1st seven words:

אתה ארור לאל יהו יהו ארור תמת ארור

Calculation:

$310 = (2 \backslash \text{נ}) + (2 \backslash \text{לאל יהו}) + \text{ישראל}$

$310 = 10 \times \text{אל}$ ("God").

2nd seven words:

ארור מת תמת ארור אתה ליהו ארור

Calculation:

$248 = (2 \backslash \text{נ}) + \text{נ} + (\text{ישראל} \backslash 2) + \text{ליהו}$

$248 = 8 \times \text{אל}$ ("God").

Ten is the value of *yod* and eight is the value of *cheth*. Together this spells the word חי, "Chai", which means "life", but in reverse, symbolically implying its opposite, "death".

248 is the number of positive mitzvoth (commandments) followed by Jews, and it is the sum of האור + החשך (the light + the darkness) from Genesis 1:4.

I find the curse tablet to be a wonderfully romantic bit of true history. In my mind's eye I can imagine an ancient Israelite secretly preparing a potent curse using all his knowledge of the hermeneutic arts of his day. He writes on a tablet so tiny it was designed to be overlooked, and he works in secret so that only himself and God are privy to its contents, making it potent and magical. I imagine the scribe, perhaps Naphtali or one of his brothers, creeping out in the dead of night under the light of a full moon to bury his tablet on the mountain of Ebal, leaving it active and potent beneath the sands … until 2019 when it was discovered and the power of the curse presumably dissipated.

To be able to read the rhetoric math of the Bible takes time and practice. It took a great deal of work and research before I could get to the stage of analyzing an ancient text and could confidently tell you whether there is gematria in it or not. Firstly, I needed to find out what the correct cipher was, and that took the most time. Finding the (main) Biblical cipher took working through a series of hypotheses and deductions and testing them.

Consider that all Hebrew scripts have twenty-two letters, and if we were to assume that Standard Gematria was the original cipher with these scripts then it would have a numeral system that ranged from 1 to 400 in decimal, which is exceptionally strange. A unary numeral system that counts from 1 to 22 is equally unusual because naturally occurring numeral systems almost universally reflect their origins from a common system of counting parts of the body (fingers, toes, finger joints). Since the Alphabet originated on the Egyptian Sinai Peninsula, and because the Egyptians counted in decimal, then we would expect the alphabet to represent 20 values, not 22.

A key insight into the biblical cipher came to me after I made the hypothesis that this was actually the case. I posited that if 22 letters were representing 20 values then it followed that 2 letters must repeat one of the values already represented by 20 letters. This narrowed the field down to the last two letters of *shin* and *tav*, which in Standard Gematria represent 300 and 400. So I followed this up with yet another hypothesis—that their original letter values had been multiplied by 100. What if the *shin* was really 3 and the *tav* was actually 4? And voila! I had found the correct cipher for both the Bible and *The Book of the Law*.

Finding the ciphers also made a harmony of the numerical set of the Seven Palaces. This has a constructed symmetry to it.

When the gate of the path that has four letters (*shin*, *tav*, *tsade*, and *qoph*) is added to its opposite gate of the *cheth*, the result is 217, and on the opposite side, when the gate of the *resh* is added to the gate of the *vav* then the result is 218.

The diagonal gates each sum to 285 when calculated as one gate across, and when each letter of the diagonals are doubled each has a gate value of 365:

$$\text{ד} + \text{ע} + \text{ר} + \text{י} + \text{א} = 285$$
$$\text{ד} + \text{נ} + \text{ר} + \text{ל} + \text{א} = 285$$
$$\text{ד} + \text{ע} + \text{ע} + \text{ר} + \text{ר} + \text{י} + \text{י} + \text{א} = 365$$
$$\text{ד} + \text{נ} + \text{נ} + \text{ר} + \text{ר} + \text{ל} + \text{ל} + \text{א} = 365$$

365 is the number of negative mitsvot, as well as the number of days in a year. When added to 248 positive mitsvot, you get the number of total mitsvot, which is 613. This is a calculation found in Genesis 1:2–3:

אור + וחשך – פני תהום = 365
Face of the deep – and darkness + light

There are prominent correspondences in the verses to the combinations of letters on the Seven Palaces called Gates. The midrash of Genesis

Rabbah says: "The Patriarchs—they are the Chariot", and other texts qualify that they are the legs of the Divine Throne.

האור + החשך = 248
[The light + the darkness]
365 + 248 = 613.

248 is 31 × 7, and is the number of the name of Abraham. When multiplied by ten, 248 is the sum of the two middle gates on the Seven Palaces. For this sum we take the value of the large *beth*—2,000 rather than 2:

ב + ג + ה + ז + ר = 2215
ה + ס + ר = 265
2215 + 265 = 2480.

Prior to discovering the cipher, the path with four letters had appeared to pull away from the rest of the diagram with a gate value of

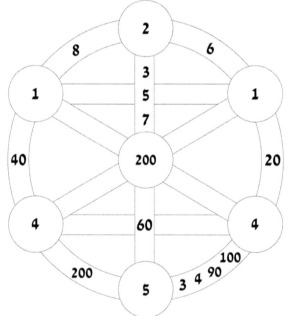

Left Column: 2 + 8 + 1 + 40 + 4 + 200 + 5 = 260.
Middle Column: 2 + 3 + 5 + 7 + 200 + 60 + 5 = 282.
Right Column: 2 + 6 + 1 + 20 + 4 + 100 + 90 + 4 + 3 + 5 = 235.
260 + 282 + 235 = 777.

The three columns.

899, but now it produced gate values which appeared on other areas of the Wheel. Moreover, when the Biblical cipher was used on the Seven Palaces it made the three columns sum to 777, and turned the section of the *vav* from the Holy Name to a sum of 480.

When I tested my newly discovered cipher on Genesis 1:1 and *Liber AL vel Legis* 1:1, I was amazed to find that both yielded a result of 700.

הארץ + השמים + אלהים + [220] בראשית = 700.
220 + Had + Manifestation + Nuit = 700.

I had discovered that Aleister Crowley had re-created the gematria sum in the first line of his *Book of the Law* to exactly mirror the calculation of Genesis 1:1, and thus I realized that he had been working with the biblical cipher over a hundred years before I discovered it. He had transliterated it into the Latin script, resolved to keep it a secret, yet written *The Book of the Law* with it.

Though Aleister Crowley is often dismissed by many as a charlatan and worse, in regards to his cryptography and his knowledge of the Bible, he evidently had the inside track. According to Henrik Bogdan, Crowley's detailed knowledge of and fascination with the Bible remained with him throughout his life.

I can empathise. One lifetime is hardly enough time to properly study the Bible, especially when everything has to be checked for mathematics. To say I was stunned by the implications of my findings would be an understatement. Crowley left us a record of how he felt at the discovery. He stayed up all night in awe and adoration. For him, this was the Lost Word, and this was *it*. This was the key to all the canon, to all the writings of the ancient mystics, and to all the secrets promised to the aspirants of esoteric magical societies.

It took a lot more testing to rule out chance and coincidence before I was certain of what I'd found, and could rule out confirmation bias and chance. I've seen a lot of people go off the deep end trying to convince themselves and others that they've found a valuable cipher, and these are sad and cautionary lessons. Many of them hold private delusions about being chosen by a higher power to reveal some great wisdom to the world from their private and usually arbitrary numerology systems. It's a massive ego trip, and I wanted no part of it.

I had the entire virgin landscape of biblical and occult cryptography before me, but I didn't trust it. I needed to be sure that I had the keys, but as then I knew practically nothing of the art or conventions of gematria. I had not then realized that gematria was an art with strict conventions, and was in fact, a form of ancient rhetoric mathematics.

It has been several years since my initial discovery of the Seven Palaces. During that time, I have done thousands of gematria sums and I have developed an appreciation for the full extent of the art. It wasn't practiced in any free-form way, but in a way that allowed a calculation to be decoded exactly as it was encoded by the original scribe. The habit of taking a professional approach to research has served me well here. It has allowed me to understand the architecture of the system, and to arrive at results using the scientific method.

Every calculating word or mnemonic that I admitted to the list of reserved words has only gotten onto that list after first being checked against multiple instances where it appears in a book, and then it is investigated in other books, before it has finally proven itself to be a convention or rule of the system.

Where there were no names to classify something crucial to a section of the system I encountered, then I was forced to invent new ones. I've tried to make these as reflective of their properties as possible, but I make no claim that they were ever terms used in ancient Hebrew.

In the modern world there is an abundance of numerical ciphers, and though most of them are clearly useless for gematria, we need to be able to clearly distinguish which one we are talking about. Ancient scribes during biblical times do not appear to have named their ciphers, and knew of four at most, so it was never an issue for them. Biblical Gematria was likely just *manah* ("counting"), and the Reversal Cipher something like "turn" or "back". If there were original Hebrew names for the ciphers, that is a matter for linguists to sort out, but the Greeks called these scribal arts *gematria*, *notariqon*, and *temurah*, which are what we call them today. Although these names are Greek, the Greeks didn't invent the arts to which they referred, and the modern practice of gematria is very far from the ancient practice of mathematics in the Bible. As this book demonstrates, gematria was first practiced by the Hebrew speaking peoples, and the Greeks came to know of it only after they borrowed the Hebrew alphabet from the Phoenicians.

בראשית ברא את אלהים השמים ואת הארץ

In the beginning (220) [created] Elohim (86) the Heavens (98) and
the Earth (296) = 700.

Genesis 1:1

CHAPTER 3

About ancient Hebrew rhetoric mathematics

God doesn't speak Hebrew—God speaks numbers.

Lon Milo Duquette.

What is gematria?

Gematria is a formal system of rhetoric mathematics—that is, mathematics that is done without math notation—that was used by ancient scribes to supply key pieces of information to their writings so they could be understood in a spiritual context. It was a way of reading and writing texts embedded with mathematical calculations.

Features of Biblical Gematria:

- Each letter is also a number.
- Each letter has a place in creation.
- Each letter has a placement in a special priestly ordering of the alphabet that reflects its place in creation.

The priestly ordering of the alphabet was used by the first Temple cult as a type of table of verses for Genesis 1–2. Every verse corresponds

31

to the mythic qualities of every letter. For instance, the letter *beth* corresponds to Genesis 1:2. The letter *aleph* corresponds to Genesis 1:3–4, and so on.

The letters themselves were believed to have been created in spirit or principle by Elohim. The practice of Gematria in biblical times included a number of conventions, such as:

– Reserved prepositions and verbs to indicate types of arithmetic.
– Nouns reserved to represent numerical values.
– Reserved words as mnemonics—usually relating to the pictographic origins of a letter.
– Flagwords in the text, e.g. "behold!".
– The use of notariqon and temurah and using the cipher values in reverse.
– Standard rhetorical features, such as the use of gematria with an alphabet acrostic.

The conventions that govern the art and the practice of Biblical Gematria were so systematic that a scribe knew that whatever sum he embedded in a text would be read and understood in exactly the way he intended it should be understood. This is why I say "there is no guessing with Biblical Gematria."

Gematria appears to have flourished during the time of the first Temple. The Book of Genesis was probably written at the first Temple, using the writings of Moses as a guide, and it is absolutely stuffed with rhetoric math. The first book of Kings also contains information about the Temple that is supplied by the gematria of the text, and that's something we will explore in more depth later.

Though gematria was first invented by the Jewish people, it was carried into Christianity by Jews that converted, and therefore we find calculations in rhetoric math scattered across the New Testament. It's used in some of the Gospels and in the book of Revelation, and, when the correct ciphers are used, it resolves questions about the meaning of the 153 fish and the number of the Beast.

General knowledge of this type of math was lost during the early Christian period, but knowledge of it may have been fostered outside of the purview of the Catholic or Protestant churches by members of esoteric societies and groups identifying within western esoteric and occult fraternities.

Western hermeticism rather shamelessly appropriated the spiritual architecture of Jewish mysticism, but there was little awareness that this might have been a culturally insensitive move at the time. Hermeticists employed the spiritual architecture of the ancient Temple religion but provided alternative rituals and meditative work so that gentiles might partake of comparable results.

The study of the Torah in the context of ancient first temple Jewish mysticism can be a very instructive spiritual vehicle. It encourages self-reflection. It can deepen a feeling of connection with God, and lead to a better appreciation of the purpose of our lives. Non-Jews don't have hundreds of mitzvoth to obey but the great takeaway from Torah study is the importance of adhering to the will of God (the will of the divine spark in each of us) in our thoughts and actions, because doing that is the foundation of all ethical conduct.[12]

Even if you just want to learn to practice gematria for use with texts in English, it is still necessary to learn the Hebrew alephbet as a foundation to your studies so that you will be alive to the cryptic portions of the gematria that you will find in Greek and English writing scripts. Whether you write the word "fire" in English, or Hebrew (אֵשׁ) or in Greek (πῦρ) all these words have the mnemonic value of 3, but it is only by studying Biblical Gematria with the Hebrew script that you can come to appreciate why "fire" has the value of 3 and what place it took in the ancient architecture of the universe.

"In the Beginning…"

בראשית = 220

ב בר ברא בראש בראשי בראשית = 2000

(Reversal Cipher)

ב × ר × א × ש × י × ת = 48000

CHAPTER 4

Learning the Hebrew alephbet

Come and see: The first subject of the Torah we give to children is
the Alphabet. This is a matter that mankind cannot comprehend,
nor can it rise in their minds, not to mention saying it with their
mouths. Even supernal angels and the most sublime can not comprehend it, as these matters are the mysteries of the Holy Name.

Zohar, Acharei 73

תשרקצפעסנמלכיטחזוהדגבא

Assuming you don't already know them, the first step in learning
gematria is memorizing the twenty-two letters and five final forms of
the Hebrew writing script.

When I was studying western Hermeticism I got along for years just
using English transliterations of the Hebrew alphabet, i.e. a = *aleph*,
b = *beth*, c = *cheth*, and so on. However, this simply won't work for studying the rhetoric math of the Bible, chiefly due to the fact that although
transliterated Bibles exist, they are IPA phonetic transliterations, rather
than letter-for-letter substitutions. I've provided a pdf with a letter-for-
letter transliteration of the first two chapters of Genesis on the Shematria Gematria Calculator site as a stop gap, but there's no substitute for
learning the Hebrew alphabet.

https://www.shematria.com/assets/images/Genesis_transliteration.pdf

The good news is that the Tanakh was written before the Hebrew system of vowels (Niqqud) was invented, so you don't need to learn the vowels and they have no value or part in the practice of Biblical Gematria.

The best way to learn the alephbet is to engage your muscle memory and write it out. Readers can download a workbook for this which is hosted on the Shematria site. You can print out your own sheets and trace each letter until writing the letters feels natural and you recognize them easily:

https://www.shematria.com/assets/images/Workbook%20~%20The%20Hebrew%20Alephbet.pdf

Testing yourself with flashcards is another method that is useful in solidifying character recognition. Online flashcards with correspondences for Biblical Gematria can be found on the Sanctum Regnum website.

https://thesanctumregnum.pythonanywhere.com/hebrewtest

There are also many free apps available for phone, tablet, and PC which allow you to practice writing and learning the letters. When you can comfortably recall the name and number of each letter, come back to this section.

* * *

Although hand-writing the Hebrew letters is the best way to learn the alephbet, once it is memorized you'll probably want to be able to practice typing it into a phone, tablet, or computer.

This will help you use a gematria calculator, and to take notes of gematria. If you participate in a social media group and want to share your gematria findings, you'll find it easier if you have a Hebrew keyboard set up on your device. This next section will explain how to set up your devices to use Hebrew and Greek writing scripts alongside your QWERTY keyboard. Don't forget—Hebrew is written from right to left!

Setting up your keyboards on android
1. Select "Settings", then "General Management", then "Language and Input".
2. Select "On-screen keyboard" and then tap on your default keyboard.

3. Tap "Languages and types" and select "Manage input languages".
4. To activate a Hebrew keyboard, scroll down until you see "עברית", and turn it on.
5. To activate a Greek keyboard, scroll down until you see "ελληνικα" and turn it on.
6. Open up a browser or note app to bring up the on-screen keyboard. Swipe right along the space bar to bring up your Hebrew and/or Greek keyboards.

Just swipe the space bar again when you need to return to the English alphabet.

Setting up your keyboards on windows
1. Select the Start button, then select Settings > Time & Language > Language.
2. Under Preferred languages, select the language that contains the keyboard you want, and then select Options.
3. Select Add a keyboard and choose the keyboard you want to add. If you don't see the keyboard you want, you may have to add a new language to get additional options. If this is the case, go on to step 4.
4. Return to the Language settings page, and select Add a language.
5. Choose the language you want to use from the list, then select Next.
6. Review any language features you want to set up or install, and select Install.
7. An icon will appear on your toolbar that allows you to select the language you wish to use with your keyboard. However you will have to practice before you learn which letters are mapped to your keyboard.

Prefixes and Suffixes
Translators try their best to parse biblical Hebrew into English, but the two languages are structurally different which means that a translation is always an approximation at best. Sometimes translations contain words that aren't actually in the original text but are put there to make the sentence conform to the rules of English grammar.

Though it is not necessary to learn the biblical Hebrew language in order to practice gematria, is highly useful to know the Hebrew prefixes and suffixes. The value of prefixes and suffixes are included as part of the nouns value and they take no other place in gematria than that, but knowing them will help you navigate the source text and check the translation.

Open up Biblehub's interlinear feature here:

https://biblehub.com/interlinear/genesis/1-1.htm

You'll see that it displays the Hebrew bible by its Strong number, which is above a pronunciation guide, which is above the written Hebrew, and underneath that there is a translation and a designation of the words by grammar into nouns, verbs, adjectives, prepositions and all the other parts of speech.

The first word is "בראשית" which means "in [the] beginning". The first letter, *beth* (ב), is a prefix with the meaning "in" which is followed by the main word, "ראשית", meaning "beginning" or rather more literally, "at the head", since "ראש" means "head". If we wanted to change this word to say simply "the beginning" we would remove the letter *beth* as the prefix and replace it with the letter *heh* like so: הראשית. We can also observe that the suffix to the word is a feminine plural, so the word is more like "beginnings" than "beginning" (singular).

There are eleven prefixes which are made by single letters placed at the beginning of a word. Each prefix letter introduces a new meaning. They are:

aleph (א), *bet* (ב), *heh* (ה), *vav* (ו), *yod* (י), *kaph* (כ), *lamed* (ל), *mem* (מ), *nun* (נ), *shin* (ש), and *tav* (ת).

Together with the suffixes, these letters are called the Otiyot HaShimush. To give you another example, the letter ו (*vav*) is a common prefix which means "and", so if you read וחשׁך with the translation "and darkness" you will know that the "and" is part of the word rather than a liberty taken by the translator to parse the sentence into English. Bear in mind that there can be more than one prefix attached to a word, so you ought to know the order that prefixes are combined too. As a general rule, the *vav* always comes first and *heh* always comes last. The *heh* is often absorbed into the *beth* or *lamed* prefix.

Prefixes and their meanings:
ו (*vav*). Meaning: "and", "but". If used with other prefixes the *vav* comes first. The *vav* can change past tense to future tense and vice versa, for instance changing "he loved" to "he shall love".

ל (*lamed*). Meaning "to", "for".

ב (*beth*). Meaning: "in", "with", "by".

כ (*kaph*). Meaning: "like", "as".

מ (*mem*). Meaning: "from". If used with the heh prefix, mem comes before it.

ה (heh). Meaning: "the". *Heh* is always the last prefix before the root word. If used with the *beth, kaph* or *lamed* prefixes the *heh* is omitted but the other prefix takes on its meaning. For instance; וביומי means "in the days". *Heh* can also be used to indicate a question.

א (*aleph*). Meaning: "I will" when attached to a verb.

י (*yod*). Meaning: "he will", or "they will" when attached to a verb.

נ (*nun*). Meaning: "we will" when attached to a verb.

ת (*tav*). Meaning: "she will", "you will", or "they will" when attached to a verb.

ש (*shin*). Meaning: "that", "which", "who" and "whom".

Suffixes and their meanings:
Every Hebrew noun is either masculine or feminine; however, it is impossible to determine the gender of some nouns due to their lack of a suffix. For instance, the Hebrew word for God, אל, has no suffix. A common suffix that denotes a masculine plural is ים, for instance מי (water) becomes מים (waters). The feminine plural is ות making a אפשר (possibility) into אפשרות (possibilities). To change a masculine noun to a feminine we need only add the ה (*heh*) to the end, for instance מלך (king) becomes מלכה (queen) with the simple addition of the *heh*.

Possessive pronouns are also written as suffixes:

י : of me.

נו : of us.

ך : of you (masculine, singular).

ך : of you (feminine, singular).

כם : of you (masculine, plural).

כן : of you (feminine, plural).

ו : of him.

ה : of her.

ם : of them (masculine).

ן : of them (feminine).

(220 with the Reversal Cipher)
  — "YHVH" in Paleo-Hebrew
בראשית (220)
  — "In the beginning" in Hebrew
התורה (220)
  — "The Torah" in Hebrew
Λογος αΛ (220 with the Reversal Cipher)
  — "Word of God" in Greek

CHAPTER 5

Writing scripts

The Hebrew alphabet today is written in an Aramaic writing script that was borrowed from the Babylonians after the fall of the first Temple. The proper name for this script is *Ktav Ashuri*, but is commonly called the "square script", and it was used to write Aramaic.

Ktav Ashuri is derived from the Paleo-Hebrew alphabet and its Phoenician stylistic variants, which in their turn were derived from the Proto-Consonantal Script (PCS), which is the earliest known alphabetic writing script in the Levant. Ancient Near East scholars are certain that the Proto-Consonantal letters were derived from a set of specific Egyptian hieroglyphs, and that each letter carried a meaning in their names.

Today, most Hebrew writings are made in the *Ktav Ashuri* script, and so even though some biblical works would have originally been composed in the Paleo-Hebrew Script (*Ktav Ivri*), you should begin by learning the Hebrew Alphabet in the square script. Once you have that under your belt, you can set yourself the goal of learning these other older writings scripts too, so that you'll be able to appreciate the way that the memory of the earliest letter-pictures and their role in creation was kept alive in the mind's eye of the scribes, no matter what writing script they used.

a. The Proto-Consonantal Script

The Proto-Consonantal Script.

The Proto-Consonantal Script was used by Hebrew-speaking people and was formed in Egypt (between 1859 and 1842 BCE) by using twenty-two Egyptian hieroglyphs. Through the study of the origins of each letter, we can learn about the many of the words that are reserved to represent set values (mnemonic words), since most of these hold a letter value. The PCS was written both left to right and right to left, and it is believed to have been formed by acrophony, meaning that each pictographic letter has a phonetic sound associated with the initial consonant in the word that is represented by the pictograph. By the middle of the fifteenth century BCE, inscriptions with PCS were being composed by Hebrew speaking herders and miners, particularly in the Wadi el Hol region of Egypt, but also in the Southern Levant.[13] Professor Lemaire (2017) suggested that early alphabetic writing was developed during "the period of Hyksos domination in the south of Palestine", which would have been the Egyptian Delta around the 18th–17th centuries BCE.

It is not known whether any numerals were associated with these letters, yet it's possible. As an explanation for the origins of the alphabet it goes a long way towards explaining why it was those twenty-two letters in particular, coming from twenty-two particular hieroglyphs out of the 700 that existed in ancient Egyptian, that were chosen to represent phonetic sounds and numbers.

It may be the case that these characters represented numerals before they represented phonetic sounds. There's no intrinsic reason that this shouldn't be the case, because while reading and writing is undoubtedly useful, numeracy was absolutely essential to the type of sophisticated and cosmopolitan civilization that Ancient Egypt was.

The acrophony that we see in the alphabet could simply be an effect of needing names and sounds for numeral characters that for all practical purposes suitably distinguished them from one another, which led naturally to their phonetic associations and the development of writing and reading. But on the other hand, it could be that these twenty-two signs had a ritual use association with the creation myths of the Hebrew speaking peoples. Such devices would be useful for remembering and reciting oral history.

Think of a place in ancient Egypt where numbers would need to be clearly distinguishable—if you were buying or selling something in a bustling, crowded market, then the more differentiated the names of the numeral characters are from one another, the easier will go the sale and purchase of items. Or if you are at a cattle market, or at a crowded state sponsored public event. There would have been numerous noisy work situations, or work situations that required land or cattle to be measured or counted, and numbers to be exchanged over a distance, or from within mines, from men and women shouting. Over time, and from constant common usage, the language would quickly evolve and adapt to make the numbers more distinguishable from one another.

If our hypothesis about the mathematical basis of the alphabet is correct, then evidence to prove the case may be discovered if special attention is given to PCS texts that don't seem to make sense, because such "texts" are likely candidates to be calculations.

There is a lack of consensus in the academic community over the meaning and origin of some of the PCS letters and their original names. On the other hand there is broad agreement for most of the letters. This becomes relevant to the art of gematria because many mnemonic words have their origin in the pictograms of the PCS. For instance, the word for "doors" in Hebrew is "daleth" which is the name of the letter, and it has a set or given value of 4.

Regular use evolved the PCS script into Paleo-Hebrew, which is more formally known as *Ktav Ivri*, but however removed from their original shape the letters became, their origins were remembered in the letter names and their mnemonics. This is why a good working knowledge of the conventions of gematria, in particular those of the mnemonics words, comes in very handy.

b. The letters and their sources

The following monograph draws on the work of current scholars in the field, such as Douglas Petrovich,[14] Judith Dillon, Brian Colless, and Jeff Benner, and their attempts to refine our understanding of the origins of the alphabet. I have compared the Mnemonic Words of the scribes with the original names of the letters and their hieroglyphic source. The alphabet charts they compiled were especially useful, and they allowed me to successfully collate a list of potential mnemonic words that were tested against the gematria of the Tanakh. Their research has shaved years from my own.

Beth (2) B

The pictogram is of the floor plan of a house or tent. The original name is thought to be *bayith* (בית) which means "house" and is a mnemonic word with the gematria value of 2. Such words tend to confirm the original name of each letter.

In the order of the alphabet presented in Genesis 1–2, the *beth* takes first position and it is attributed to the highest position of the Seven Palaces (the Seventh Palace). However, abecedaries found at Sinai show the letter occurring in the more familiar second place, suggesting that the alphabetic order of Genesis was arranged according to the narrative structure of the creation myth, and most likely had a practical mnemonic function in the memorization and the recitation of the oral law.

The verses of Genesis 1:1–2 correspond to this letter and begin with a *beth* in the word בראשית, *brashith* (220) The verses display an admirable density of gematria calculations.

בראשית (220) has the same value as התורה, *HaTorah*, and יהוה, YHVH, when the Name is calculated with the Reversal Cipher. Also קדש וקדש ("Holy of Holies"), and Λογος + אל[15] *logos* ("Word of God"), again using the Reversal Cipher. It is also the value of the combined letters that the letter *yod* of YHVH represents on the Seven Palaces.

בראשית + אלהים + השמים + הארץ = 700

In the Beginning + Elohim + the Heavens + the Earth = 700.

אלהים + השמים + הארץ = 480

Elohim + the Heavens + the Earth = 480

Which is the value of the *vav* of YHVH on the Seven Palaces.

Notariqon of 1:1 (with the Reversal Cipher):

ב + כ + א + א + ה + ו + ה = 800.

Genesis 1:2 (with the Reversal Cipher):

פני – וחשך + תהום + ב + אלהים אלהים + פני המים = 800

Face – and darkness + of the deep + and the spirit + Elohim Elohim + face + the waters = 800.

And the first part of this sum (with ordinary Biblical Gematria):

והארץ + היתה+ תהו + ובהו = 360.

And the earth was formless and void = 360.

Which is the number of degrees in a circle, which has an inside, and an outside (thus 2) even though the line is closed. The letter *beth* is used as a prefix with the meaning "in" or "inside".

Let's look at the sentence as a whole:

והארץ היתה תהו ובהו וחשך על פני תהום ורוח אלהים מרחפת על פני המים

    And the earth was formless and void and darkness [was] upon [the] face of the deep and [the] spirit Elohim [was] hovering upon [the] face [of] the waters.

Note that the word "and spirit" is a mnemonic word with the value of 2, and the word "hovering" is a calculating word that indicates the value of the previous noun should be duplicated. While there is a על "upon" that follows "hovering" we do not subtract it from the sum because the word is a verb which renders the "upon" as inert.

Other mnemonic words that represent the value of 2 are באפיו, *beap-paw*, which means "nostrils", and "wings".

These numbers carry with them universal ideas of wholeness in all creation, both manifest (700) and universal (800). The multiples of 7 and 8 are common measurements in Ugaritic literary texts.

2 + 800 = the total sum of the values of the letters of the Hebrew alphabet:

ב   +   רקצפעסנמלכיטחזוהדשגא = 802

All these numerical constructions try to show that everything created is from God.

Aleph (1) A

The pictogram of the *aleph* is of an ox head. The original name of the
letter is thought to be אלף, *eleph* (111), which means "cattle", but also
"leader" or "teacher". It is one half of the word אל, *al* or *el*, which means
"God".

This letter corresponds with Genesis 1:3–5:

> ויאמר אלהים יהי אור ויהי אור
>
> And said Elohim Let there be light and there was light.

From which we have the following sum of the nouns:

> 500 = אלהים אור אור

Genesis 1:4:

> וירא אלהים את האור כי טוב ויבדל אלהים בין האור ובין החשך
>
> And saw Elohim the light because good and divided Elohim
> between the light and between the darkness.

From which we have the sum:

> 500 = אלהים האור טוב גם וק ול'

So Genesis 1:3–4 is 500 + 500 = 1000, which is the value of the *aleph* when
it is written larger than the normal size.

There are two *alephs* on the Seven Palaces, one symbolizing light and
day and the other symbolic of darkness and night.

And Genesis 1:5:

ויקרא אלהים לאור יום ולחשך קרא לילה ויהי ערב ויהי בקר יום אחד

And he called Elohim to light; day and darkness called night and there was evening and there was morning a day One.

Gimel (3) G

According to Douglas Petrovich,[16] the original name of O38 is thought to be גהר (208) which means "bend".

According to Jeff A. Benner the pictogram of origin was a picture of a foot, but it is difficult to imagine a less likely origin for this letter because according to Genesis its power was over the creation of שמים ("sky"). Brian Colless thought it might have been a boomerang, and Christopher Rollston ventured the idea that it might be a *gami* ("throw stick"), which does have the virtue of getting thrown into the sky. Likewise, something can be said for "bend" which may be an allusion to the traditional pose of the Goddess Nwt as the night sky, bending over the earth. The picture is probably connected to a door lintel, since the word: המשקוף ("the lintel") branches into related words suggesting the supporting of weight.

Shin (3) Sh

There is some controversy about this one. Douglas Petrovich believes the origin of the Shin to be from this sign D27, שדים (57), which means "breasts", but I have my doubts about whether a symbol for a pair of breasts was employed to represent the value of three.

[illegible] I have an alternative suggestion that fits the pattern of the available data. To me, this sign looks remarkably similar to N25: ⌒⌒⌒ which means "hill-country", usually in the sense of "foreign lands" and "desert lands", and it appears to have a continuity of meaning in Genesis. Verses 1:9–10 are corresponded to the *shin*, from which we learn a key thing about the qualities of the letter, namely that it's power is fire, heat and "drying out" land, separating it from the waters and seas:

ויאמר אלהים יקוו המים מתחת השמים אל מקום אחד ותראה היבשה ויהי כן

ויקרא אלהים ליבשה ארץ ולמקוה המים קרא ימים וירא אלהים כי טוב:

And said Elohim, "Let the waters under the sky be gathered into one place, so that the dry land may appear." And it was so.

And called Elohim the dry land "earth," and the gathering of waters He called "seas." And saw Elohim it was good.

In the *Ashuri* script, the letter *shin* would be associated with fire and heat, and I think it stayed true to the attributes of its parent and grandparent script in this. The *shin* was needed to dry things out after the primordial waters had receded. Perhaps the ancients imagined the bumpy, hilly nature of the world like bread rising in an oven.

We can see three hills (or mountains) in the hieroglyph, so the number is right for the letter value, but if we consider that the hills on either side are truncated in half, then we have three hills from two triangles, which may carry a numerical perspective about the creation of the cosmos therein. In Genesis, creation begins from the House of God, which is the *beth* (2) and this separates into two *alephs* (1) + (1) and from this emerges the 3.

The fiery quality of the letter *shin* may also be corroborated by the *Sepher Yetzirah*:

[*Beth*] First, is the Spirit of the Living God ...
[*Aleph*] Second, from the Spirit he made Air ...
[*Gimel*] Third, Primitive Water ...
[*Shin*] Fourth, from the Water, He designed Fire ...

The author of the *Sepher Yetzirah* had an obvious bias towards Greek and was attempting a depiction of ten ineffable existences, but it's interesting that a list of the priestly order of the alphabet places *shin* as the fourth letter in the alphabet which corresponds to Fire in the SY list. The clincher in Genesis 1:9 is that היבשה ("the Dry Land") is a mnemonic word for the letter *shin* and carries the value of 3.

Daleth (4) D

There is a broad and long standing consensus about this sign that it is the drawing of a door to a building or tent. The original name in Hebrew is דלת, *daleth*, which means "door", and there are known mnemonic words meaning "door" or "doors" that carry that value of 4, such as דלתות ("doors").

This letter was represented in Temple architecture by the two "doors" of the first temple, one of which was open during the day while the other door opened only at night. These two doors represented the two Palaces of the Daleth; one on the daylight side and the other on the nightside, and through them the souls of all beings passed each way between the planes of heaven and earth. This belief guided the creation of the daily door-opening rituals at the first Temple that occurred at dusk and dawn.

These are quite esoteric and abstract concepts that are difficult to convey in a narrative about creation. The scribe of Genesis 1 has had to fall back on allusions. In the narrative plan, God has made the heavens and the earth and produced light and dark and the sky, the dry land and the seas. But this is the first time that anything living has existed on earth, thus it is the first time that living beings pass through the door between heaven and earth to inhabit the material world, and they are given the ability to reproduce their material form too.

> Then Elohim said, 'Let the earth bring forth vegetation: seed-bearing plants and fruit trees, each bearing fruit with seed according

to its kind.' And it was so. The earth produced vegetation: seed-bearing plants according to their kinds and trees bearing fruit with seed according to their kinds.

Genesis 1:11–12

But 1 Kings 6:31 offers us a more direct insight in the narration of the design elements and craftsmanship that went into the Temple doors. Solomon carves angels and palm trees and open flowers into the doors, and then covers the whole thing in gold:

> In the same way he made four-sided doorposts of olive wood for the sanctuary entrance. The two doors were made of cypress wood, and each had two folding panels. He carved into them cherubim, palm trees, and open flowers; and he overlaid them with gold, hammered evenly over the carvings.

They must have been impressive doors to walk through, knowing that they symbolized crossing over from the earth into the realms of heaven and the afterlife.

Tav (4) Th

Again, there are ongoing discussions over this sign. Is the origin of the *tav* a four-petaled flower M42 as suggested by Douglas Petrovich? ✣

Or two crossed sticks as suggested by Jeff Benner? (Z9–11) Could Christopher Rollston be correct in his guess that it was an owners mark?

I take my starting point from the relevant verses for the *tav* which concern the power of "time" and the calendar:

לאתת והיו הלילה ובין היום בין להבדיל השמים ברקיע מארת יהי אלהים ויאמר
ושנים: ולימים ולמועדים

[and let them be] for signs and for seasons and for days and
years.

Genesis 1:14

(7 * 70) 490 = לאתת ולמועדים ולימים ושנים

490 is ten Sabbatical (49) years, which is a full span of time. It may be
that the original name of the letter *tav* was עת, *eth* ("time"), but unfortunately we cannot check the name by testing it with the set value of 4,
because measuring words by convention do not hold any value.

The four petals of the flower, or four mouths, depending upon
how you see it, appear to represent "the signs", "the seasons", "the
days", and "the years", and it's inclusion suggests that the alphabet
(the "signs") was used in time-keeping and identified primarily by
the scribe with time-keeping rather than writing. Perhaps the *tav* sign
acquired those meanings in a place where numeracy for time-keeping,
money, and keeping a tally of things were ubiquitous, but reading and
writing skills were less known in the wider population.

If the *tav* sign originated as four mouths, then because one of the
meanings of the mouth in Egyptian mathematics was to indicate fractions, here it may signal the how the signs, the seasons, the days and the
years were split up into four divisions—four fractions of a whole circle
for the seasons and the years—the spring and autumn equinoxes and
summer and winter solstices. And for the days, dusk and midnight, and
morning and noon.

Finally, I think we should compare this sign with the sign for eternal
life, the ankh. If the *tav* cross indicates time, then the loop must represent life, which is made eternal from being bound to the cross. The very
similarity of the ankh with the cross is extra corroboration.

Heh (5) H, E

The sign of the *heh* is believed to come from the A28 sign in the Gardiner list. Rollston believes this little man is calling out. Petrovich thinks his arms are raised in praise. Other authors suggest "jubilation". I think this little man has his arms raised to the sky in a prayer of thanks for the light.

The Hieroglyphic source of the Heh.

That's very specific, but my conjecture comes from Genesis 1:16b–17:

> And the stars and set them Elohim in the expanse of the sky for the light upon the earth.

This is more important than it sounds at first. In the Genesis narrative, the hidden portion of the story indicates that the fruit of the tree of knowledge was "light", and by "eating" it (adding it to their own number and taking on its qualities), Adam and Eve became subject to the divine decree that Elohim made in 1:17 for light, and had no choice but to go forth to incarnate into the earth below, carrying their inner light with them.

On the Seven Palaces the *heh* appears high up on the diagram before the throne of God, but the *heh* also governs the first Palace below where the earth is—the object of illumination.

As the *Bahir* says, "There is a Heh above and a Heh below".[17]

There are actually two egyptian Hieroglyphs for the Heh. Besides the hieroglyph of a man with his arms raised to the sky, there is also an alternative version of a man sitting.

Vav (6) U, V, W

The PCS *vav* is believed to have come from the pictogram O30. Suggestions for this picture are: a tent peg, mace, and a pillar support. The Genesis verses associated with the *vav* concern the creation of birds and sea creatures of all kinds.

Whereas in the verses for the *daleth*, where every bit of vegetation was given a seed with the potential for generation within itself, in the verses of the *vav* God gives an active commandment to "be fruitful and multiply" (ברו). If this was a tent peg, perhaps the item was suggested for its sameness to others of its set, thus carrying the idea of replication and multiplication. The use of the *vav* as a prefix means "and".

These verses written for the *vav* are also the first time God gives his blessing. In gematria terms, a "blessing" means that the value of the noun next to it is to be multiplied by 2.

Elohim goes on to give his second blessing to the creation of man, which occurs under the domain of the *cheth*. Both of the paths of the *cheth* and the *vav* are connected to the Palace of the Beth and are at the top of the Seven Palaces.

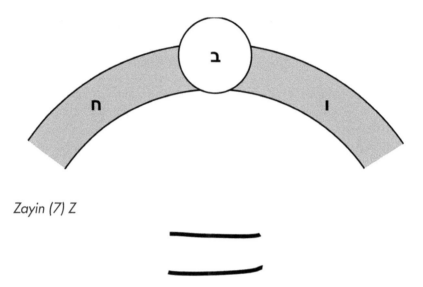

Zayin (7) Z

The *zayin* is thought by Petrovich to have come from sign D13 in the Gardiner catalogue: ⌒‿‿, and he suggests that the original name of the letter is זעה, which means "sweat" (i.e. "from the brow"). Jeff Benner suggests a "mattock" (a primitive type of ax), or a "hoe" or a "plow". I favor the latter suggestion because the Genesis verse for the *zayin* concerns the creation of cattle and bugs which are primary symbols of fertility, but perhaps the brow is a factor as lines in it can be likened to a furrow in a field.

> And said Elohim, "Let the earth bring forth living creatures according to their kinds: livestock, land crawlers, and beasts of the earth according to their kinds." And it was so. Elohim made the beasts of the earth according to their kinds, the livestock according to their kinds, and everything that crawls upon the earth according to its kind. And saw Elohim that it was good.
>
> Genesis 1:24–25

Cheth (8) Ch

In the Genesis verses associated with this letter, human beings are created. "Male and female he created them", and "in the image" of Elohim. People have suggested the pictogram is of a tent wall, a fence, or a hut, and may potentially have been from V2, which is a stylized candle wick twisted or bound together.

I could easily see in the candle wick a symbol of the human being, still and virgin before receiving the flame (consciousness), then living while lit (with consciousness), but then being snuffed out by an invisible hand leaving only the candlewick (the charred body) in its place. Perhaps the three twists represent the three parts of the soul—*nephesh, ruach* and *neshamah*—or have some relevance to the five parts of the Egyptian soul.

Of these five parts, the *ren* was the name. The *ba* was the personality. The *sheut* was the shadow twin. The *ib* was a metaphysical heart that felt and thought, and was endowed with will and intention. The *ka* was the vital spark of living flame that warmed you and kept you alive, thus the way the aging of David was described in 1 Kings was that he grew cold.

Teth (9) T

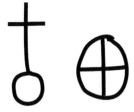

Petrovich thinks this sign is from F35, which is a picture of a heart and windpipe. Phonetically it represents the word *nfr*, which means "good" or "beautiful". The Hebrew version would be *tov* ("good"). Benner suggests the origin of the sign was a basket. Rollston thinks a spindle. I think it is a heart, windpipe, and a stomach attached, because the theme of this letter in Genesis 1:29–30 is all about food:

> Behold, I have given you every seed-bearing plant on the face of all the earth, and every tree whose fruit contains seed. They will be yours for food. And to every beast of the earth and every bird of the air and every creature that crawls upon the earth—everything that has the breath of life in it—I have given every green plant for food.
>   [The word for 'food' is also used to mean "for fuel" (i.e. for a fire).]

Aleister Crowley felt the macrocosmic associations to this letter, and thus to the tarot, were awfully pedestrian, and so he widened the definition to be "all material delights and things which are a pleasure to the senses."

Yod (10) I, Y

Everyone agrees that the Yod comes from the pictogram of an arm (D36) and hand (D47).

The name "*yod*" means "hand". The arm and hand were associated with work, and thus implicitly rest from work, and the Genesis verses that are associated with this letter speak of the completion of creation and God resting from work. In Genesis 2:3 it says:

ויברך אלהים את-יום השביעי ויקדש אתו כי בו שבת מכל-מלאכתו אשר-ברא אלהים לעשות:

And blessed Elohim + day the seventh and sanctified it for in it Shabbat (he rested) from all the work that created Elohim to make.

This gives us the following calculation:

אלהים אלהים ז ז מלאכתו אשר ברא אלהים לעשות = 900

This calculation includes everything in the line after "מכל" ("from all"), and note the 7 7 7 in there, because the seven has been "sanctified" (multiplied by two). The word "Elohim" is also written twice because to bless something is to multiply the next word by two. We will cover these conventions later, but the illusion drawn by 90 (*tsade*) multiplied by 10 (*yod*) may be to a woman resting after laboring to birth a child. The thirty-nine categories of activities that Jews refrain from on Shabbat are called *avot melachot*, which means "parent labors".

> One of the themes that appear on many different levels in the Torah
> is the process of birth, whether of the universe, an individual or
> the Jewish people. ... The creation of the cosmos can be seen in the
> allegorical context of G-d giving birth to the world.
>
> Rabbi Avraham Arieh Trugman

With these verses for the *yod*, all the letters of the holy Name YHVH have been described, and so the scribe only begins to write the name YHVH for the first time after these verses. This is why only "Elohim" is written in chapter one and in 2:1–3.

Kaph (20) K

This probably comes from pictogram D28 which shows 2 hands and arms connected.

The word כף, *kaph* means "palm branch" as in the tree. The Genesis verses are rather obscure but may be related to the fertility of water (and the water cycle) in the form of a primordial mist rising from the earth prior to vegetation being created on it, and to rain. Exactly how or why these ideas are related to two hands is unknown to me, but palm trees have a relatively high water use compared to other desert trees.

There is an example of notariqon in Genesis 2:6 that includes the name of the letter כפה (*KPH*):

‫ואד יעלה מן הארץ והשקה את כל פני האדמה‬ =
‫וים הוא כפה‬

Which means "And the sea is a *kaph*."

The word ‫וְהִשְׁקָה‬, meaning "watered" or "rained" has the set value of 20 for the Kaph.

‫האדמה פני כ הארץ + ואד‬ = 500 − (b.g)

The gematria sum of the verse replaces the word for "watered" or "rained" with the *mem* (40), and subtracts the mist from the ground:

‫הארץ – ואד + מ פני האדמה‬ = 520

$520 = 26 \times 20$.

In the Zohar the mist is interpreted to mean the yearning of the female for the male.

Lamed (30) L

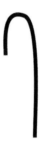

This is one of the more mysterious letters in the alphabet. It is the second letter of the Hebrew word for God, ‫אל‬, and the word ‫למד‬, *lamad*, means "to teach" or "to learn". The pictogram is thought to be a shepherd's crook or a goad by most authorities. The Genesis verse for this letter is 2:7:

> Then YHVH Elohim formed man from the dust of the ground and breathed the breath of life into his nostrils, and the man became a living being.

From which we extract the following sum:

‫יהוה אלהים + האדם + עפר – האדמה + ב נ חיים האדם נ חיה‬ = 700.

This is quite a complex sum with calculating words and mnemonics and we won't go into the technicalities here, but translated, the sum says: YHVH + Elohim + the Adam + Dust – the ground + B + N + Life + the Adam + N + to live. The value of 700 is probably there to emphasize that this letter was there at the beginning of all creation. Through the power of the letter *lamed* all living things possess a soul that can both learn from its mistakes and be instructed from the divine blueprint within us all.

Now you might imagine that the word למד, *lamad*, would be a mnemonic word (see Ch. 4 d.) with the value of 30, and it's the first thing I checked out when I studied this letter, but no! למד is indeed a mnemonic but it carries the value of the *aleph*, 1, like the word אהב, *ahab*, which means "love". The theological implications are fascinating and may point to an early period of ancient Near Eastern history when God had a wife—his Asherah.

In simple mathematical terms it draws a numerical equivalence between אל ("God") and יהוה אלהים, *YHVH Elohim*.

"God" is אל = *aleph* + *lamed*. *Eleph* = 111. *Lamad* = 1. 111 + 1= 112 which is the total of יהוה אלהים, *YHVH Elohim*. The gematria encapsulates the idea of God as being the great teacher of all.

אל God
AL
AΛ
Aleph Lamed
teacher, leader
Eleph Lamad
to teach, learn
אלף למד
(mnemonic)
111 + 1
112
YHVH ALHIM
יהוה אלהים

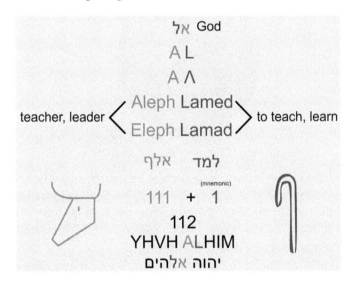

Note that 111 is the mnemonic for אשה ("woman"), and (made in God's image) originally Adam was both male and female; thus to reflect

God's divine qualities, the letters of their name must be both male and female.

The letters of the name אדם, ADM, may have been borrowed from each side of אלף, ALP, and למד, LMD.

Mem (40) M

Most authorities believe the original name of letter *mem* was מים, *mayim*, which means "waters". Yet *mayim* isn't a mnemonic of the letter *mem*, and the Genesis verse for the *mem* doesn't mention water at all:

ויטע יהוה אלהים גן בעדן מקדם וישם שם את האדם אשר יצר

And planted YHVH Elohim garden in Eden east and he placed the name + the Adam that he formed.

The symbol of Shamash.

We need to delve a little into ancient Egyptian solar mythology to appreciate this letter. Each day, the Goddess Nwt gets pregnant with the sun and delivers in the East. The rising Sun emerges from the waters of the seas at dawn. In the picture below, the Goddess Nwt is attended by two midwives, probably Isis and Nephthys.

The main theme of this letter is more complicated than a simple water symbol. It's the fertility of water that is key here, and the pregnancy of the Goddess who carries the sun child within her waters each day and is delivered of the infant Ra/Shamash.

From the book of day—the astronomical ceiling tomb of Ramses IV.

40 weeks is roughly the length of a human pregnancy.

In the Bible, the creation of Adam has a parallel gestation in the context of Semitic myth. No Goddess is mentioned but the name of the Adam (his image) is placed in the east until such a time in the biblical narrative that he ingests the fruit of the tree of knowledge (light) and is thus obliged to descend to earth, as is the divinely decreed purpose of all light.

The Hebrew Word for "sun", שמש, shamash, represents two parts fire and one part water, but the common symbol for shamash is a four pointed star with four rays of light shining from it. These rays are reminiscent of the proto-consonantal mem. Might this letter have been first associated with shamash, and then later with Adam, the biblical hero of the solar journey?

The mem is central to the name shamash, with the two shins surrounding it, and no doubt it was thought that the face of the sun had a reflective, shining, watery quality about it, within its fiery ball. Fire by itself emits light, but not in the same reflecting, shining way of water.

The Pillar of Jachin is associated with the mem on the Seven Palaces, which may explain a verse in the Yalkut Shimoni, Bereshit 1:3, which describes how God created the heavens with pillars of water.

Nun (50) N

The original name of this letter is believed by Petrovich to be *nachash*, which means "serpent". Other authorities have suggested the pictograph to be plant shoots, but I concur with Petrovich because *nachash* is a mnemonic with the value of 50 for this letter.

This letter concerns mortality, death, and the afterlife.

The Genesis verse for the *nun* is 2:9:

> ויצמח יהוה אלהים מן האדמה כל עץ נחמד למראה וטוב למאכל ועץ החיים בתוך הגן ועץ הדעת טוב ורע:
>
> Out of the ground the LORD God gave growth to every tree that is pleasing to the eye and good for food. And in the middle of the garden were the tree of life and the tree of the knowledge of good and evil.

The theme of the letter is taken up in Genesis 3, where the serpent denies to Eve that eating the fruit of the tree of knowledge would lead to her death. Note that the words "die" and "death" carry the set value of 50 for the letter *nun*, so the phrase מות תמתון, ("die, you will die") in Genesis 3:4 is 100.

Samekh (60) S

There were two signs used for this letter in different localities. Petrovich thinks the original names of these letters were ס\שער, *sear*, and סרה, Sarah, with the first symbol representing "hair", and the second symbol being a fish with the projected original word meaning "stink".

Jeff Benner thinks the letter may have come from the pictogram of a thorn, and may carry the meanings of "grab" and "protect". But the Genesis verses for this letter leave no doubt that the first sign is a branching river and the fish sign refers to the river connection:

> Now a river flowed out of Eden to water the garden, and from there
> it parted and became four heads.
>
> Genesis 2:10

I like the suggestion of the word Sarah for the original letter *samekh's* name because it has the value of 265, which is the gate value of the *samekh* on the Seven Palaces. I don't think it carries as much weight as a name that is a mnemonic, but then again, perhaps not all of the original letter names were used as mnemonics for one reason or another.

Ayin (70) O

There's little doubt about the original name of this letter. *Ayin* is עין ("eye"). The pictogram for the letter looks like an eye, and the word עין is a mnemonic of the letter with the value of 70, as are words that mean "eyes", "the eye", and variations.

The Genesis verses (2:15–16) for this letter involve the temptation of the fruit (the light) of the tree of knowledge of good and evil, and it is here that God delivers his warning to Adam:

> And took YHVH Elohim the man and put him in the Garden of
> Eden to tend and to keep it. And ordered YHVH Elohim to the
> Adam saying "Every tree of the garden all they shall eat. but of the
> tree of the knowledge good and evil not shall eat from his number,
> for in the day that you shall eat from his number die shall die!"

By analogy, the word עין ("eye") can also imply a fountain or spring (as the "eye" of the landscape) as we see in Genesis 16:7 about the flight of Hagar:

> And found her, the Malak [angel or spirit-king] YHVH by an eye
> of the waters in the wilderness by the eye on the way to Shur.

The phrasing of this may suggest either that the Malak and Hagar were besides the eye of the waters, but it could also be that the Malak was the letter *ayin* itself. Ancient superstitions and beliefs are attached to such springs of water that emerge from the earth, and inevitably in most cultures these places became sacrosanct and were imagined to be the domain of spirit beings.

Peh (80) P

There is no difficulty about this letter either. It is a picture of a mouth, and פה, *peh*, means "mouth".

The Genesis verses for the *peh* discuss the will of God to find a companion for the Adam. So he creates all the beasts of the field and birds of the air and brings them to the Adam to name them, but among them there couldn't be found a suitable companion. Is this to be wondered at? The Adam was both masculine and feminine, but the other beings made by God were either male or female.

The concepts that surround the naming of other beings denotes a type of superstition around the spoken word. To know the name of a being loaned some type of power over it. It was fitting that higher beings should know the name of lower ones, but if a lower being knew the name of a higher being or a God, then this was thought to be against the natural order of things—it could invoke chaos because it was by the mouth of god and through the speech of God are things brought into this world; into manifestation.

Tsade (90) Ts

   This letter is eighteenth in the priestly order of the alephbet, and it corresponds to Genesis 2:21–23. The pictogram of the *tsade* is thought by Petrovich to be from V33,[18] which is the image of a sack, while Benner believes this letter comes from a different hieroglyph which is something to do with following a trail or a hunt.[19] I see it as a newborn baby wrapped in swaddling, or even the placenta.

   At the current time of writing, the known mnemonic words for the *tsade* are: "Corners" (obviously for the 90 degrees), "Bone" (or "Marrow" would be more accurate), "Flesh", and "Sack". Petrovich comes closest to establishing a hieroglyphic origin for the *tsade*, but if we think of a "fleshy sack" we arrive at the idea of the placenta, and this is perfectly in keeping with the Kabbalistic tradition also. In Kabbalah, the separation of the first woman from the first man that occurs in Genesis (2:21–23) is regarded as the first "birth".

   Verse 2:21 of Genesis describes the powers of the *tsade*, employs the *mem* (pregnancy) and the *tsade* in the word מצלעתיו to mean "from their ribs" or "from their side" to explain the birth of "this one" (Eve). In 2:23 Adam describes the Woman as "עצם מעצמי", the "bone from my bones":

> And made fall YHVH Elohim a deep sleep on the Adam and he slept and took one from his ribs (or his side) and closed up the flesh in its place. And made YHVH Elohim + the rib (side) that he's taken from to Woman and brought her to the Adam. And said Adam "This one is the now bone from my bones and flesh from my flesh to this one be called Woman because from man was taken this one."

The phrasing of עצם מעצמי ובשר מבשרי ("Bone of my bone and flesh of my flesh"), uses four mnemonic words, each with the value of 90, and for a total of 360—the value of degrees in a circle, which makes both a numerical allusion to the *tsade* and a visual one. The symbolic and magical value of a circle for birth, divinity and beginnings shouldn't be overlooked either.

Giving birth in ancient Egypt was a magical process for women. The birthing bricks of Abydos depict women in labor as having sky-blue hair rather than the normal Egyptian black, indicating that the woman had taken on a divine role, possibly emulating the Goddess Nwt in her daily birthing of the sun.

The placenta had its own hieroglyph, and in royal processions, a standard bearer would carry the symbol of the placenta aloft. According to the magical thinking of the Egyptians, the placenta was believed to be inhabited by a twin soul which could pose a danger to the newborn, so disposing of it safely was a priority. Some scholars suggest that royalty had a second tomb made for the placenta. But while it is possible that high-borns may have built tombs, common people typically buried the placenta somewhere secret to protect the child, or else they threw it in the river (where it was probably eaten by a crocodile).

There are several biblical Hebrew words using the *tsade* in their root that suggest a connection with birth.

צא, *TsA*, means "go", "go forth", "go out", "come out" or "leave". In Genesis 8:16, Noah is told to "go out" from the Ark with his wife and sons, and this may be seen as symbolic of leaving the womb.

יצא, *ITsA*, also carries the sense of "bringing forth", often the bringing forth of life. In Genesis 15:4 it is used directly in the sense of an emission in the phrase "brought forth from your body", and in Joshua 6:4 the phrase "… nor shall be brought forth from your mouth a word …" is used in the sense of a birth metaphor. To speak, "to say something" was to bring that "something" into manifestation (even if only slightly).

מצה, *MTsH*, is a word that comprises both the *mem* of pregnancy and the *tsade* of childbirth. The word has two senses with this spelling. For one, it can mean the unleavened bread or cake—the Matzah that was eaten prior to the exodus of the Hebrew people from Egypt. The other meaning is strife or struggle, possibly originating from the pain and struggle of women in childbirth. Rabbi Yitzchak Luria conceptualized the exodus as the birth of the Hebrew people and likened Egypt to a womb,[20] which makes sense because the word for Egypt is מצרים which is a plural of מצ.

Qoph (100) Q

According to Jeff Benner, "when all of the words derived from this parent root Φ [qoph] are compared the common theme of a circle or revolution is found." Benner also theorizes that the line was probably originally horizontal and represented the horizon. Douglas Petrovich thinks V25 (a spun fiber) is the origin of the pictogram and puts forward *qur* as the original name of the letter.

Other suggestions have been that it's a sewing needle, the eye of a needle, or that it's a monkey from the fact that קוף means both "monkey" and "needle". קף has the value of 180 which is the number of degrees in half a circle.

קו, *qav* means "a line", or "a cord". It is sometimes translated as "measuring line".

Might the word קוף, *qoph*, come from קצף, *qatsaph*? When we apply the Reversal Cipher it spells אשת meaning "women". *Qatsaph* carries the meanings of "to break off" or "splinter" as well as "to anger" or "to make furious". Now as we'll see later, the words אשה ("woman") and אשת ("women") are mnemonic words, not with the value of 100 for the *qoph* but with the value of 111, which is the same value as the name אלף, *aleph*. In verse 21 (the birth of Eve) the narrative makes a bit of wordplay out of this value; Adam calls Eve three times by the term "this one" as he is proclaiming her to be "Woman".

It's possible that the Hebrew characters of Adam and Eve were partially based on, or at least inspired by, Egyptian creation myths. קף carries the meaning of "to bend" or "to arch", which may be connected with the blue Sky Woman, Nwt, who is depicted bending over the red male earth, Geb. The name אדם, Adam, is the same word for "red" or "scarlet" which would identify his mythological origins with Geb, and this would of course link "the Woman"[21] with the Goddess Nwt.

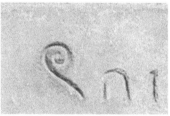

The Egyptian hieroglyph that represents 100 is a spiral. For 10 there is a heel shape but it takes little imagination to see in it a simplification of the "bending over" of the Goddess Nwt. The last sign for 1 is just a vertical line or a cord. If we dig a little deeper into Gardiner's sign list we discover that the spiral (Z7) is a hieratic variant of G43, which is a picture of a quail chick and we see that two quail chicks carry the sense of "end". The biblical Hebrew word for "end" is קֵץ, QTs.

111 is this context represents more than the cumulative increase of the number 1 by a factor of 10 and 100, but is relative to concepts about the relationship between the microcosm and the macrocosm—between the individual and the cosmos.

The Genesis verse for the *qoph* is 2:24:

> Therefore shall leave a man + his father and mother and he is joined in his wife and become flesh one.[22]

In the next verse we learn that "the Woman" and "the Adam" are naked, which may suggest that "the Woman" is associated with the Moon as counterpart to the masculine associations made to the Sun.

Resh (200) R

The origin of the *resh* has never been in dispute. It is D1 on Gardiner's sign list. The original name of the letter was ראש, which means "head", and was sometimes used in the sense of "to lead", "top", "to be first/ chief", and "beginning".

The Genesis verse for the letter *resh* is the last verse in the chapter, 2:25:

ויהיו שניהם ערומים האדם ואשתו ולא יתבששו

And then those two were naked the man and his wife and not ashamed.

ערומים (meaning "were naked") is a mnemonic for the letter *ayin* (70), and ואשתו (meaning "and his wife") is a mnemonic word with the value of 111.

By multiplication the sum is:

2 × 70 × 50 × 111 = 777,000.

Or rather:

איק × נ × ע × ב = 777,000.

I'm guessing that the scribe wanted to give us a grand finale as he finished off his scroll.

By addition it is 2 + 70 + 50 + 111 = 233, which is the gate value of the Palace of the Letter Beth.

777 + 233 = 1010, which is the total value of all the letters upon the Seven Palaces, minus the *beth* as that is reserved for the beginning of creation from within the house of God.

Using the Reversal Cipher, the value of the letter *beth* is 200, which is the Biblical Gematria value of the letter *resh*. The first word of the Bible is composed of the prefix *beth* (meaning "in") and the word *Reshith*, which is derived from the word *rosh*, which is the original name of the letter *resh*. In this fashion the end and the beginning are united.

c. Paleo-Hebrew/Phoenician/Ktav Ivri

2	1	3	3	4	4	5	6	7	8	9
૭	⟨	٦	w	◁	✕	⋽	Y	ㅍ	੪	⊗
2	1	3	3	4	4	5	6	7	8	9

10	11	12	13	14	15	16	17	18	19	20
┭	㇠	∠	⅋	㇆	〒	o	㇉	㇫	ㇷ	٩
10	20	30	40	50	60	70	80	90	100	200

Inscriptions made with Paleo-Hebrew appear in the archaeological record from around the tenth century BCE. In 1979, two tiny silver scrolls were discovered at Ketef Hinnom, inscribed with Paleo-Hebrew extracts from the Book of Numbers. They were dated to the end of the seventh century BCE and preserve the earliest known citations of texts that are also found in the Hebrew Bible.[23]

Some letters of the Paleo-Hebrew script are visually similar to their PCS origins, only more stylized. Others bear only a brief resemblance. They represent their alphabetic order value as well as a Biblical Gematria value.

Like the PCS script that came before it, Paleo-Hebrew was written both left to right and right to left, but unlike the *Ashuri* script that would come after it, it possessed no *sofit* forms. These are special forms of some letters that are used at the end of words. It is likely that many biblical texts were originally composed in the Paleo-Hebrew script but were later written, letter-for-letter, in the Assyrian script.

Starting with the return of the captives from Babylon, the Paleo-Hebrew script was gradually replaced with *Ktav Ashuri*, although we can tell by the Dead Sea Scrolls that it continued to be written by small pockets of people right up until the first century CE. In some of the scrolls found in the Quram cave, the Ashuri script was used for most of the document but the name of God was written in Paleo-Hebrew.

d. Modern Hebrew/Ktav Ashuri

The main difference between Paleo-Hebrew and its descendent *Ktav Ashuri* in terms of the gematria of the scripts, is that Paleo-Hebrew had only twenty-two characters and no *sofit* forms.

The earliest adoption of *Ktav Ashuri* happened following the exile of the Kingdom of Judah in the sixth century BCE. By the first century BCE, *Ktav Ashuri* had become the dominant writing script and eventually became today's normative Jewish Hebrew script:

זקףותסרקצפעסנמלכיטחזוהדגבא

Ktav Ashuri has some features that are not present in the Paleo-Hebrew alphabet, namely the *sofit* forms (or final forms).

In some late gematria ciphers, these final forms are given different numbers ranging from 500–900, and this gave rise to the mistaken idea that Hebrew gematria was copied from Greek Isopsephy, however in the Bible the *sofit* letters are numbered the same as their counterparts, because they first acquired their value with the Paleo-Hebrew writing script.

The extended form of gematria was never actually used, except as a guide to which letters of the Greek alphabet should represent what Hebrew letter and Biblical Gematria value. Rather than seeking to find a letter-to-letter correspondence that was based on any historical origin of the Greek letters, the ancient scribes mapped the Hebrew cover-cipher

("Standard Gematria") to the Greek cover-cipher ("Standard Isopse-phy") and then used the mapping of the cover-cipher to the Biblical Gematria cipher to determine the numerical value of the Greek letters.

e. The Galay writing script

I can't end this section without mentioning a new writing script of my own design that works for Hebrew even better than it works for English. I created Galay from the spatial arrangement of the Seven Palaces. The letter positions on the Seven Palaces creates a writing script that is both logographic and alphabetical.

An example of the Galay writing script.

Logographic scripts have thousands of word glyphs to memorize, so before you read a word you have to remember it. Therefore it can take more than a decade to properly read a logographic script, whereas you can read Galay from the moment you can recall twenty-two spatial positions, which takes days at most, or hours—not years.

With practice, Galay readers move from deductive reading to glyph recognition until it becomes automatic, which makes the process of reading much faster!

אשת בטח גמלתהו דרשה היתה היתה ותקם זממה חגרה טעמה ידיה כפה לא מרבדים נודע סדין עז
פיה צופיה קמו רבות שקר יהוה תנו = ‎777.

The Alphabetic Acrostic of Proverbs 31:10–31.

CHAPTER 6

Ciphers

There have been a great many ciphers invented in diverse writing scripts over thousands of years; however, it is the ones that were actually used that are of special interest to us.

There is simply no point to using a cipher that is different from the one which is embedded in a text. If you're not working on a text like the Tanakh or the New Testament or the Talmud or the Zohar or one of Aleister Crowley's voluminous works, and if you're just cherry picking correspondences out of a hat, what you're engaged in is numerology, not gematria.

a. The Genesis Order

Although it is rarely used, the Genesis Order begins this list because we see in it the origin of ancient Hebrew rhetoric math. Biblical Gematria and the Reversal Cipher were preferred for their higher value spreads, but the Genesis Order Cipher is a simple numerical sequence for the Hebrew letters between 1 and 20, in this order, from right to left:

באגשדתההוזחטיכלמנסעפצקר

The sum of all the letters in the Genesis Order is 217, which is אל ("God"), 31 × 7.

1 + 2 + 3 + 3 + 4 + 4 + 5 + 6 + 7 + 8 + 9 + 10 + 11 + 12 + 13 + 14 + 15 + 16 + 17 + 18 + 19 + 20 = 217.

Some people don't accept this cipher simply because it is not in the usual alphabetic sequence of *aleph, beth, gimel, daleth, heh,* and so on. They argue that various stele have been discovered with the regular alphabetic order on them, which is true. But the Genesis Order reflects the categories by which God created the world, arising from within the House of God (*beth*), and then dividing between the day and the night (*aleph*). It was a priestly order, rather than being a general order that was allowed to be known by other peoples outside of the tribes, such as the Canaanites and the Phoenicians.

The Genesis order has a low value numerical spread, which makes the likelihood of you finding domain-related values in a small piece of text increase exponentially. The Genesis Order Cipher is used sparingly in the Tanakh—only twice that I know of: as a type of "table of contents" for Genesis 1–2, and in the context of an alphabetic acrostic in Proverbs 31 that spanned twenty-three words to produce the value 777.

Genesis 1–2 instructs us on the identity of the letters and their heavenly qualities as spirits of God. Every verse is about the qualities of a letter of the alphabet, and every verse has gematria as a comment upon the letter. It uses the Genesis Order as an index that corresponds to an underlying ancient map of the cosmos (the Seven Palaces). Though the verses are laid out according to the Genesis Order, the gematria of the verses are composed in Biblical Gematria, as is true for most of the Tanakh.

The following sum is composed using the Genesis Order with Proverbs 31:10–31, which have an alphabetic acrostic. The first word from each verse is counted, as well as the name of God, יהוה, which is in verse 30. The calculation has 86 characters, and 86 is the sum for אלהים, Elohim. Proverbs 31 declares itself to be the Words of King Lemuel, and the Oracle taught to him by his mother. No other mention is made of this King in the Tanakh, but Jewish legend identifies him as Solomon, taking this advice from his mother Bathsheba:

אשת בטח גמלתהו דרשה היתה ותקם זממה חגרה טעמה ידיה כפה לא מרבדים נודע סדין עז פיה צופיה קמו רבות שקר יהוה תנו [= 777].

It's an interesting and comparatively rare example of the Genesis Order Cipher being used, and in both cases it is only used when it can be supported by another feature of the text to define all the elements in the composition, such as an alphabetic acrostic. Note also that the sum is quite long, because only by using the cipher on such a long sum can the result be non-suspect.

Using the Genesis Order with numerology is a bit too simple. There's nothing particularly meaningful about a mass of coincidental number matches from phrases and keywords when you're using such a low value spread. That's probably why the ancients didn't make much use of it for math, except in specific places.

b. Biblical Gematria

The Bible is by far the largest repository of gematria and the most used cipher in it is the Biblical Gematria cipher.

The number values of each letter are:

ב Beth = 2, א Aleph = 1, ג Gimel = 3, ש Shin = 3,
ד Daleth = 4, ת Tav = 4, ה Heh = 5, ו Vav = 6,
ז Zayin = 7, ח Cheth = 8, ט Teth = 9, י Yod = 10,
כ Kaph = 20, ל Lamed = 30, מ Mem = 40,
נ Nun = 50, ס Samekh = 60, ע Ayin = 70, פ Peh = 80,
צ Tsade = 90, ק Qoph = 100, ר Resh = 200.

The number sequence runs thus: 2 + 1 + 3 + 3 + 4 + 4 + 5 + 6 + 7 + 8 + 9 + 10 + 20 + 30 + 40 + 50 + 60 + 70 + 80 + 90 + 100 + 200 = 802.

On the Seven Palaces the letters of the Holy Name represent all the letters of the alephbet except the letter *beth*. *Beth* appears to be in a category of its own, as the "House of God", and the place from where God conducts the work of Creation.

When we remove the initial letter *beth* from the rest of the alphabet:

ר ק צ פ ע ס נ מ ל כ י ט ח ז ו ה ת ד ש ג א = 800.

In ancient Ugarit, the Baal texts tell that EL, the Bull God, lifted up his voice in seven chambers and eight openings. When Baal came to earth he brought with him seven servitors and eight boars. Seven and seventy times he loved a heifer by the edge of the stand of death, eight and eighty times.[24] The themes of the seven and eight, 70 and 80, 700 and 800 are ubiquitous to the texts, which suggests the Canaanites and the Ancient Hebrews shared a common numeral system and similar mythological beliefs about it.

In Biblical Gematria, the value of the *shin* is 3 and the value of the *tav* is 4. The *shin* is placed behind the *gimel* and the *tav* is placed after the *daleth*, although in actual fact they share the third and fourth place positions. This is an impossible aspect to represent in a list format however.

All the other well-used ciphers are offshoots of this one. The Reversal Cipher attributes these values in reverse. Biblical Gematria has been transposed over to the Greek alphabet to be used in the New Testament, and transliterated to the Latin alphabet to be used with English in the writings of Aleister Crowley.

The Biblical Gematria cipher is also the one which has traditionally been the most secret. It was only brought to the light of public knowledge six years ago, and a gematria calculator for it (Shematria) wasn't brought online until 2019. Initially it was received with little fanfare. That can perhaps be explained by the rash of so called Bible codes in the last decade that people were excited about for two hot seconds before they were proven to be phantoms of the imagination. Nevertheless, an almost aggressive disinterest in the true biblical cipher has made me question at times if the fundamental calculus of truth in our society is broken? Does it have to trend on TikTok before people take an interest?

Although the vast majority of studies into gematria were done using Standard Gematria (a cover-cipher), there were some researchers that anticipated the finding of gematria in a unique cipher in the bible. Lieberman admitted that it is possible gematria was employed in biblical texts. Knohl noted that "it is not out of the question that this technique was already known in the biblical period and was used specifically in religious contexts". He also hypothesized "the fact that the representation of the numerical values of letters is not demonstrated in mundane use in ancient Israel before the Hellenistic period may point to the possibility that this method was first a sacred secret knowledge that was kept in closed circles". As they knew well, an absence of evidence is not evidence of absence when it comes to codes and ciphers.

Biblical Gematria was a very strong cipher because it is counterintuitive. Our brains are hard-wired to think of numbers in a linear fashion, stepping up along a line. Having two characters with the same value appears to be initially redundant, and having this happen twice in the same alphabet appears doubly redundant. But that's only because we don't understand why the alphabet is set the way it is. The most likely explanation for it involves the ineffable holy name of YHVH, יהוה.

So far, a record of biblical calculations is being kept in the Shematria database. If you find a calculation in the Bible you are encouraged to share it with the database. Please include the biblical verse you are investigating, the calculation in the original language (Hebrew or Greek), the transliteration of the language and the translation of the verse and/or the calculation, your name or pseudonym, and the date on which you discovered the calculation. Please add a special note for any calculating words or mnemonics that you use. If approved your calculation should appear within the database within 24 hours.

The study of Biblical Gematria is as new as it is ancient and thus it is as exciting as an undiscovered land. You can be a part of building a community that works on decoding the Bible by publishing your results to social media and explaining the differences between gematria and numerology.

c. The Reversal Cipher

This cipher is the biblical equivalent to the Atbash cipher. The order and value of the Biblical Gematria cipher has been reversed. It's more than likely that the Reversal Cipher gave birth to the Atbash cipher. Instead of the values running from 2 to 200, the Reversal Cipher runs the values down from 200 to 2. With this cipher the first letter is substituted for the last letter of the Hebrew alphabet, the second letter for the next-to-last letter, the third letter for the third-to-last letter, and so on:

> Beth = 200, Aleph = 100, Gimel = 90, Shin = 90,
> Daleth = 80, Tav = 80, Heh = 70, Vav = 60, Zayin = 50,
> Cheth = 40, Teth = 30, Yod = 20, Kaph = 10,
> Lamed = 9, Mem = 8, Nun = 7, Samekh = 6, Ayin = 5,
> Peh = 4, Tsade = 3, Qoph = 1, Resh = 2.

For example, the Notariqon of Genesis 1:1 would be בבאאהוה, and the Reversal Cipher-word would be ררקקעסע, which sums to 800. In Genesis 1:2 there is: פני המים + פני אלהים + ב + אלהים אלהים + תהום + וחשך – פני which also sums to 800 with the Reversal Cipher.

The Reversal Cipher word value for YHVH is 220, which is the value of the words בראשית, *brashith*; התורה, HaTorah, Λoγoς + αΛ, *logos* אל, and οδον ιεϝε (way of YHVH). It's the value of the combined letters under the *yod* of YHVH on the Seven Palaces.

It's likely that the first word of the Bible is *bereshit* precisely because it is a word with the value of YHVH via the Reversal Cipher, in order to show that all things come from inside the House of God.

It also has various occult associations, being the value of the identifying seal of the Brothers of the Rosy Cross, and the sub-figura number of the typeset manuscript of *The Book of the Law*, and the total of the book's paragraphs.

The Reversal Cipher is itself somewhat symbolic and carries with it ideas of being "before" or "inside", suggesting an inner meaning. It was sometimes a way for scribes to express impolite feelings or judgments that they might have wished to conceal or at least speak of circumspectly. For instance, while listing the names of the offspring of Esau, the concubine of Éliphas is called תמנע, Timna, which with the Reversal Cipher spells out פחזה, *pachazah*, which means "wantonness", and the name of her son עמלק, Amalek, is a cipher of החטא, *haChet*, which means "the sin".

d. Greek Gematria

Greek Gematria is found mostly embedded into the Christian New Testament. The values of Biblical Gematria were transposed over to the Greek writing script by adjusting the letters with the value of 300 and 400 in the standard system to 3 and 4 respectively. One of the reasons why we know that Hebrew gematria was ported to the Greek script and not the other way around, is because Greek gematria has no letters with a value over 200.

Greek to Hebrew letter correspondences for Biblical Gematria:

β Beta = Beth (2),
α Alpha = Aleph (1),
γ Gamma = Gimel (3),
τ Tau = Shin (3)
δ Delta = Daleth (4),
υ Upsilon = Tav (4),
ε Epsilon = Heh (5),

F Digamma = Vav (6),
ζ Zeta = Zayin (7),
η Eta = Cheth (8),
θ Theta = Teth (9),
ι Iota = Yod (10),
κ Kappa = Kaph (20),
φ Phi = Kaph (20),
λ Lamda = Lamed (30),
μ Mu = Mem (40),
χ Chi = Mem (40),
ν Nu = Nun (50),
ψ Psi = Nun (50),
ξ Xi = Samekh (60),
ο Omicron = Ayin (70),
π Pi = Peh (80),
ω Omega = Peh (80),
ϙ Koppa = Tsade (90),
ϡ Sampi = Tsade (90),
ρ Rho = Qoph (100),
ς Sigma & Stigma = Resh (200).

There are two letters (kappa and phi) with the value of the *kaph* (20), two letters (mu and chi) with the value of the *mem* (40), two letters (nu and psi) with the value of the *nun* (50), two letters with the value of the *peh* (80), and two letters with the value of *tsade*. It is not a coincidence that *kaph*, *mem*, *nun*, *peh* and *tsade* are the letters of the alphabet which have *sofit* (final) forms in the *Ktav Ashuri* writing script.

At the present time of writing there hasn't been enough research into the use of gematria in Greek religious life for me to be able to say that the ancient Greeks used this cipher outside of the New Testament, but Judith Dillon reminds us that the roots of Greek literacy are Semitic roots, and there are some interesting sums that emerge from natural combinations of the names of various Greek gods and goddesses. For instance, the twins αρτεμις (Artemis) and απολλων (Apollo) sum to 700. ωγην (Oceanus) and τηθυς (Tethys), who were (according to Homer) the primeval parents of the Gods, sum to 365. And κοιος (Coeus) and φοιβη (Phoebe) sum to 480.

I can say the following with certainty, however: the practice of gematria was in vogue centuries before Pythagoras was even born, and before the Zodiac settled down into twelve distinct signs. Early astronomy was important to the ancient Hebrew people in terms of its uses to the calendar and for time-keeping, but there was no concurrent believe attached to the planets as influencers of human events and destinies.

Instead, the people of ancient Israel thought that the entire reason why the Sun and the Moon existed was to shine their light upon the earth, so that time-keeping (the quality of the letter *tav*) might be established. "Let them be for signs and seasons and days and years" it tells us in Gen 1:14, but "signs" didn't mean zodiac signs; it meant the holy letters of the Hebrew alphabet. The Hebrew word which is being translated as "signs" is אתת, which is the Hebrew word for the Hebrew alphabet. The gematria of 1:15 and 1:17 both result in calculations for 482, which is the decimal sum of 802 in the base 60 of time measurement, and 802 being the sum total of the alphabet. To the Sun and the Moon they assigned roles under the letter *tav*, which governed time, and to the stars they assigned the letter *heh*, which was represented in two places on the Seven Palaces: on the bottom palace, which is on the earth, and to a path that is high in the heavens and directly before the throne of God.

These letters have no natural association with zodiac signs nor planets, despite the arduous work of Golden Dawn type organizations to create a tarot system that combines Hebrew letter associations with zodiacal attributions. These late artificial systems must be viewed as separate and contained systems that, while borrowing elements from Hebrew, Greek, Egyptian, Hindu, Norse, and other types of mysticism, are really doing their own thing. They've attempted to craft artificial systems of mystical attainment via an attempted synthesis of many diverse systems.

If you were able to chat to an ancient scribe of the First Temple, using some type of time travel machine, he would have no idea what *chakras*, asanas, or sun signs were, but he might be enchanted to see the Tree of Life. Next time you see a picture of the Tree of Life laid over a picture of the seven *chakras*, remember that the only place where they really interpose themselves for such inspection is in you.

e. English Gematria

Crowley used a form of transliteration that was taught in the Golden Dawn, thus he employed digraphs to transliterate the Hebrew letters as well as single letters. They are:

Beth = B (2)
Aleph = A (1)
Gimel = G (3)
Shin = Sh (3)
Daleth = D (4)
Tav = Th (4)
Heh = H, E (5)
Vav = U, V, W (6)
Zayin = Z (7)
Cheth = C, Ch (8)
Teth = T (9)
Yod = I, J, Y (10)
Kaph = K (20)
Lamed = L (30)
Mem = M (40)
Nun = N (50)
Samekh = S, X (60)
Ayin = O (70)
Peh = P, Ph, F (80)
Tsade = Ts, Tz (90)
Qoph = Q (100)
Resh = R (200).

In English alphabetic order, the cipher is:

A=1, B=2, C=8, D=4, E=5, F=80, G=3, H=5, I=10, J=10, K=20, L=30,
M=40, N=50, O=70, P=80, Q=100, R=200, S=60, T=9, U=6, V=6,
W=6, X=60, Y=10, Z=7.

Including the digraphs:

Sh=3, Th=4, Ch=8, Ph=80, Ts or Tz=90.

This transliteration is useful for working with Crowley's Hebrew compositions. For instance, the word *ARARITA* is notariqon for the phrase "One is His Beginning; One is His Individuality; His Permutation is One". In Hebrew, Crowley said this was:

אחד ראש: אחדותו ראש ייחודותו: תמורתו אחד [777 =]

This transliterates to:

AChD RASh: AChDVThV RASh YYChVDVThV: ThMVRThV AChD
[= 777]

As for other writers of gematria in the Latin writing script, although theories abound there's very little else to speak of at the moment that can be proven and what little exists amounts to no more than numerology, and the speculative work of amateur cryptographers.

Generally people used private ciphers to record things of a sensitive or even dangerous nature, and in the days of John Dee and Edward Kelley, they were the hallmarks of the royal Spymaster General and the diplomat. I deeply suspect that his language of "Enochian" is a ciphered language, but as far as I can tell they don't appear to have employed biblical ciphers.

It is possible that the three Rosicrucian anonymous manuscripts, called the Fama Fraternitatis, the Confessio Rosae Crucis, and the Chemical Wedding of Christian Rosenkruetz, may have used Biblical Ciphers.

f. Standard Gematria

During the writing of the Talmud and the Mishnah, the dominant form of gematria in use among the Rabbis of the time appeared to be "Standard Gematria" (*Mispar Hechrechi*).

1. Aleph – A, א
2. Beth – B, ב
3. Gimel – G, ג
4. Daleth – D, ד
5. Heh – H/E, ה
6. Vav – U/V/W, ו
7. Zayin – Z, ז
8. Cheth – C/Ch, ח
9. Teth – T, ט
10. Yod – I/J/Y, י
20. Kaph – K, כ
30. Lamed – L, ל
40. Mem – M, מ
50. Nun – N, נ
60. Samekh – S/X, ס

70. Ayin – O, ע
80. Peh – P/Ph/F, פ
90. Tsade – Ts/Tz, צ
100. Qoph – Q, ק
200. Resh – R, ר
300. Shin – Sh, ש
400. Tav – Th, ת
20. Kaph sofit – K, ך
40. Mem sofit – M, ם
50. Nun sofit – N, ן
80. Peh sofit – P, ף
90. Tsade sofit – Ts/Tz

Standard is sometimes extended by giving the *sofit* forms values in the hundreds: *kaph* = 500, *mem* = 600, *nun* = 700, *peh* = 800, and *tsade* = 900.

There's very little evidence that biblical scribes used the Standard cipher. If they ever used either Standard or the extended version of Standard with hundreds for the *sofit* forms then they did it so vanishingly rarely that there's almost no record of it. There's not enough evidence to show or prove the use of this cipher to anyone. There is Genesis 1:1:

אלהים + השמים + הארץ [= 777]

This uses Standard Gematria, but that's about it in the Tanakh, as far as I can see. In the Talmud, Standard Gematria appeared to be the main cipher of the Jews because it was being used as a way to hide calculations made in biblical ciphers. This is what I call a cover-cipher, which is a published cipher that is used to mask a hidden cipher. For example, when asked why the fire festival of Lag Ba'omer was thus named, the Rav Shmuel Baruch said:

> We call it ל"ג בעומר Lag Ba'omer because the letters between the ל
> and the ג [when you continue from the end to the beginning] is מ נ ס
> ע פ צ ק ר ש ת א ב, which is the gematria of 1393 …

He goes on to compare the value of 1393 with another phrase of the same value and seems to explain it. However, the worthy Rav is using Standard Gematria as a cover-cipher to hide his real calculations which are composed in Biblical Gematria:

מ נ ס ע פ צ ק ר ש ת א ב [= 700]

Using a cover cipher is like being a stage magician who distracts your attention from one hand to another so that he can pull off an illusion. There are also cover-ciphers for Greek (Standard Isopsephy) and cover-ciphers for English occult texts composed in the last century by Aleister Crowley and the Golden Dawn.

One of the reasons why people get into gematria is because they see "something in it". That is because all words and phrases without a *shin* or a *tav* will work with the cover cipher, so they can see some of the mathematics. However, because the *shin* and the *tav* do have different numerical values, all but the simplest calculations are hidden from sight. Whatever gematria people think they see in the Bible, the truth about it is far greater.

When academic scholars questioned whether there was gematria in the Bible they used the Standard Gematria cover-cipher to assess the question and (naturally) came up virtually empty-handed. If the Standard Cipher was ever used in the Tanakh it was employed even more sparsely than the Genesis Order Cipher.

Scholars such as Israel Kholn and Stephen J. Lieberman were careful not to assume that there was no gematria in the Bible just because there was a lack of evidence for the Standard cipher.

The difference between Standard Gematria and Biblical Gematria is that in Biblical Gematria the *shin* is 3 and the *tav* is 4. This made Standard Gematria a very convenient cover-cipher to conceal calculations in Biblical Gematria. Standard Gematria could be quickly worked out by subtracting and replacing the values of any words containing *shin* and *tav* letters.

The gematria of any Hebrew text written after Talmudic times should be assessed using both the Standard Gematria cover-cipher, and then popping the lid and taking a look under the hood with Biblical Gematria. The same is true for any English gematria written by Aleister Crowley after 1900. Greek Isopsephy flourished for so brief a time that the Standard Isopsephy cover-cipher is mainly of ritual interest to latter day occult and fraternal societies. It is well worth checking all the major elements for ritual papers that include Greek names and calls with the Greek version of the Biblical Gematria cipher.

It's useful to know these cover-ciphers, and to pay attention when you see them in the Talmud and in Kabbalistic texts, because there's usually something interesting to find underneath them.

g. Pseudo-ciphers

Pseudo-ciphers are ciphers that don't belong to a fully fledged gematria system or that haven't actually been used in any known written document. They're usually used by numerologists. There are plenty pseudo-ciphers out there, so I'll quickly describe the ones which are popular at the moment.

The Agrippa Cipher

The Agrippa Cipher									
Numerical Values	A	B	C	D	E	F	G	H	I
	1	2	3	4	5	6	7	8	9
	K	L	M	N	O	P	Q	R	S
	10	20	30	40	50	60	70	80	90
	T	U	X	Y	Z	J	V	Hi*	W
	100	200	300	400	500	600	700	800	900

This one is popular at the moment, due to the conspiracy theories of the man behind the misnamed "Gematria Effect". Mr. Hubbard strongly suspects that the world is being run by a secret brotherhood of Jesuits who are using numerology to stage news events. He uses the Agrippa cipher, although there are no known documents to be written in the Agrippa cipher.

The Agrippa cipher that is provided by some calculators is derived from the original Agrippa cipher but extra letters have been added and the sequence has been disturbed. This cipher is only of interest to numerologists and some conspiracy theorists.

This is the same cipher which is touted by the Gematrix calculator as "Jewish Gematria", despite there being a total lack of Jewish heritage behind it.

English Gematria

Another pseudo-cipher is the so-called "English Gematria" which is featured on the Gematrix site. This one numbers the Alphabet from A–Z in multiples of 6: A = 6, B = 12, C = 18, until Z = 156. There is no evidence that this cipher has ever been embedded in any written text. It was apparently based on a cipher used in the medieval period when the alphabet had twenty-four letters, but evidence for this original cipher is scant, amounting to a single example showing number equivalence in a poem. There's nothing to suggest the original had a gematria system behind it, and this cipher is not the same as the original; it is only based on it.

Simple gematria

The last semi-pseudo-cipher is called "Simple Gematria" by Gematrix. Here they accidently hit on a cipher that has been used. It's basically A = 1, B = 2, until Z = 26, and it is used once in Aleister Crowley's *Book of the Law*. You sometimes see it popping up in children's literature, and as I recall it was also used in a Sherlock Holmes story. It has never had a fully fledged gematria system behind it (with conventions for mathematics) but at least it has been used.

‏[360 =] והארץ היתה תהו ובהו

And the Earth was formless and void.

‏וחשך על פני תהום ורוח אלהים מרחפת על פני המים

"And darkness was upon the face [of] the deep and spirit Elohim
were hovering upon the face of the waters."

Genesis 1:2

‏800 = פני – וחשך + תהום + ב + אלהים אלהים + פני המים

Note that the letter *beth* is included because it is the value of ורוח ("and
spirit"), and אלהים ("Elohim") is used twice because the word מרחפת
("hovering") indicates it. The subtraction occurs to וחשך ("and darkness") because על ("upon") indicates the subtraction of the previous
word.

CHAPTER 7

Conventions of the art of gematria

Conventions (plural noun) are a way in which something is usually done, especially within a particular area or activity.

Methodology (noun) a system of methods used in a particular area of study or activity.

Gematria is a formal system of math, which means that each element of it is consistent wherever it is used.

a. Methodology

Hebrew is an exact language. A few years ago I created a dual logographic and alphabetic writing script, and consequently hung out for a while with a nice bunch of peeps who create their own languages as a hobby. It wasn't unusual to hear people voice the opinion that Hebrew struck them as being very similar to a constructed language. Now I don't believe that, but I think I can explain where this common perception comes from.

The letters of the alphabet from the very earliest times (Egypt) were more that simple glyphs that represented phonics. The people of ancient Egypt were used to glyphs that represented things, and each of the letters of the Hebrew alphabet represented a distinct aspect of creation: *beth*, the house of God; the *alephs*, the day and the night; *gimel*, the sky; *shin*, heat/dry land; the *daleths*, the doors of souls; *tav*, time and the calendar; *heh*, the stars and the purpose of light (to come to earth); *vav*, birds and fishes; *zayin*, cattle and insects; *teth*, food and sustenance; *yod*, work and rest from work; *kaph*, mist (representation of the water cycle involving ancient concepts of water and fertility); *lamed*, spirit or soul; *mem*, pregnancy; *nun*, life and the afterlife; *samekh*, the bounty from heaven (symbolized by the four rivers from Eden); *ayin*, the temptations of the mortal life for souls; *peh*, courting and mating; *tsade*, childbirth; *qoph*, woman; and *resh*, man/the solar journey.

If you memorize this list, as an ancient scribe would have done, you will have the backbone of the ancient Hebrew worldview. It's possible that, as words changed in the spoken language, as words are wont to do over decades and centuries, they would be more likely to change to incorporate whatever letter they were most closely related to.

In the following pages you'll learn about different categories of words that are used in gematria, but you also need to know about words that are typically excluded from gematria sums.

Measuring words, such as days, nights, weeks, months, years, etc. are exempt from calculations even though they are nouns. When a number of days or years is specified in the text then we do not calculate the name of the number, but simply add the number to the sum. For instance, "four hundred and eighty years" is simply 480. Also excluded are the nouns "sons", "daughters", and "name" or "the name" as these words seem to have fallen under the class of "measures" according to Temple conventions (it is the rule throughout the Book of Genesis). However, be aware that in the Book of Job there are exceptions to this rule. In Job 42:13 there is this calculation:

[בָנִים ("sons") × 7] + [בָּנוֹת ("daughters") × 3] = 900.

This shows us that gematria conventions are not always uniform. While most conventions are followed by all scribes, what was a particular convention to the Temple scribes may not have been known or practised among people in a more rural setting, away from the royal and priestly center of business in Jerusalem.

If you're wondering where to start, keep in mind that Biblical Gematria has "flagwords" that are intended to draw your attention to specific bits of gematria. הנה ("behold!") is one such flagword, as is the word

ממנו, *minmennu*, which is usually just translated as "from" in the Bible. It comes from the root מנה, *manah*, (Strong's 4487) which means "to count", "to number", or "to reckon". ממנה is a preposition that means "from the number", or "from the count". It is also a flagword. But when biblical translators use ממנו or ממנה they tend to only translate their prefix *mem* ("from") and ignore the rest of the word. *Minmennu* actually means "from his number/portion/measure" so watch out for these words as you work. They aren't included in gematria sums but they usually appear when the scribe wants to draw your attention to a particular number, and they are used over a thousand times in the Hebrew Bible. They can be good places to start working on.

Gematria is not present in genealogies, so all the material on who begat whom should be passed over. This isn't to say that these genealogies don't feature numerological work, only that gematria sums are not embedded into these parts of the text.

Gematria is not present in all books of the Bible. In some books (especially Genesis, Exodus, 1 Kings, Job, and Ezekiel) it is a densely woven part of a text. In other texts it is used sparsely or sparingly.

Readers should be wary of scribal interpolation. For instance, in Exodus 7 it is clear that the original calculations were composed using the three lettered name of God: YHV, rather than YHVH, and they should adjust their calculations accordingly when using the name of God in that section. Again, this demonstrates the usefulness of gematria as a tool to track various minor cases of scribal interpolation as well as providing an extra method of dating the original composition.

Books that are written with gematria have stylistic differences in their composition from books that do not. The practice shapes the way of the written word.

In the New Testament there is a similar patchwork. In the gospels, especially John, there is a lot of gematria, and John 1, 2, and 3 are good sources. The author of the book of James tends to only add it if he is explicit about it, signaling it with the Greek version of the flagword "behold!", ἰδού. I once thought the Book of James was devoid of gematria until I actually checked his "hinney" declarations and was pleasantly surprised. Despite being more sparing in his use of gematria, he was obviously a scholar and is well aware of the Reversal Cipher, and of mnemonic words. With an explicit declaration of gematria in 5:9, he creates a sum that is intended to be read with the Reversal Cipher to reveal the name of a "judge" to be—Abraham—and so cleverly constructed is it that he also managed to draw 451 in Biblical Gematria which is the

value of the Hebrew word אדרגזר meaning "judge" as a confirmation.
All the best gematria has this multivalent feature that speaks to the time
and contemplation that the scribe put into making it.

Imagine for a moment our scribes, in their various places of business across times and places, from Canaan to ancient Egypt and then
back to Canaan they dwelt. They lived in ancient Israel and Judah and
in ancient Greece and Rome and in Babylon. They were taught their
scribal skills and knowledge by priests, and by their mothers[25] and
fathers. It was mandatory instruction for Kings of Israel. Bringing with
them the matriarchal attitudes of Egypt, it was the royal family matriarchy that decided whether an heir was fit to be invested and his knowledge (about the Chariot and Creation) could be tested by her.[26]

Attached to the side of the first Temple in Jerusalem, we would find a
community of scribes working in their scribal quarters. We can imagine
Solomon visiting his scribes, walking out of the bright sunshine into the
windowed gloom to address his chief scribe about preserving the documentary record of his people. We can imagine that they had shelves of
neatly stacked papyrus, which had a special section containing lists of
calculating words and mnemonics. We can imagine them at their desks,
blue and white tassels resting gently upon the papyrus as they drew the
pen neatly into each letter. In the quiet afternoon the room would be
filled with the gentle music of quill against paper. On holy days, there
may have been singing.

For most, being a scribe would have been an occupation that took up
their morning, leaving afternoon and evening for farming and family.
Even full time scribes would be obliged to leave the Temple grounds
before the sun was set. Entry to the compound was regulated by the
door-opening and -closing rituals that were performed by the priests to
greet the new day.

Even the chief scribe would ready himself to leave the Temple rather
than be obliged to stay within the courtyard for the night. He would
walk home—perhaps a mile or two—to his wife and his children,
with a scroll wrapped safely in a shawl in his large leather bag, and
later on, by candlelight he might retire to his study and smoke a little
בשם קנה (200) and begin to write …

Scribes in rural areas were probably more dependent upon the oral
law that was passed along to them from their parents, and learned from
local teachers. On the Sabbath we can imagine these scribes meeting at
the village square to discuss Torah and God and the word of God, and
then going to the Temple wall to *daven* (pray). And perhaps it was on

those days that their teacher would set them some homework, and if a teacher felt someone's contribution was good enough it would be sent to the Temple, copied and distributed. It may even have been seen by the King himself. Small towns were equipped with scriptoriums and oversaw the flow of practical information to and from the government.

In the rural areas the women would still practice the rituals of their mothers. Groves were set aside and prayers to "YHVH and his Asherah"[27] were made for the protection of women in childbirth, which suggests that both women and men were literate in word and number. In the royal household it was the role of women to educate their children in the royal art.

King Solomon inscribed a huge alphabetic acrostic notariqon that summed to 777, but he confessed to having learned these teachings from his mother. Eventually it would become common for scribes to commission other scribes to make copies of their writings. Imagine Ezekiel, the firebrand, rushing into the scriptorium for five new copies so that he could hand them to his friends before Shabbat. Slowly and organically they would be copied and his literature would spread from one town to the next. By contrast, imagine Job, writing for his children at night while working his farm during the day. He writes his gematria sums out with a smile on his lips and he thinks to himself, "I wonder whether young Jacob will get this one?" Job just wants to inspire his kids and interest them in the eternal verities of life. His gematria is fun and inventive, in the style of a cryptic crossword creator rather than a priest. Obviously, the last few chapters are the best. Perhaps, if it wasn't for the village elder that would make a point of going to visit Job at regular intervals, then he may never have shown him his writings, or have been eventually persuaded by him to have them copied for a larger audience? Upon such overlooked and unrecorded everyday events the course of history is set.

Imagine James, hiding his Jewishness and his Jewish thoughts behind gematria. "Behold!" he writes "The Judge before you is standing!" But what he means is that Abraham (under the name of Immanuel (248)) is your judge, for it was Abraham (248) that interceded for the righteous when God proposed to entirely destroy all living in Sodom and Gomorrah.

Imagine old John, living alone on an island, with too much time on his hands to brood over his exile. He cannot sleep at night so by candlelight he writes a book that is almost a spell. Genesis is about creation but Revelation is the exact opposite; it is an apocalypse in twenty-two chapters.

Early tradition says that John was banished to Patmos by the Roman authorities. This tradition is credible because banishment was a common punishment used during the Imperial period for a number of offenses. Among such offenses were the practices of magic and astrology. Prophecy was viewed by the Romans as belonging to the same category, whether Pagan, Jewish, or Christian. Prophecy with political implications, like that expressed by John in the Book of Revelation, would have been perceived as a threat to Roman political power and order. Three of the islands in the Sporades were places where political offenders were banished (Pliny, Natural History 4.69–70; Tacitus, Annals 4.30)

It could be that John corresponded each of the verses beginning with a "behold!" in Revelation to a letter or a palace/path, to compose the very opposite of Genesis 1–2, but if so I think he may have jumbled up their sequence. Perhaps he feared that he would not only be accused of prophesy, but also of sorcery?

There are 885 instances of הנה ("hinney") or והנה in the Tanakh and 200 instances of its Greek counterpart, ἰδοὺ, in the New Testament. Not all of these will be followed by gematria because not every scribe knew gematria. Scribes that do not use gematria may still use the word as a simple literary device.

Every 1,085+ instances are worth investigation however. We can break down the use of these flagwords in the Tanakh, book by book, as follows;

Book: no. of instances of הנה or והנה.

Bereshit (Genesis): 120.
Shemot (Exodus): 36.
Vayikra (Leviticus): 28.
Bamidbar (Numbers): 26.
Devarim (Deut): 9.
Yehoshua (Joshua): 18.
Shoftim (Judges): 44.
Shmuel I (1 Samuel): 77.
Shmuel II (2 Samuel): 47.
Melachim I (1 Kings): 45.
Melachim II (2 Kings): 48.
Yishayahu (Isaiah): 64.
Yirmiyahu (Jeremiah): 77.

Yechezkiel (Ezekiel): 84.
Hosea: 2.
Yoel: 1.
Amos: 13.
Ovadiah: 1.
Yonah: 0.
Micha: 1.
Nachum: 2.
Chabakuk: 3.
Zephania: 0.
Chaggai: 1.
Zechariah: 18.
Malachai: 4.
Tehillim (Psalms): 29.
Mishlei (Proverbs): 8.
Iyov (Job): 15.
Shir HaShirim (Song of Songs): 4.
Rus (Ruth): 5.
Eicha (Lamantations): 0.
Kohelet (Ecclesiastes): 6.
Esther: 3.
Daniel (Doniel): 12.
Ezra: 0.
Nechemia: 4.
Divrei HaYamim I (1 Chronicles): 8.
Divrei HaYamim II (2 Chronicles): 22.

When you're actually working on sums in the Bible then you have to pay very special attention to the relationship that words have to one another. You must progress along the calculation, word by word in their proper sequence. Give yourself a license to be pedantic and keep a record of your work in a notebook.

If you come across a calculating word that is usually relevant to the next word, but the next word is not a noun, then ignore it. It doesn't count. This is also true of calculating words that are relevant to the prior word. Calculating words either have a specific noun of reference, or they don't. They are not left hanging unless the scribe doesn't want you to calculate with them but they are necessary to express something in the open text.

Don't fall into the trap of believing that a calculation has ended because you reach a new line number. There are many calculations that run on for several verses, and some special ones that run for several pages. Some calculations begin by referencing a prior word that is in a previous line. Simply apply the calculation to the last word of the prior verse.

If you run into difficulties try considering things from a research perspective (see Chapter 8). The scientific method is the best tool for the job and your best friend in the end.

Finally, never try and force a result, and don't fudge it. Don't try and cheat. You're only cheating yourself if you do. There is no such thing as a colel[28] rule in Biblical Gematria, so you cannot add or subtract 1 willy-nilly to your sums. The gematria that's in the bible is more interesting than anything you could invent, so if you have a sum that's not working but you're sure there's something there (either because there's a flag-word, or because you have a verse that is surrounded by other verses with gematria), note down your thoughts about why it might not be working. Look for other things that may be going on, such as notariqon and temurah. Flag any suspected calculating words and mnemonics for research in your notebook. These may be throwing your calculations off. If you can't find anything in the verses you're working with, go on to another verse and allow yourself to sleep on the matter. But if you're sure there's something there, there's one more thing you can do, and that's check whether the verse is suspected by scholars to have some degree of scribal interpolation. If that is suggested, but it's a matter of single word interpolation, then you can check both suggestions to find the original version.

b. Conventions of structure

The historical development of mathematical notation can be divided into three stages: the rhetorical stage, the syncopated stage and the symbolic stage. The rhetorical stage is where calculations are performed by words and no symbols are used. All Biblical Gematria was composed during the rhetoric stage.

The syncopated stage is where frequently used operations acquire symbolic abbreviations. It is a mix of the rhetoric and symbolic stages.

The symbolic stage is where we find ourselves in today's modern world; comprehensive systems of notation have completely superseded rhetoric notation. However, it was not until the fourteenth century that this stage began, and the two most widely used arithmetic symbols for addition and subtraction, + and –, were invented. The plus sign was used by 1360 by Nicole Oresme as an abbreviation for "et", meaning "and". The minus sign was first used in 1489 by Johannes Widmann.

Biblical Gematria used conventions of language to describe the mode or logic of the calculation. Biblical authors and *sopherim* used nouns (the names of things or people) to carry numerical value, and verbs (action words), and some prepositions (small connecting words) to represent the type of calculation to be performed. However, not every verb or preposition indicates a calculation, even within the middle of a sum. Many verbs or prepositions mean nothing to the gematria of the sum and they are omitted or ignored, just like adjectives (describing words) are. One must also remember that there were no dictionary definitions of nouns, verbs and the like for an ancient scribe to refer to, and sometimes the designation must be decided by the sense in which a word is being used, or in sympathy for the mindset of the scribe rather than the modern perspective. For instance, time is a noun and one of a static class of fundamental physical qualities, but time can also be thought of as a verb since it is eternally following one moment to the next.

The features of gematria don't stop at strict mathematical operations. There are certain advantages to using a rhetoric system of math notation which have been lost upon the adoption of the symbolic systems. Biblical Gematria carried cryptic elements that made words mean things like "don't count the next word" or "count the next two words even if they're adjectives", or "take only the first letter of the next word".

As gematria used these features of the natural language, it was easily embedded into texts. Interesting, intriguing, and sometimes beautiful or horrifying stories were the result. It was at once a delightful and reverential form of art among the scribes of the ancient Near East, used to create spell-binding and entertaining texts. We will cover the more cryptic elements in the next chapter, but for now I'm going to give you a list of operating words, starting with the common ones. Try to memorize the most common words so you are able to follow the calculating syntax in your practice. I also encourage you to start a list or a database of your own common calculating words to help you in your practice.

c. Calculating words

אהב : aheb (verb)
Meaning: "love"; indicates the addition of 1.
Example: ישראל ויהודה א דוד ("Israel and Judah loved David")
Symbolic notation: Israel and Judah + 1 + David

אכל : a'kal (verb)
Meaning: "eat"; indicates subtraction.
Example: שבעת ימים תאכל מצת ("seven days they will eat matso")
Symbolic notation: $(7 \times \text{days}) - \text{matso}$.

Note: This notation caused some difficulty for scribes that wanted to mention eating in their narrative but didn't want to use it to subtract. Therefore, it often appears at the end of sentences, or is followed with an את which cancels it out.

את, ואת : et, v'et (preposition)
Meaning: "and" or "add"; indicates addition.
Example: השמים ואת הארץ ("the heavens and the earth")
Symbolic notation: the heavens + the earth.

Note: When את is preceded by a calculating word, such as: לשחט את ("to slay") then the calculation of the preceding word applies. For example, in Genesis 22:10:

וישלח אברהם את ידו ויקח את המאכלת לשחט את בנו

And stretched out Abraham + his hand and took + the knife to slay + his son
This resolves to the following calculation:

אברהם ידו המאכלת – בנו = 310

Abraham + Hand + Knife – his son = 310 [31×10].
In this case, the last את acts as a signifier of a direct object.

על : al (preposition)
Meaning: "on" or "upon"; indicates subtraction.
Example: וחשך על פני תהום ("and darkness on face of the deep")
Symbolic notation: face of the deep – and darkness.

ובין, בין : ben (preposition)
Meaning: "between", "and between"; indicates division by 2.
Example: בין עיניך ("between your eyes")
Symbolic notation: your eyes / 2.

ברך : barek (verb)
Meaning: "bless" or "blessed"; indicates the value of the word following should be multiplied by 2. However, in Daniel it is used to denote the word prior to it.
Example: ברך יהוה את יום השבת ("bless YHVH and day Sabbath")
Symbolic notation: (YHVH × 2) + day Sabbath.

ברא : bara (verb)
Meaning: "created"; indicates addition.
Example: בראשית ברא אלהים ("in the beginning created Elohim")
Symbolic notation: in the beginning + Elohim.

תחת : tahat (preposition)
Meaning: "under", "below"; indicates subtraction.
Example: ידך תחת ירכי ("your hand under my thigh")
Symbolic notation: my thigh – your hand.

הרה : harah (verb)
Meaning: "pregnant" or "conceived"; indicates duplicating the value of the previous word (if a noun).
Example: ויבא אל הגר ותהר ("And went in to Hagar and conceived")
Symbolic notation: (Hagar × 2)

טרם : terem (adverb)
Meaning: "before"; indicates that the value of the word immediately preceding it should be multiplied by 2.

יָדַע : yada (verb)
Meaning: "knew"; indicates that the value of the word previous to it should be replicated (multiplied by 2).

Example: והאדם ידע את חוה ("And the Adam knew [+] Eve")
Symbolic notation: (And the Adam × 2) + Eve

ילד, תלד : yalad (verb)
Meaning: "she bore", "birthed"; indicates that the value of the word previous to it should be replicated (multiplied by 2).

תהר, הרה : harah (verb)
Meaning: "she conceived", "pregnancy"; indicates that the value of the word previous to it should be replicated (multiplied by 2).

לִשְׁתּוֹת : lishtot (preposition/verb)
Meaning: "to drink"; indicates subtraction.
Example: והמן לשתות אסתר ("and Haman to drink Ester")
Symbolic notation: and Haman – Ester.

מעל : me'al (preposition)
Meaning: "above"; indicates addition.
Example: המים מעל הארץ ("the waters above the earth")
Symbolic notation: the waters + the earth.

מאד : me'od (adverb)
Meaning: "greatly" or "exceedingly"; indicates multiplication by 10.
Example: יפה הוא מאד ("beautiful she was exceedingly")
Symbolic notation: beautiful (she was × 10).

מַגִּיעַ, נֹגֵעַ : nogia, maggia (verbs)
Meaning: "reaching", "touching"; indicates addition.
Example: וראשו מגיע השמימה ("and its head reaching the heavens")
Symbolic notation: and its head + the heavens.

מרחפת : rachaph (verb)
Meaning: "hovering", "moving"; indicates the previous word value should be used twice.
Example: ורוח אלהים מרחפת ("and the spirit of Elohim was hovering")
Symbolic notation: b Elohim Elohim.

קדש : qad'des (verb)
Meaning: "consecrate"; indicates multiplication by 2.

Example: יום השבת לקדשו ("day the Shabbat consecrate")
Symbolic notation: day Shabbat × 2

ילוד : ye'lud (verb)
Meaning: "born of"; indicates subtraction.
Example: אדם ילוד אשה ימים רגז ("man born woman day trouble")
Symbolic notation: (man − woman) + days trouble

שחט : sachat (verb)
Meaning: "kill"; indicates subtraction.
Example: צאן למשפחתיכם ושחטו הפסח ("lambs according to your families and kill of him the Passover")
Symbolic notation: lambs according to your families—the Passover

נתתי, נתן : Nathan (verb)
Meaning: "to give", "put", "set"; indicates addition.
Example: קשתי נתתי בענן ("my bow I set in the clouds")
Symbolic notation: my bow + in the clouds

גהה : ghar (noun)
Meaning: "medicine"; indicates multiplication by 2.
Example: לב שמח ייטב גהה ורוח נכאה תיבש גרם ("A heart merry does good medicine and spirit broken dries the bones")

נְכֵאָה : nekeah (adjective)
Meaning: "broken"; indicates division by 2.
Example: See above.

d. Mnemonic words

At Wadi El-Hol near the Nile River, ancient inscriptions show us how the first alphabet emerged from Semitic people who drew simple Egyptian pictograms that represented sounds. These people were not trained scribes of the day. Those needed decades of training to memorize the thousands of different pictographic and logographic signs. The inventors of the alphabet were ordinary folks groping towards another form of literacy that would be accessible and useful to them in their daily lives. They chose pictograms of highly memorable images, such as eyes and mouths, snakes and heads, and a little stick man with his arms raised to receive light from the sky. Each picture was not only a mnemonic for a phonetic sound, but also for a number.

While writing is useful, in a largely illiterate society knowing your numbers is even more so. They can be used record the tally of a flock or a harvest, of simple items bought and sold, the measures of land and property, of time passing (days and weeks), and of distance, so alphabetic literacy likely arose from numeracy.

The first use of written numbers likely emerged when the alphabet acquired a more or less standardized order, with the first letter representing "one", the second "two", the third "three" and so on to a count of twenty. The need to record larger numbers saw the development of a larger number system, so the value of each letter after the tenth was increased tenfold: *yod* (10), *kaph* (20), *lamed* (30) to *resh* (200).

An illiterate people using numbers in this way quickly becomes literate, as they would pick up the sound of the letters that distinguished each number from one another. For example, the letter *nun* (50) which carried an *n* sound was depicted as a snake, *nachash*. As time passed these pictograms became simpler and more stylized as the people grew better accustomed to writing. By the time the Kingdom of Israel was founded, pictograms had become conventional Paleo-Hebrew letters but the images they originally represented continued to be taught across the generations. This should be unsurprising to us as the practice is still in use to teach children today. It is the equivalent of "*a* is for apple, *b* is for bee".

The Hebrew tribes settled in the land of Israel and erected temples and military outposts. Their kings trained scribes which became essential to the day to day infrastructure of the country. They regularly sent letters to the rulers of neighboring lands, and they set to recording much of the oral wisdom and history of their people. It is at this point in history that the cultural memory of the pictograms was put to a new purpose, embodied in an art form that had emerged from the dual use of signs (אתת) as letters and numbers. Today we call it gematria, but that name has a Greek origin. Though it was a deeply embedded part of Temple Mysticism, we don't know what it was called by the ancient Hebrew speaking peoples themselves.

If I had to take a guess, I'd suggest they called it the word מנה, *manah*, which means "to count". It is easy to see how a word like *nachash* ("serpent") came to hold the fixed value of 50, because we know that the pictogram of the letter *nun* was a serpent. However, there are many mnemonics with fixed values where it's not immediately clear how they came to hold them. Rather than being rooted in their pictographic origin, they take part in the story of creation, which suggests that the alphabet may have been used as mnemonics to remember the stages of creation in oral story telling. For example, the word רקיע ("expanse") holds the value of 3 instead of 380. אשה ("woman") holds the value of 111, and she is called "this one" three times by Adam. Regardless of how these mnemonics came into use, they added an extra layer of secrecy to biblical texts. To verify each new mnemonic, these examples have been cross-checked against multiple examples in the Tanakh (see "Gematria Research").

Mnemonics list

באפיו, *beappaw*: Meaning "nostrils". Representing the value of 2 and the letter *beth*.

בשר, *basar*: Meaning "flesh". Representing the value of 90 and the letter of *tsade*.

בית, *bith*: Meaning "house". Representing: the value of 2 and the letter of *beth*.

אמ, *am*: Meaning "mother". Representing the value of 1 and the letter *aleph*.

אש, *ash*: Meaning "fire". Representing the value of 3 and the letter *shin*.

אשה, *issah*: Meaning "woman". Representing: the value of 111. Usually the letter *qoph* has the value of 100 but its value on the Seven Palaces may be 111 instead.

איש, *aish*: Meaning "man". It represents the value of 45, identical to that of אדם Adam which can mean either "man" or "scarlet".

אהל, *ohel*: Meaning "tent". Representing the value of 111.

דלתות, *dal'towt*: Meaning "the doors". Representing: The letter *daleth* and the value of 4.

יבשה, *yabbashah*: Meaning "the dry ground". Representing: the letter *shin* and the value of 3.

יד, *yad* (noun): Meaning "the hand". Representing: the letter *yod* and the value of 10

כנפות, *kanpowt*: Meaning "corners". Representing: the value of 90, from the degrees in a square's corner. Sometimes in reference to the corners of the earth represents the value of 4 × 90 = 360 which is the degrees of a circle.

לחם, *lechem*: Meaning "bread". Representing the value of 40 and the letter *mem*. Evidently the metaphor of "a bun in the oven" for pregnancy is a very ancient one.

למד, *lamad*: Meaning "to teach". Representing the value of 1 and the letter *aleph*.

נחש, *nachash*: Meaning "serpent". Representing the letter *nun* and the value of 50.

נפש, *nephesh*: Meaning a (higher) part of the soul. Representing the letter *nun* and the value of 50.

נשמה, *neshamah*: Meaning a (lower) part of the soul. Representing the letter *nun* and the value of 50.

עיני, *e'ne* (noun): Meaning "the eyes". Representing: the letter *ayin* and the value of 70.

עצם, *etsem* (noun): Meaning "bone". Representing: the letter *tsade* and the value of 90.

פיה, *pi'ha* (noun): Meaning "the mouth". Representing: the letter *peh* and the value of 80.

צְרוֹר, *tsrwr*: Meaning "sack". Representing the letter *tsade* and the value of 90.

רוּחַ, *ruah* (noun): Meaning "spirit". Representing the letter *beth* and the value of 2.

רָקִיעַ, *raqio* (noun): Meaning "expanse". Representing the letter *gimel* and the value of 3.

Like any other type of art form, some writers of gematria are more skilled than others and everyone has their own style. Ezekiel delights in creating texts that are densely embedded with long and complex gematria that uses many cryptic elements, but other authors use gematria sparingly, or prefer short sums. Aleister Crowley is strict in some texts but throws away the rule book in others to go free-styling. By working with each individual author and text at a time, you can acquaint yourself with their particular individual style.

e. Notariqon and temurah

So far everything has been quite straightforward, but now we turn our attention to the element of wordplay in gematria. I tend to think of this as the fun part of Biblical Gematria.

Although the cryptic crossword puzzle was first invented in the 1920s, some examples of ancient gematria bear a close resemblance to its abstract and cryptic clues. Generally, it is possible to deduce the answer to the sort of wordplay you encounter in the Torah, and this may be proven or disproven by testing. In the Torah, general arithmetic is combined with cryptic wordplay and mnemonics, so many texts are a form of art that combine narrative with number. There is a certain amount of innate skill that comes with being "good" at wordplay, but just like cryptic crosswords, it helps to know what types of puzzles to expect too. Here are some examples of things you may encounter.

Notariqon is a method of deriving a word or sentence or gematria calculation by using each of its initial or final letters. Not all compositions with notariqon form another word or sentence that is meaningful when read rather than counted. Although rare in the Torah, it is used more by Kabbalists and extensively in the Thelemic *Book of the Law*.

One well known example in Kabbalah is the word ישראל (Israel) that can be read as an acronym:

יש שישים ריבוא אותיות לתורה

Meaning: "There are six hundred thousand letters in the Torah".

When the word שישים (sixty) is replaced by the letter *samekh* which holds the value of 60, the gematria of the verse sums to 600:

יש ס רנוא אתיות לתורה = 600

The most obvious piece of notariqon in the Bible is discovered in Genesis 1:1: בבאאהוה =   800 (with the Reversal Cipher).

There is also an intriguing calculation in Numbers 8:2 which directly refers to notariqon by the word בהעלתך meaning literally "in the ascending" or "when you arrange", pronounced roughly as *beha'aloteka*. This may have been the original name for notariqon.[29] It's from the root עלת meaning (alternatively) "go up", "ascent", or "burnt offerings":

נהרות שבעת יאירו המנורה פני מול אל הנרת את בהעלתך אליו ואמרת אהרן אל רבד

"Speak to Aaron and say to him, 'in the mounting + the lamps,
to on face of the lampstands gives light seven lamps."

אהרן האמ פה ז הנרות = 700 (via the Reversal Cipher).

It's a very interesting notariqon because it spells out the words "The Mother Here". Fascinating really, especially in context of the plan of the Temple and Tabernacle and their symbolic representation of the Seven Palaces. "Mother" is a mnemonic word with the value of 1, as we see in Genesis 3:20:

And called Adam the name of his wife "Eve" because she was the mother of all living things.

חוה = 19 = "Eve".
אמ = 1 = "Mother" (mnemonic) for the *aleph*.
חי = 18 = "Living".
חי + אמ = 19.

On the Seven Palaces, אמ, AM ("Mother") is a gate comprising the left side Palace of the Aleph which has the path of *mem* descending from it to meet the door (Palace of the Daleth) into the world below.

Notariqon also exists in Genesis 2:6 to add to the mystery of the letter *kaph*:

A mist went up from the ground and watered + all face the ground.

ואד יעלה מן הארץ והשקה את כל פני האדמה

The word "mist" becomes "and his ground" and the second part of the sum reveals the name of the letter *kaph* but with a feminine *heh* at the end. Sometimes this word is translated as "compelled", and the Zohar (1:35a) explains this verse as "and the mist rising is the yearning of the female for the male."

ואדמהו כפה

Letter interpolations are something that I don't support the use of in an exegete of the Bible. I'm including it, but the greatest caution must be made with it. A great many things that were not deliberately embedded by the author may be found with it. I'm including it because it can sometimes be found in combination with other scribal devices, such as the alphabetic acrostic.

Letter interpolations are a simple method of removing letters to reveal a hidden sentence. For instance, lets go back to the alphabetic acrostic sum from Proverbs 31:10–31. If we remove every second letter:

נ רההה רויש פהמ זיצ עדן דמו האר ייכ רטמ זמח תוק דשה גלה אתט

and then every third letter, we are left with the sentence:

את גל דשת וזמר טי יהאדם עד זיף הר ורהן.

I translate this as:

[alternate suggestions in brackets]

+ Rolled in threshing and mountain sheep [and great music] nine and ten will the men upon Ziph mountain and mountain N [and mountain of them]

"We rolled in, threshing and great music we made, nineteen men will go upon Ziph mountain and their mountain!"

And from this we can extract another gematria sum of the same value of the previous notariqon, but this time with Biblical Gematria:

דשת וזמר – האדם + זיף הר ורהג = 777.

Threshing great music – the Adam + Ziph Mountain and their Mountain = 777.

If this was an intentional message embedded in the text then the significance of "Ziph" to Solomon and Bathsheba may have been that it was the place where David hid when Saul set out to murder him, but it was also the site of an ancient (even then) religious settlement. In 2018 a 9,000 year old stone mask was discovered Pnei Hever region (ancient Ziph).

As interesting as all this is, this kind of work is only of suggestive value when it comes to their exegete.

Temurah is a technique for the permutation of letters, where the letters in a word or phrase are exchanged with other letters, usually according to a precise rule. We find the temurah cipher in the Torah uses the Reversal Cipher, but in the Talmud they apply the Atbash cipher, although in all likelihood it is being used as a cover cipher. The Atbash cipher is arranged according to the usual order of the alphabet from *aleph* to *tav*, while the reversal cipher used the Genesis Order from *beth* to *resh*.

f. Flagwords

Alongside these methods of cryptic wordplay there is also a set of notational words that exist in the body of gematria to indicate cryptic operations. These are the bread and butter of gematria practice.

You need to familiarize yourself with these and there are exercises in the workbook to help you get the hang of working with them. Note that some of these special cryptic words are nouns but they should not be counted. They are exceptions to the usual rule. I have listed as many as I have encountered but you should be aware that there are probably more that are not yet on my radar. If you think you have found one of these, please refer to the chapter "Gematria Research" for pointers on verification.

כל, meaning "all", is a wonderful little noun and instruction. It has individual and perhaps regional conventions, however. It means in some cases, according to some scribes, to count the next two words (even if they are adjectives) until you reach the next verb or preposition. But in some other cases it can mean to count all the words afterwards whatever they are. For instance, in Genesis 2:3 the מכל in the verse is used in the latter fashion.

לא, meaning "not", indicates that you should not include the next word in your calculations.

הנה, meaning "behold!", and you may also see הנני meaning "they will behold" which is also translated sometimes as "here", indicates that there is gematria in the following text.

ראש, meaning "Head", indicates that the initial letter or syllable should be taken from a word so indicated, for instance in Genesis 48:14 when Israel lays his right hand on the head of אפרים, Ephraim, the syllable אפ is taken. ראש is sometimes followed and qualified by עַל ("on"). However, note that the use of this term is not consistent across the Tanakh. Sometimes a head is only a head! The use of this word in Genesis 48:14 is certain as it is used twice for the purpose, but special care must be taken when analyzing any calculation where it is used to determine whether it is being used in its cryptic sense or whether it should simply be counted as a usual noun with the value of 204.

דבר, can refer to several words with the same spelling and is translated diversely as "word", "speech", "a portion", "thing", "because" or even "pestilence". I think this word, more than any other, meaning "word" but indicating that you should count the next word, illustrates how writing and math were of one thing in the minds of the ancients.

Although these words are nouns, they are not counted, but rather direct the reader to count the word immediately after them.

הַשְּׂמָאלִית, meaning "left", indicates the letter on the far left side of the previous word.

הַיְמָנִית, meaning "right", indicates the letter on the far right side of the previous word.

g. Alphabetic acrostics

In Biblical Hebrew, alphabetic acrostic verses use the structure of the Hebrew alphabet to demarcate a new line or paragraph.

The acrostic in Proverbs 31:10–31 also provides the structure of a gematria sum that is composed with the Genesis cipher. There are about a dozen or so alphabetic acrostics in the Bible, but the strange thing is that many of them miss letters from the alphabetic order, or else they switch the order of the letters, and this is more often the case than not.

I have often wondered at the motivations of a scribe to remove a letter or change its placement in the alphabetic order. This was the magic of the scribe. Writing the holy letters upon blessed pale parchment must have felt subtly empowering to them, after all; these symbols represented vast and intelligent forces abroad in the cosmos. Each letter they inscribed partook in the Holy Assembly of the God. These "signs" were believed to be the symbols that God himself used to create the entire macrocosm of things that were resonant in the soul of God, and also in God's image—the Adam (the microcosm). So why would a scribe exchange letters? To take a real example, why would a scribe exchange a *peh* for an *ayin*?

Might a scribe write the letters in this order to symbolically dethrone some letters from their domain, perhaps, or to strip them of power. The letter *ayin* represented the temptations of the world and the flesh and the letter *peh* represented the consummation of those desires, so we might expect that person who has been taught to repress their desires for the good of their tribe might express them in such personal symbolism as letter reversals. Or letter omissions may have been a way to express grief. It is an old custom to tear a small part of your clothes to express grief in Judaism. Perhaps a similar practice pertained to writing, leading to letter and line switches and omissions as symbolic for loss? We just don't know.

Some letters cover single lines (Psalm 25, 34, 145, Proverbs 31:10–31). Others cover half a verse (Psalm 111, 112), or two verses (Psalm 37), or even eight verses (Psalm 119).

Psalms 9 and 10 are linked together by an irregular acrostic. Each letter covers two verses but several letters are either missing or appear in the wrong order.

In Lamentations 1–4, chapters 1 and 2, each Hebrew letter heads one verse, which consists of three stanzas. In chapter 3 each letter heads three stanzas/verses, and thus it has sixty-six verses. In chapter 4 there are twenty-two verses and each letter consists of two stanzas beginning with that letter of the alphabet. Chapter 5 also has twenty-two verses, but is not thought to be a regular alphabetic acrostic. However, it has been observed that the text displays signs of further arrangement.

It has been noted that in Lamentations 1 the alphabetic order is the one known today, but in chapters 2–4 the letter *peh* precedes *ayin*.[30] Assis provides the argument "that the order of the letters pe and ayin was not fixed at the time or, alternatively, that there were two traditions of alphabetic order" and provides support for their assertion with inscriptions found at vIzbet Siartah and Kuntillet i vAjrud, and a wealth of evidence from the documentary and archeological record.

Proverbs 31:10–31 is one of the thirteen alphabetical acrostic poems in the Bible, where each line begins with a successive letter in the Hebrew alphabet. It is called חיל אשת, *Eshet Ḥayil* ("The Woman of Valor", WV). Professor Victor (Avigdor) Hurowitz noted:

> WV contains a chain of eleven words and phrases repeated in reverse order, overlapping the entire hymn. Another chain of eight repeated terms runs through the entire chapter, overlapping v. 1–9 and then the second half of WV (v. 20–31). Finally, two themes arranged chiastically overlap the entire chapter (women-wine// wine-women). Undoubtedly the units were intentionally molded into a tightly knit composition, either by an author or a thorough editor. Unified ch. 31 constitutes the seventh major unit of the Book of Proverbs, balancing chs. 1–9 in theme, and deserving the title "the Seventh Pillar of Wisdom's House".[31]

These verses have an interesting history. Proverbs 31 declares itself to be the Words of King Lemuel, who says it is an oracle taught to him by his mother. No other mention is made of this King in the Tanakh, but Jewish legend identifies him as Solomon, taking advice from his mother Bathsheba. This chapter is often recited on Friday night before Shabbat dinner in some Jewish homes as a praise directed from the husband to his wife:

> Who can find a virtuous wife? For her worth is far above rubies. The heart of her husband safely trusts her; so he will have no lack of gain. She does him good and not evil all the days of her life ... Her husband is known in the gates, when he sits among the elders of the land ... she opens her mouth with wisdom, and on her tongue is the law of kindness. She watches over the ways of her household,

and does not eat the bread of idleness. Her children rise up and call
her blessed; her husband also, and he praises her: many daughters have done well, but you excel them all. Charm is deceitful and
beauty is passing, but a woman who fears the Lord, she shall be
praised. Give her of the fruit of her hands, and let her own works
praise her in the gates.

Proverbs 31:10–31

Its notariqon is 777 by the Genesis Order:

יהוה תנו זממה חגרה טעמה ידיה כפה לא מרבדים גמלתהו דרשה היתה ותקם אשת בטח
777 = נודע סדין עז פיה צופיה קמו רבות שקר

This calculation contains 86 characters, corresponding with 86 as the
value of אלהים, Elohim. The Genesis Order is a simple numerical system
that we might expect to have been taught to children (see pg. 25), but
there are layers within layers for these verses.

In Nahum 1:1–9 The *aleph* covers three lines. There seems to be an
interjection of 2 lines before the rest of the consonants, which cover
only one verse each. The letter *zayin* appears in the second position
of the line.

777 = ראשון שני שלישי רביעי חמישי שישי שבת

Translation:
Sunday + Monday + Tuesday + Wednesday + Thursday + Friday + Shabbat = 777
The Days of the Week

CHAPTER 8

Gematria and the Hebrew Bible

Gematria has been root and stem, brick and mortar, blood and bone to Hebrew Mysticism down through the ages since the earliest times. From out of ancient Egypt it emerged into the Southern Levant during the fifteenth century BCE[32], with the spread of the proto-consonantal alphabet.

It was German Stenographer Carl Faulmann who first recognized that, rather than numbers being assigned to letters, it was the other way around, with phonetic sounds being attributed to characters for numerals. In his 1880 work *Das Buch der Schrift* he wrote of the early alphabet:

"I have shown, by comparison with the hieratic scripts of the Egyptians, that these names [of the letters] correspond to the characters and that the arrangement of the alphabet does not owe its existence to chance. The alphabet consists of three sections: of which the first contains 8 characters, namely the basic sounds, while the second, also containing 8 sounds, lists the four sounds related to the first, with only a rearrangement of the last two rows, the throat and tongue sounds has taken place. **It is worth noting that these phonetic signs are also numerical characters, which explains the faithful transmission of the character string. My guess is that the invention of alphabetic writing consisted** in using these signs, which were known much earlier as numerals, to write words without mixing them with the syllable signs customary in Egypt or adding determinatives. Since this procedure did not result in the ambiguity that the Egyptians wanted to prevent with their determinatives, it was imitated by the neighboring peoples, who, however, mostly retained their usual numerals. In any case, this is the only way to explain the character change that is evident in some alphabets. Since it cannot be assumed that civilized peoples would have dispensed with the use of writing at all, but rather knew communication by means of individual signs, albeit imperfect and ambiguous, the use of numerals for sound designation seems to have been an invention that is reminiscent of the well-known story of the Egg of Columbus."

But before the days when temples and cities were built, the tribes of Israel travelled between the sacred places of their lands, carrying with them the Ark within the Tabernacle. They would pitch camps at traditional spots, usually having a water source such as a spring or river nearby, and then they would set up the curtained enclosures of the Tabernacle with the Ark residing in its inner sanctum (the "Holy of Holies"). They would set up their tents in ritualized arrangement around the Tabernacle.

The legendary architect of the Tabernacle, Betzal'el, was said to have known "the combination of letters with which heaven and earth were made", and to have fashioned the Tabernacle in accordance with them.[33]

The well-spring or river would symbolize God's bounty coming down from heaven, springing forth from the Garden of Eden. Later on, Solomon designed the Temple with this symbolism in mind and appointed a massive water basin to the south of the Temple. It was accompanied by ten water carriages, to represent these heavenly waters flowing to earth.

A visitor to the temple would enter the outer court, and see people on the flagstones who were reciting prayers and preparing sacrifices, and we might see people passing by on their way to the various chambers that were attached to the outside of the Temple. These would have been various scribes and secretaries engaged in the business affairs of the Temple.

The inner court was only permitted for priests. They tended to the fires of the altar with bronze implements and splashed the blood of the sacrifices upon the feet of the altar.

Absolutely no-one went into the Hekhal except for the high priest once a year, to speak the name of God. Inside the Hekhal rested the Ark of Testimony with the wings of the cherubim covering either side to prove seating for God.

The texts of this period show a gematria that is more sophisticated and formal than earlier times, probably due to an explosion of literacy in the population and an increase in the amount of scribes working at close quarters together in the temple.

The sons of these scribes would have been instructed in reading and writing just as a carpenter's son would learn carpentry or a blacksmith's son would learn his trade at his father's anvil. According to legend, it was Moses that wrote the whole of the Torah, but it's more probable that the scribes of the Temple took the ancient parchment scrolls as their basis and applied a more formalized style of gematria and storytelling to them that was more decorous for the royal House of David.

Certainly there are parts of Exodus that could not have been written by Moses because they describe his death and subsequent events. Many of the oldest texts (for instance, the Book of Amos) mostly refer to God as simply "El" rather than YHVH or Elohim.

The gematria of Genesis 1–2 is impressively crafted. Each verse was composed to describe the qualities of a letter on the Seven Palaces (Ashe, 2019). For instance, the third verse of Genesis 1 is attributed to the letter *aleph*:

ויאמר אלהים יהי אור ויהי אור

And said Elohim 'Let there be light' and there was light.

The verbs of this verse aren't significant and the nouns are: 500 = אור אור אלהים. And since there are two palaces of the *aleph*, one for day and one for night, 500 x 2 = 1000, which is the value of a large *aleph*. Each verse of Genesis 1–2 is embedded with gematria that relates to a letter, and I have published an analysis of it in my previous work *The Genesis Wheel & other hermeneutical essays*.

a. Talmud & Hekhalot

The Talmud compares Ezekiel and Isaiah's visions of God's Chariot-Throne, noticing that Ezekiel gives a lengthy account of details, while Isaiah is very brief.

It gives an exoteric explanation for this: Isaiah prophesized in the era of Solomon's Temple, while Ezekiel's vision took place in the exile of Babylonian captivity. Rava states in the Babylonian Talmud that although Ezekiel describes the appearance of the throne of God, this is not because he had seen more than Isaiah, but rather because the latter was more accustomed to such visions:

> ... for the relation of the two prophets is that of a courtier to a peas-
> ant, the latter of whom would always describe a royal court more
> floridly than the former, to whom such things would be familiar.
> Ezekiel, like all prophets except Moses, has beheld only a blurred
> reflection of the divine majesty, just as a poor mirror reflects objects
> only imperfectly.

In the Talmud we find examples of Rabbis that appear to be using Standard Gematria, but they are using it to cover work in the Biblical Gematria cipher. Thus demonstrating that Standard Gematria is a cover-cipher. For example, the reason why Lag Ba'omer is so named.

Talmudic hermeneutics are the rules and methods for determining the meaning of scripture. It includes the rules by which the requirements of the oral law are derived and established by the written law, and relates to grammar and exegesis, prepositions, prefixes and suffixes, gematria, notariqon, and temurah. Compilations of such hermeneutic rules were made during the first century BCE, namely The Seven Rules of Hillel,[34] The Thirteen Rules of R. Ishmael,[35] and the thirty-two Rules of R. Eleazar b. Jose ha-Gelili. It should be noted that neither Hillel, Ishmael, nor Eliezer b. Jose ha-Gelili sought to give a complete list of the rules of interpretation. They omitted many rules from their compilations and restricted themselves to elucidating the principal methods of logical deduction, which they called *middot* ("measures"). They did not invent these rules; they simply collected them. All these hermeneutic rules in the Talmud and Midrashim were themselves collected by Meir Loeb ben Jehiel Michael Weisser (Malbim 1809–1879) in his special work *Ayyelet ha-Shahar*.

Malbim's commentary to the Bible is established upon three fixed principles: in the text of the Torah and the figurative language of the prophets there are no repetitions of mere synonyms; consequently every word in a sentence is essential to the meaning in accordance with the rules of the language, despite the fact that they seem to be mere synonymous repetitions; and every statement conveys a sublime thought—all the metaphors are of importance and replete with wisdom for they are the words of the living God. Malbim believed the sages had "important principles and fixed rules for the grammatical forms and

the foundations of the language and of logic" by which they understood all the words of the revelation transmitted at Sinai.

The *Geonim* believed that the *middot* originated from Sinai and are
הלכה למשה מסיני, the law given to Moses at Mt. Sinai. According to Rabbi
Akiva, the divine language of the Torah is distinguished from the speech
of men by the fact that in the former no word or sound is superfluous.
His teacher was Nahum of Gimzo, who said that certain prepositions
like את, גם, and או were inclusive, while others such as אך, רק, and מן were
exclusive. He stated that "one inclusion added to another is equivalent
to an exclusion". He also said an infinitive before a finite verb was an
amplification, and so was the doubling of a word or the repetition of a
term by a synonym.

In the Baraita of R. Ishmael is a contrasting view: "the Torah speaks
in the language of men", therefore the Bible may have superfluous
words and it is his view that values should not be assigned to them for
the purpose of deducing new rules. I happen to think they are both correct. Proverbs 25:2 says:

כבד אלהים הסתר דבר וכבד מלכים חקר דבר

It is the Glory of Elohim to conceal a matter and the Glory of Kings
to reveal a matter.

A matter is concealed alongside other words that also better express
the narrative—the verbs without function or the adjectives. So even
though we may not assign values to some words of the Torah, they are
not superfluous. On the contrary, they are essential to conceal the sacred
Glory of Elohim. In respect of the repetition of entire sections of the
Torah, Rabbi Ishmael is of the opinion that "the Torah at times repeats a
whole section of the Law in order to give a new application to it".

I discovered when working with Genesis 1–2 that although there
are sections which appear to be repetitions, they have very minor differences in the repeat which produce a different gematria sum. Those
instances where single words are repeated are like those words which
are blessed, and thus multiplied by two. Rabbi Akiva basically agrees
with Rabbi Ishmael and said that "Everything that is said in a section
so repeated must be interpreted". He said that new deductions may
be drawn from it. According to Akiva, "every passage which stands
close to another must be explained and interpreted with reference to its
neighbor", but according to Ishmael nothing may be inferred from the
position of the individual sections.

Calculations in the verses of Genesis 1–2 sometimes run on from one verse to the next or occasionally are intended to be calculated across several chapters. I can cite a calculation between Genesis 1–2 to illustrate this. Eleven times does God declare that what he sees is טֹוב ("good"), and the letters that represent these verses are: *aleph + shin + daleth + heh + vav + zayin + teth + nun + samekh + ayin + peh* = 295, which is the gate value of one of the palaces of the letter *aleph*. In this case, and it is not a rare occurrence, single verses cannot be considered in isolation.

The Seven Rules of Hillel and The Thirteen Rules of R. Ishmael deal mainly with the interpretation of the narrative relative to Halakha[36] and thus they fall outside the scope of this work. It is the thirty-two Rules of R. Eliezer b. Jose ha-Gelili that dealt with the subject of gematria and other aggadic measurements. It was highly regarded, though it no longer exists, except in references by later authorities. Samson of Chinon wrote of it "Whenever you come across the words of R. Eliezer b. Jose ha-Gelili, make a funnel of your ear."

Though no longer extant, it was incorporated into later medieval handbooks on Talmudic method and biblical exegesis. Rules 27 to 31 deal with *mashal* or "allegory", *remez* or "paranomasia", gematria, temurah and notaqiron. Allegory has been part of language since the earliest times, and there are many allegorical instances used in the Tanakh, such as the prophet Nathan who warned David that Uriah was a poor man with only a single lamb, with the lamb being an allegory for Bathsheba.

Paronomosia (*remez*) is a play between two rhyming words or words that have a close sound pattern. In the Bible whole passages are based on it, such as the Blessing of Jacob where the futures of the sons of Jacob are based on a long series of puns. Obviously this form of interpretation is largely closed off to the non-Hebrew speaker, who must rely on second hand knowledge to learn of it.

There is a form of Temurah called Atbash which we've covered earlier. The Midrash cites the use of Atbash in Jeremiah 51:1 for the words לב קמי ("the heart of my assailants") standing for כשדים ("Chaldeans"). Atbash is also thought to be behind the word בבל as ששך in Jeremiah 25:26 and 51:4. An example of Rabbinic gematria that is discussed is an interpretation in Bereshit Rabbah (43:2) that Eliezer went alone with Abraham to rescue Lot from capture. In Genesis 14:14 the number of "his trained servants who were born in his house" were said to be 318, which is the gematria value of the name of אליעזר (Eliezer).

This gematria is the same in Standard Gematria as it is in Biblical Gematria because the name does not contain *shin* nor *tav*. According to

Exodus 18:4 the meaning of Eliezer's name is אלהי אבי בעזרי ("the God of my father is my help"), and when this is added to the name it results in 666 which is a number of good omen and fortitude, attaching as it does to the *sephiroth* of Tiphareth. Again, this calculation will work in either the Standard Gematria cipher or the Biblical Gematria cipher because it contains no *shins* nor *tavs*.

The Talmud also comments on the notariqon of the Torah, citing the 600,000 Israelites who are said to have left Egypt as an example by calculating with the initial letters of the names of the tribes. Alternatively Gen. Rabbah gives an example of the name Isaac as a word where every letter has a distinct relevance: י for the ten commands that tested his father Abraham, צ for the age of Isaac's mother, ח for the amount of days old he was when circumcised, and ק for the age of his father.

Equivalents are sometimes shown between words, using one or more types of gematria (sometimes Standard Gematria openly but Biblical Gematria concealed).

The numerical value of a word may have an intrinsic value. For instance, in Standard Gematria the number of *haSatan* is 364 which is taken to mean Satan cannot accuse anyone on the one day of Yom Kippur. A technique drawn from *midrashim* is to ignore the place value of numbers and use only their absolute value, and sometimes a further reduction is made that reduces the entire sum to its base value between 1 and 10. However there is nothing to say these later variations and many more minor variations besides were ever used by writers of the Torah, and any exegesis made with them would be a post hoc ergo propter hoc fallacy were it not for the principle that God exists across all time, therefore leaving open the possibility of prophetic or inspired exegesis, although that might qualify as an "appeal to God", which is another type of logical fallacy, supposedly, depending on your conceptualization of God.

Given the secrecy with which the Merkabah was kept, there is a limit on how informative the Talmud can be on the matter of the scribal conventions and methodology of the *sopherim*. However we can learn some things from the Sages and Rabbis from the examples they give. Another source of information we have about it comes from the Merkabah Mystics.

Although at first the Merkabah was a sacred secret knowledge that was kept in closed circles, in the 130 years after the fall of the second Temple (70 CE) there was a period of relative openness where the great Tannaic sages taught the Oral Law, discussed the Merkabah, and passed from teacher to student the basis for the Mishnah, Tosefta and

Talmud. Around 30 years after the fall of the second temple, the works of the Hekhalot (Palaces) began to appear. These describe spiritual travels across the Seven Palaces to reach the throne of God. In comparison to the practices of the first temple, where the priestly secrets were only taught to scribes of the temple, priests, and members of the royal family, Jewish men during the first few centuries of the common era had far greater access to teachers and sacred knowledge.

The knowledge was still secret, but it was not so secret that it could not be learned from a teacher of the Oral Law.

> Ben 'Azzai was once sitting expounding the Torah. Fire surrounded him. They went and told R. 'Akiba, saying, 'Oh! Rabbi! Ben 'Azzai is sitting expounding the Torah, and fire is lighting him up on all sides.' Upon this, R. 'Akiba went to Ben 'Azzai and said unto him, 'I hear that thou wert sitting expounding the Torah, with the fire playing round about thee.' 'Yes, that is so,' replied he. 'Wert thou then,' retorted 'Akiba, 'engaged in counting the secret chambers of the Merkabah?'
>
> Midrash Rabba on Canticles, i. 12

The temple was gone, but the ancient map of the temple survived in the idealized format of the Seven Palaces. Each part of the Temple, from the Palace of the King to the Holy of Holies had been associated with a letter, so the architecture which reflected God's creation was not lost.

With the loss of the physical temple, the conceptual temple took up a greater role in the consciousness of the Jewish people, as did the practice of magick (practical Kabbalah). Magical incantations were composed which the Talmud and Midrash call "using the Divine Name". Perhaps for the first time, the sole focus was shifting from the macrocosm of God to include the microcosm of man. It was around this time, that the *Sepher Yetzirah* which was written under the influence of Greek philosophy appeared to take the tradition in a new direction. Instead of Seven Palaces, it discussed ten *sephiroth* (emanations), and both the macrocosm and the microcosm were viewed as products of the combination and permutation of the holy Hebrew letters.

When the Tannaic stage ended (200 CE), teaching and discussion of the Merkabah became mostly prohibited, except for those people who had discovered it for themselves. The reasons for this development were complicated and not entirely clear. The secret knowledge of the Merkabah was an oral tradition, and the Sages may have been offended by texts that purported to be initiated knowledge being written down at all.

My theory is that they forbade their students to write of it or discuss it with others, and these instructions came to hold added weight once they were written down in the Talmud, which was modified in the Mishnah.

> One does not expound upon the subject of forbidden relations in the presence of three. Nor the Work of Creation in the presence of two. Nor the Chariot in the presence of one, unless he is a Sage and understands from his own knowledge. One who contemplates four things, it would have been better had he not come into the world: what is above, what is beneath, what came before, and what came after. All those that take no thought for the honor of their Creator, it would have been better that they not come into the world.
>
> Mishnah Haggidah 2:1

Once the Mishnah, Tosefta, and Talmud were published the culture became increasingly dependent upon these works and the time of the Sages came to an end (220 CE).

Earliest Rabbinic Merkabah commentaries were exegetical expositions of visions of God riding upon his chariot in the heavens, accompanied by all the divine assembly.

One mention of the Merkabah in the Talmud notes the importance of the passage: "A great issue—the account of the merkavah; a small issue—the discussions of Abaye and Rava [famous Talmudic sages]." The sages Rabbi Yochanan Ben Zakkai (d. circa 80 CE) and later, Rabbi Akiva (d. 135) were deeply involved in Merkabah exegesis. Rabbi Akiva and his contemporary Rabbi Ishmael ben Elisha are most often the protagonists of later Merkabah ascent literature.

Verman delineates four periods of early Jewish mysticism; from 800–500 BCE involving Chariot mysticism, to 300–100 BCE developing apocalyptic trends, to 100 BCE and the development of early Rabbinic Merkabah mysticism such as the *PaRDeS* ascent; also related to early Christian mysticism, and until 200 CE, continuing till circa 1000 CE, Merkabah mystical ascent accounts in the Merkabah–Hekhalot literature. Merkabah exegesis was also present in some of the texts that were unearthed at Qumran, indicating that the Dead Sea community were Merkabah exegetes. There were Merkabah homilies with detailed descriptions of Seven Heavens, encircled with lightning and flame and guarded over by cherubim. These heavens contain Seven Palaces (Hekhalot), and in the highest palace resides God's glory that is visualized as being seated upon the wings of the cherubs atop of the Ark of Testimony as a throne. But these divine visions are twice described as coming after looking down into the waters of a pool or lake and seeing the Chariot pass by in a reflection, and so the individual ascent is often called a descent.

The rabbis used the term *Ma'aseh Merkabah* for the various texts, homilies, and visionary narratives connected with the Chariot and *Ma'aseh Bereshit* for texts connected with the Creation narratives of Genesis 1–2. However these studies were not mutually exclusive, and were (in fact) interdependent with the Chariot providing a map of creation.

Essentially the accounts of the Hekhalot literature are part of the *Ma'aseh Merkabah*, being accounts of visions of spiritual ascents into heaven with the aid of angels, usually to gain insight into Torah. They are different from the Qumran homilies and apocalyptic literature in that they have no interest in eschatology, fallen angels, or demonology, and they open up the possibility of divine ascent to all comers. Through prayer and fasting, the recital of hymns, and the magical intoning of the secret names of God, the mystic would travel in their mind's eye through the heavenly Palaces. At each gate he would give the relevant incantations, seals, and angelic names that were needed to get past the *malakim*.

While I am sure that in some of these texts gematria was embedded, I haven't attempted a proper study of them because in most cases the language is written in Aramaic and also because they were all redacted after the third century.

Texts that are part of the Hekhalot works include *Hekhalot Rabbati*, *Hekhalot Zutarti*, 3rd Enoch, and *Ma'aseh Merkabah*. Many other fragmentary manuscripts seem to belong to this genre:

1) *Hekhalot Zutartey* ("The Lesser Palaces") describes the ascent of Rabbi Akiva;
2) *Hekhalot Rabbati* ("The Greater Palaces") describes the ascent of Rabbi Ishmael;
3) *Ma'aseh Merkabah* ("Account of the Chariot") is a collection of hymns to be recited during the ascent;
4) *Sepher Hekhalot* ("Book of Palaces") is a narrative in the name of Rabbi Ishmael which describes an ascent and a divine transformation of Enoch into the archangel Metatron. It is also known as Enoch 3.
5) Shi'ur Qomah ("Measurement of the Body") describes the Creator as seen at the end of the ascent. It is an exegesis of the Song of Songs.

The *Sefer Yetzirah* ("Book of Creation") describes a mixed cosmogony inherited from the Merkabah tradition but with Neoplatonic influences.

It presents a linguistic theory of creation by which God creates the universe by the combination of the twenty-two letters of the Hebrew alphabet which emanates into ten *sephiroth* belonging to the Tree of Life.

Elisha ben Abuyah's teachings under the heading of "The Work of the Chariot" was regarded as heretical. Both Rabbi Akiva and the "Akher" use motifs with "two-thrones" referred to by Daniel in Chapter 7. But by the time of the final editing of the Mishnah the study and practice of Merkabah-oriented work was officially frowned upon by Rabbinic authorities and those who pursued learning of this sort were marginalized over the next several centuries until men like Joseph Gikatilla and Moses Ben Leon brought it back to the table under the Kabbalah movement.

b. Kabbalah

Gematria is just one of the ways by which Kabbalists interpreted the Tanakh. The writings of Kabbalists are highly visual and descriptive, involving the relationships between all things and God in creation. Authors such as Joseph Gikatilla and Moses ben Leon invite the reader to a world of mental maps and systems of classifications.

Mystics the world over build such systems, as they can be used in meditation and philosophical esoteric reflection to reach states of spiritual union and transcendence. Hebrew mysticism distinguishes itself amongst the traditions of the world by having the most complex systems.

This is not to say such complexity is not needed. If Kabbalah is complex it is because life itself is complex and filled with contradiction. Albert Einstein once said:

> It can scarcely be denied that the supreme goal of all theory is to make the irreducible basic elements as simple and as few as possible without having to surrender the adequate representation of a single datum of experience.

It started simply enough among the ancient Hebrews: just twenty-two basic, quintessential classifications of creation which were represented by the twenty-two letters. They were things common in the lives of all people, and they were easily understood and memorized, and organized into a spatial relationship with one another.

The corresponding qualities of the letters grew over time to encompass esoteric and philosophical teachings. Take the idea of travelling souls for an instance. Souls were thought to pass between the heavens and the earth between *daleths* (4, "doors") that stood between the realms. Or take the letter *cheth* (8) which stood for the creation of human beings in the image (reflection) of Elohim. Thus there came to be a map for creation and a map for human beings. Necessarily, there emerged a further map for the relationship between all these things—between God, creation and human beings in a descending chain of existence. These maps were the Seven Palaces, the Tree of Life, and the four Worlds.

From antiquity, the *Sepher Yetzirah* had influenced the development of Jewish mysticism until a microcosmic system, suitable to describe the properties and qualities of the living human being, emerged as the Zeir Anpin (The Tree of Life).

A fifth world, Adam Kadmon, was conceptualized as divine light (or something beyond light) which exists in a state of pure potential. A reflection of Adam Kadmon exists in the human psyche as the collective essence of the soul, *yechidah*, namely the *neshamah* ("breath"), *ruach* ("wind", or "spirit") and *nephesh* ("living being"). The word *ruach* has the set value of 2, and the sum of *neshamah*, *ruach*, and *nephesh* is 233, which is the gate value of the House of God: 233 = נשמה + ב + נפש.

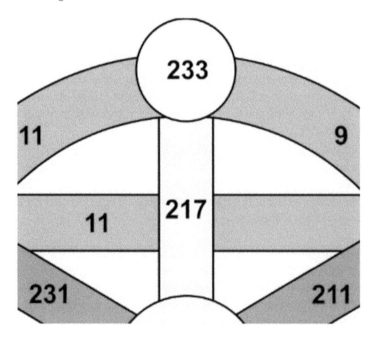

Though discussion of the Merkabah had been banned by the sages, the Provence School encouraged the private study of it:

But whoever turns his heart from worldly affairs and delves in the
Works of the Chariot is accepted before God as if he prayed all day.

The *Bahir* (1174 CE)

The *Bahir* is a book of Hebrew mysticism about the Hebrew alphabet, the
first verse of the Bible, the Chariot, the *sephiroth*, and the soul. It was published by the Provence School and it marked a new chapter of Jewish mysticism that came to be called Kabbalah. The secrecy which had shrouded the
Merkabah in earlier centuries still pervaded the subject, so their teachings
are expressed in philosophical, cryptic, visionary and theosophical ways.

> ... regarding 'The Workings of the Chariot—Ma'aseh Merkavah—
> 'מעשה מרכבה, the word Merkavah—מרכבה-chariot is related to the
> word הרכבה—which means to combine or compose, referring
> to the combinations of letters, which carry meaning, just as the
> chariot carries its rider. Primarily, the methodology of Temurah-
> letter exchange, is referred to as Ma'aseh Merkavah-the Act of the
> Chariot or the act of combining the letters.
>
> Joseph Gikatilla (Ginat Eroz)

Later Kabbalists like Isaac Luria wrote about the Tree of Life almost
exclusively, and extended the schema of the Tree by associating each of
the four worlds with it.

Earlier Kabbalists, like Joseph Gikatilla and Moses ben Leon, associated the letters of the alphabet with Beriah, the Seven Palaces with the
World of Yetzirah, and the Tree of Life with the World of Assiah.

The names of three of these worlds are mentioned in Isaiah 43:7:

יצרתיו אף עשיתיו כל הנקרא בשמי ולכבודי בראתיו

All those who have called in my name, and for my glory, I have created him, I have formed him, Yes, I have made him

And these are correlated with the words:

שמי ("my name"), ולכבודי ("Aztiluth"), בראתיו ("Beriah")

יצרתיו ("Yetzirah"), עשיתיו, and form the calculation:

שמי + ולכבודי + בראתיו + יצרתיו + עשיתיו =   777 ("Assiah").

The highest world of Aztiluth was formless, and the realm of Hashem—nothing could be said of it.

The world of Beriah was the world of the spirits of the holy alephbet, or the malakhim. Descending from Aztiluth, Hashem used these letters to create the world of Yetzirah (formation), and it is the creation of this world which is described in the first two chapters of Genesis. The map of this creation was the Seven Palaces, and every verse of Genesis corresponds to a letter from the world of Beriah and a path or Palace in the world of Yetzirah.

Lastly there is the world of Assiah (action) and the Tree of Life. The Tree became the representation of the world above from the point of view of an individual that is subject to time. In the world above and on the Seven Palaces, light and darkness, day and night are seen in balance, represented by the Palaces of the Aleph, but in the world below (in Assiah) an individual may only know day or night as reported from his senses. He cannot appreciate noon at the same time as midnight as he could from the world above.

Similarly, on the Seven Palaces there is a door that allows souls to be born upon the earth (the First Palace of the Heh) and another door that allow souls entry to heaven upon the death of the body, but in the world of Assiah, we may only appreciate the creation from one who is already living. Therefore, the *sephiroth* reflect the creation above but in a way that is relevant to the individual man or woman. For instance, the Sphere of Hod resonates beneath the Palace of the Daleth (the door into the world), and represents the idea of thoughts entering into the mind of a person. The Sphere of Netzach resonates beneath the Palace of the Daleth (the door into the heavens), and represents the idea of emotions flowing out towards others we are attached to and the communal reality of shared experience, our lives as a small mirror of the great creation.

On the Tree of Life, the left side is feminine and the right side is masculine, but on the Seven Palaces, the left side is masculine and the right side is feminine, and together they represent that backwards–forwards resonance or current between the individual and the universe.

The genius of the Kabbalists was to map a route to Hashem by aligning the microcosm of man with the macrocosm of God so that they might better serve his will on earth.

Kabbalah relates the Merkabah vision of Ezekiel, and the Throne vision of Isaiah (Isaiah 6:1–8) describing the seraph angels, to the four spiritual realms.

The highest World, Aztiluth ("Emanation"), is the realm of absolute divine manifestation, metaphorically described in the vision as the likeness of a man on the throne of sapphire.

The second World, Beriah ("Creation"), is the first independent creation, the realm of the Throne, denoting God descending into Creation, as a king limits his true greatness and revealed posture when seated. The World of Beriah is the realm of the higher angels, the seraphim.

The third World, Yetzirah ("Formation"), is the realm of archetypal existence, the abode of the main Hayyot angels. They are described with faces of a lion, ox, and eagle, and they are the archetypal origins of all creation.

The lowest World, Assiah ("Action"), is the realm guided by the lower channels of the Ophanim.

All prophecy is thought to emanate from the realm of Aztiluth, which descends to be clothed in the vessels of lower Worlds. Some Kabbalists believe that Isaiah's prophecy saw the Merkabah in the World of Beriah, restraining his explanation by realizing the inadequacy of description, and that Ezekiel saw the Merkabah in the lower World of Yetzirah, causing him to describe the vision in rapturous detail.

The two visions also form the Kedushah Jewish daily liturgy:

> We will sanctify Thy name in the world even as they sanctify it in the highest heavens, as it is written by the hand of Thy prophet: "And they (the Seraphim) called one unto the other and said, Holy, holy, holy is the Lord of Hosts; the whole earth is full of His glory."
>
> Isaiah 6:3

Those over against them (the Hayyot) say:

> Blessed be the glory of the Lord from His place.
>
> Ezekiel 3:12

And in Thy holy words it is written, saying:

> The Lord shall reign forever, thy God, O Zion, unto all generations; Hallelujah.
>
> Psalms 146:10

According to the Kabbalistic explanation, the Seraphim ("burning" angels) in Beriah realize their distance from the absolute divinity of Aztiluth and call "Holy, Holy, Holy", meaning removed or separated. This causes their "burning up" and continual self-nullification, ascending to God and returning to their place.

The lower Hayyot ("living" angels) in Yetzirah say, "Blessed" (which is a doubling) be the glory ... from "His place" of Aztiluth. Though lower than the Seraphim, their powerful desires draw down divine vitality from the supreme realm of Aztiluth, to lower creation and man. In Ezekiel's vision, the Hayyot have a central role in the Merkabah's channeling of the divine flow in creation.

Merely learning about the architecture of Jewish mysticism and the technical secrets of the art of gematria will not by themselves lead to spiritual progression. They are aids to the development of spiritual understanding, to be used in meditation, prayer, and ritual, and during the philosophical study of sacred texts. To understand this experientially then we can dwell upon each letter a day in turn; what it represents both in macrocosmic creation as well as what it means personally and individually (the microcosm). In the unity of macrocosm and microcosm the individual may attain the higher transcendental and "god-touched" levels of consciousness.

By working with the system, and ascending the Tree of Life, the system is also working upon you—pervading your unconscious and making links to your conscious awareness of your spiritual life. According to Jewish mystics, the letters of the Hebrew alphabet are vehicles of God's essence and creative power. The idea is to resonate with the macrocosm and make yourself like a Merkabah (chariot) that can be driven by God to achieve the accomplishment of the divine will flowing through you.

There were various subdivisions of the Tree of Life discussed in the *Zohar*. Accordingly, the Seven Sephiroth of Zeir Anpin, namely: Chesed, Geburah, Tiphareth, Netzach, Hod, Yesod, and Malkuth are called the Nukva. The Nukva is called the daughter of Seven, having seven sides, four aspects and twelve knots (paths) of Chesed, Gevurah, Netzach, and Hod which stand upon the body of Nukva.

Very important to the Kabbalists were the names of God upon the Tree and the Palaces, as these "gates" were used during mystical ascendance to pass the tests of the angels which guarded the House of God.

> In thirty-two most occult and wonderful paths of wisdom did Yah
> the Lord of Hosts engrave his name: God of the armies of Israel

(Tzevaot Elohai Yisrael), ever-living God (Elohim Hayim), mer-
ciful and gracious (v'Melekh Olam), sublime, dwelling on high
(El Shaddai), who inhabiteth eternity. He created this universe by
the three derivatives: Writing (SePHeR) Numbers (SePHoR), and
Speech (SiPuR).

A translation of the *Sepher Yetzirah*

The *Sepher Retzial* is a magical grimoire of practical Kabbalah about the
angel Raziel who teaches the power of speech, the energy contained
within the 22 letters of the Hebrew alphabet, and about their permuta-
tions and the meanings of the holy names.

Ginnat Egoz is an introduction to the mystic symbolism of the alphabet, vowel points, and the Divine Names. It was Gikatilla's first book,
and it greatly influenced Moses de León when he came to write the *Zohar*.

The Merkavah/Chariot, also literally means 'Composition-
Harkavah' and refers to the compositions of the letters of expres-
sion which are "vehicles" that carry meaning, as mentioned before.
[...] Primarily, what should be understood here is that although all
compositions (Merkavah) are drawn forth and rooted in Hashem's
name, the name of Hashem-יהו"ה itself completely transcends the
compositions (Merkavah). Nevertheless, it should also be understood that the 'chariot' is totally sublimated to the Rider, who conducts it according to His will, blessed is He. Allegorically, this may
be compared to how speech is totally sublimated the speaker and
cannot exist without him.

Joseph Gikatilla (*Ginnat Eroz*)

Shaarei Orah ("Gates of Light") is Gikatilla's second book. It discusses 300
names of God and is organized into ten chapters, one for each *sephirah*.
The Arizal call it "a key to understanding the mystical studies", and the
Vilna Gaon recommended that his students study it. It is written in the
form of a letter from Gikatilla to one of his disciples (Shualt Imameni)
who has asked him to help him to advance in knowledge of God:

... to shine before you a way to understand the path in the subject
of understanding the names of G-d.

Using the holy names for selfish reasons was strongly frowned
upon by all the *merkubalim* (kabbalistic teachers), but Gikatilla saw

that the disciple was deeply motivated to come to a greater closeness and understanding of God, and not driven by base or egotistic
desires (low magicks), so he allowed it and instructed him with this
brilliant work.

> Therefore I need to instruct you the way which the light falls, in
> other words to show you how to go about to actually attach to
> God, and to show you the way that God desires or conversely does
> not desire. When you reach that state of reaching that which God
> desires, then you will be able to call on God and God will answer
> you. Will be that those that are close to him, you will love God with
> all your soul, and you will take pleasure in God and he will give
> you what you desire.[37]

Shaarei Orah is a beautiful work and when it is approached after a
careful examination of the gematria of the gates of the Seven Palaces, much that is obscure about it can be seen in a clearer light of
comprehension.

c. Gates

Each part of the Seven Palaces corresponds to a letter and is part of several "gates" (combinations of letters).

Gates may also be made from combinations of two or more gates,
and each of the letters which share their paths with other letters may
contribute to the overall gate or may be calculated individually. For
instance, the gate of the four letters; *shin, tav, tsade* and *qoph* is 206,
but to get the individual gate for the *tsade* we'd add 90 to the letters at either side which are *daleth* (4) and *heh* (5) so the gate of the
tsade is 99. Another thing we can do is count the top threefold gate
thrice, and the bottom fourfold gate four times, i.e. 217 * 3 = 651, and
206 * 4 = 824.

To find a gate value for the Palaces rather than the paths between
them, then we need to add the values of the letters in the adjacent paths
AND the value of the letter on their opposite Palaces. For example (not
counting the *beth*):

> The Gate of Resh = *gimel* + *heh* + *zayin* + *aleph* + *yod* + *daleth* + *nun* +
> *heh* + *samekh* + *daleth* + *ayin* + *aleph* + *lamed* + *resh* = 450.

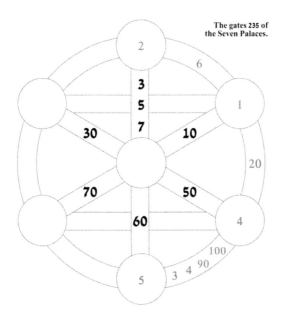

The gates **235** of the Seven Palaces.

Spokes: 3 + 5 + 7 + 10 + 30 + 50 + 60 + 70 = 235
Right Column: 2 + 6 + 1 + 20 + 4 + 3 + 4 + 90 + 100 + 5 = 235.

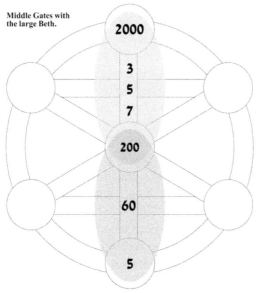

Middle Gates with the large Beth.

2000 + 3 + 5 + 7 + 200 = 2215
200 + 60 + 5 = 265
2215 + 265 = 2480 = 248 × 10.

Gates are fascinating because of the way certain numbers are reflected around the set. For instance there are two gates with the value of 235:

Nor are we restricted to using the small values of the letters. For instance, when a letter is written large it represents the thousands. Consider what happens to the gates when we do this for the letter *beth*:

In chapter 1, I presented you with two diagrams of the gates using the Biblical Gematria cipher, because I'm not sure whether it was the convention or the norm to count the *beth* into the gates or count it out, as it is left out of the Holy Name and set apart in the Seven Palace.

If we include the *beth* (2) then we can correlate the diagram with Ezekiel's gematria work involving the man, lion, ox and eagle, but if we consider the diagram once the *beth* is not included, we see a sum of 930 for the three gates above the first Palace gate (215 + 450 + 265), and when that is added to the gate of first palace (670) it gives a grand total of 1600 (800 x 2). On the other hand, consider the sum of the gates of the Palaces of the Aleph when a added to the gate of the *resh* when we include the *beth* in their gate numbers: 295 + 253 + 452 = 1000. Also, if we add together all the gates from the paths while including the *beth*, and we multiply the gate of the 3 by 3 and the gate of the 4 by 4, we arrive at the number 3108 which is 777 * 4:

$$(217 * 3) + (206 * 4) + 9 + 11 + 11 + 25 + 45 + 88 + 209 + 211 + 231 + 254 + 265 + 274 = 3108.$$

But perhaps the gates were not supposed to be either one way (with the *beth*) or the other (without the *beth*). The ambiguity suits the theology of the Palaces, showing that God is at once pervasive through creation and apart from it.

> The existence of the world is through letters, the existence of the letters through numerics, and the numerics exist through God.
> R. Joseph Gikatilia, Gināth Egōz, p. 289.

The gates of the Seven Palaces can also be represented with the Genesis Order Cipher and the reversal cipher. The Genesis Order Cipher may have been the first way that numerals were associated with the Seven Palaces, since the letter *beth* has the value of 1 for the Seventh Palace:

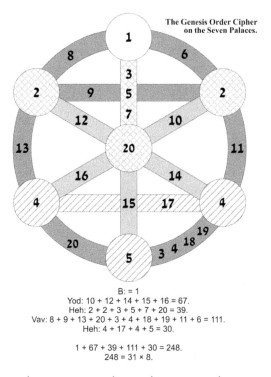

The Genesis Order on the Seven Palaces.

d. Sacred & secret

The associated oral mysticism had it that God had created everything using the letters as primordial tools, and the Seven Palaces existed as his primordial Torah.

Therefore the mysticism surrounding the letters and the Seven Palaces were holy secrets of great power in the ancient imagination. Each letter, path, and palace was the basis for ritual practices, observances, festivals, and prayers, and they remain so even today.

The Palaces have been called (from first to seventh) Vilon, Rakia, Shehakim, Zevul, Ma'on, Makhon, and Aravot, but from where the names of these come is obscure. Teachers of Kabbalah exhorted their students to be like a Merkabah, and to resonate with all that is good within creation in order to serve God.

We were never intended to take the imagery of the Merkabah literally—not by Ezekiel nor Joshua nor Elijah not Job. The chariot symbolizes the diverse ways that God manifests in this world, with all these diverse parts being represented by a letter. God is not made up of these forms, but each letter is represented by his Name, which carries his outer glory.

If you have been reading this guide in sequence, by now you are privy to a couple of technical secrets that you will not find stated plainly in other written works on Kabbalah. The priestly order of the alphabet, and the gematria values for the Bible, were knowledge that belonged to the Merkabah. This was highly secret and was only communicated orally to a restricted class of persons, or else written about cryptically in works that were not translated.

> The Gemara asks: What is the meaning of the continuation of this verse: "For stately clothing" This is one who conceals matters that the Ancient of Days, i.e., God, concealed. And what are these? These are the secrets of the Torah, the esoteric Act of Creation and the Act of the Divine Chariot, which should remain hidden.
>
> Pesachim. 119a. 2–5

The motivation of the Jewish people to keep the core of their letter mysticism a secret comes from a protective tradition surrounding the sacred and the holy. There was fear that their knowledge might be misused if it fell into the wrong hands—for instance, by people trying to use the names of God for their own gain rather than to grow closer to the divine presence. There was also a fear of being ultimately culpable for acts that lead to the disrespect of God through the profaning of his name.

> The forbidden degrees may not be expounded before three persons, nor the Account of Creation before two, nor the Account of the Chariot before one alone, unless he is a Sage that already understands of his own knowledge.
>
> Mishnah Hagigah 2:1

The most abstract motivation comes from the mystical view that God transcends all things of matter and form, and thus in narrative God is either described in terms that place the deity behind some formless effulgence, or as dwelling in a profound darkness that is beyond sight. The Hebrew letters are regarded as glyphs for the spirits of Elohim

(Malachim) who participated in the creation of the world—spirits that could be extremely dangerous if the worship that belonged to God alone came to them instead.

> ... all the Merkavot-chariots of composition are tied to the name Elo"him [אלהים] since this is the name that is used throughout the act of creation (Ma'aseh Bereshith) to compose all compositions.
>
> Joseph Gikatilla (*Ginat Eroz*)

To keep the gematria values of the Torah a secret in the Talmud and the various commentaries (Mishnah), a simple solution was applied. Because the *Ashuri* script had five more letters (the *sofit* forms ץ,ף,ן,ם,ך) than the Paleo-Hebrew script it could be extended to represent values from 1–900 by raising the value of the letter *shin* to 300 and the letter *tav* to 400. Once done, the cover-cipher resembled an extended Hebrew version of the Standard Greek cipher. However in the Talmud we find Standard Gematria (not extended) is the most used form of cipher (on the surface). Due to the counter-intuitive presence of two letters with the same value, twice, in Biblical Gematria, this "bait and switch" routine was enormously successful.

With true Biblical Gematria, the Christian is suddenly granted insights into his own scripture that has been denied him for generations, while the occultist is handed the keys they need to unite the macrocosm with the microcosm and cross the abyss—as long as they use the right gematria cipher for the text. Yet to learn and practice this ancient art we need to know a lot more about it than the value of the letters. Scribes of the ancient world weren't comparing the values of one word with another. Ancient gematria was, in every sense, the early practice of arithmetic. It has reserved verbs and prepositions to indicate mathematical operations like addition, subtraction, multiplication, or division. Sentences, verses, and sometimes entire chapters reveal number values, ranging from mundane things like the 365 days in a year, to the temple mysticism.

The Talmudic interdictions concerning Merkabah speculation are numerous and widely held. Discussions concerning the Merkabah were limited to only the most worthy sages, and admonitory legends are preserved about the dangers of overzealous speculation concerning the Merkabah.

Interdictions against speculation about the Merkabah appear in the Tanakh, the Talmud and the Mishnah. For example:

> Seek not out the things that are too hard for thee, neither search the things that are above thy strength. But what is commanded thee, think thereupon with reverence; for it is not needful for thee to see with thine eyes the things that are in secret.
>
> Ecclesiasticus 3:21

It must be studied only by exemplary scholars:

> Ma'aseh Bereshit must not be explained before two, nor Ma'aseh Merkabah before one, unless he be wise and understands it by himself.
>
> Mishnah Chagigah 2:1

Further commentary notes that the chapter-headings of *Ma'aseh Merkabah* may be taught, as was done by Rabbi Ḥiyya. According to Yer. Hagigah ii. 1, the teacher read the headings of the chapters, after which, subject to the approval of the teacher, the pupil read to the end of the chapter, although Rabbi Zera said that even the chapter-headings might be communicated only to a person who was head of a school and was cautious in temperament.

According to Rabbi Ammi, the secret doctrine might be entrusted only to one who possessed the five qualities enumerated in Isaiah 3:3 (being experienced in any of five different professions requiring good judgment), and a certain age is, of course, necessary. When R. Johanan wished to initiate R. Eliezer in the *Ma'aseh Merkabah*, the latter answered, "I am not yet old enough." A boy who recognized the meaning of חשמל (Ezekiel 1:4) was consumed by fire (Hagigah 13b), and the perils connected with the unauthorized discussion of these subjects are often described (Hagigah ii. 1; Shab. 80b).

These superstitions are like echoes of the secrecy of the priests who worshiped YHVH at the first Temple.

e. The Temple

The location of the first Temple is identical in description to that of the Temple of "El" located in the mountains, at the "source of the rivers; amidst the channels of the two oceans." It's a Temple plan that is the backbone of the garden of Eden narrative.

The very act of restricting the Hekhal (the "holy of holies") from all but one chief priest, and only once a year for the special purpose of saying "the Name", made it a special and exclusive space that would be imagined with awe by all around it. In the popular imagination, that was the house where God lived on Earth. Surely, they would imagine the space in complete darkness with the golden ark of the covenant inside, and sitting atop the wings of the cherubim, as if on a throne, with the clouds all around him, there was God, the focus of all their worship. Surely they would recreate the events that happened within the Hekhal once a year—the lighting of the lamps and the saying of the Name in their mind's eye as they celebrated.

The priests of YHVH had something else in their mind's eye too—a drawing that was revealed to each of them after initiation, that showed God's relationship to all creation through the holy letters. A new priest would have been shown by his brothers that the tabernacle before it and now the Temple was constructed according to a divinely ordained plan that portrayed everything in creation and God in everything through the Name.

> What is most amazing about Judaism is that Hashem is restricted to that holy of holies space and yet at the same time every accessible to us when we are open and mindful and embracing of God's creation.
>
> David Kolinsky

This idea is powerfully embraced in a visual way in the diagram of the Seven Palaces, because the upper *heh* is before the throne (the face of God) and the lower *heh* intersects with the Temple at its center[38] but embraces all the earth and the world of Assiah.

The priests and scribes of the Temple were fully invested in doing their duty to God, their King and their High Priest. They knew that just a few yards away was a seat for God atop the golden wings of the cherubim. On the sacred map of creation shown them, that space or interior was represented by the letter *beth*.

The Hekhal, or "holy of holies", was divided from the rest of a large room called the "holy place" by a veil that represented the *gimel* as the sky that hides the glory of God behind it. The ark represented the House of God, the *heh* was the foundation stone upon which rested

Possible correspondences to the First Temple.

the Ark, and the golden utensils represented the *zayin*. Or at least I believe those are the right attributions for 1 Kings 6–7. The study of the Temple is still one which is evolving for me. I'd advise you do your own study. Architectonic gematria is comparatively more difficult than text based work by several factors, because the link between the architectural features is symbolic.

Sometimes there is an obvious allusion. For instance, the table of shewbread and the letter *teth*, or the Sea of Bronze and the letter *samekh*, but other links are more tenuous and difficult to understand.

For those of you that would like to engage in this research area, I've included a highlighted text from 1 Kings chapter 6–7 in appendix 3. The chart above is my best estimation of the letter correspondences between the first Temple and the Seven Palaces, but I'm not so sure about letters like the *nun*, *ayin*, or *tsade* so I've left them blank for now.

Around the Hekhal were 30 chambers, fifteen to each side, which is the sum of *gimel* + (upper) *heh* + *zayin*. These provided chambers for scribes and for storage.

The holy place was lit by seven oil-lamps from their lampstands (*yod*), and it was furnished with altars for incense (*lamed*) and tables for shewbread (*teth*).

Outside of the Holy Place, a path that traversed the inner court to the Palace of Solomon (lower *heh*) represented the *samekh*.

The Temple could be entered through a number of gates by those who were ritually pure, and visitors participated in sacrificial meals. It was built very closely to the Kings palace, actually within earshot. The Kings palace may have functioned to parallel the bottom palace on the Wheel of the Chariot where the earthy domain and the physical creation of the world were manifest. In the Hall of Pillars (*heh*) the King sat in judgment on his throne. Further back from the King's Throne room was his palace and living area, and a hall like this was also made for the Queen.

An outer court connected the royal palace to an inner court with the Temple located in the center. Only priests were allowed in the precinct of the inner court which symbolically represented the Garden of Eden. The inner court parallels the rectangular section of the wheel of the chariot, bounded by the cross beams and the circumference.

The outer court was surrounded by service chambers used by priests, prophets, and courtiers, and they served for storage, for the eating of the sacrificial meat, and other functions.

In the inner courtyard stood a large bronze altar with a fire burning on top of it. Several types of sacrifice were performed atop this altar and the blood was collected and poured into the base of the altar with special bronze implements.

To the left and right of the entrance to the Temple were placed ten enormous bronze vessels filled with water and mounted inside wheeled stands. Each stand had four wheels and was decorated with cherubs, cattle, and lions. A huge basin, 'the Sea' (*yam*), was placed slightly to the left of the entrance, and this rested on twelve bronze cattle which were aligned to the north, south, east, and west. The ten vessels were used for washing meat and the priests used the Sea for washing themselves.

Symbolically the Sea represented the river flowing from the Garden of Eden, to water the garden before branching into four rivers. These four heads are metaphorical for the four spokes of the wheel that branch to the northeast, the northwest, the southeast, and the southwest from the axis, distributing the life-giving grace of the divinity from his residence.

The entrance to the house of God was flanked by two immense and freestanding bronze pillars that were topped with floral motifs of a lotus-shaped capital, decorated with pomegranates, and intertwined, tangled branches. Some writers have raised the possibility that they represent the two trees which grew in the middle of the Garden of Eden—the Tree of Knowledge and the Tree of Life.

The pillars have a likely correspondence with the path connecting the bottom palace with the solar palace at the axis of the wheel. If so, the symbolism of the two pillars may be related to the injunction of silence during the sacrifice, represented by the two letters *heh samekh*, meaning "silence" and *heh samekh resh*, meaning to take away or remove. As Zephaniah declared: "Be silent at the presence of the Lord YHVH—for the day of YHVH is at hand—for he has prepared YHVH a sacrifice and He has consecrated His guests." The pillars were named Yakhin and Boaz.

The entrance of the Temple is framed by four stepped and interlocking door frames. The entrance is usually portrayed as having double doors but there is nothing actually in the literature to definitively indicate this:

> For the entrance to the inner sanctuary he made doors out of olive wood that were one fifth of the width of the sanctuary. And on the two olive-wood doors he carved cherubim, palm trees and open flowers, and overlaid the cherubim and palm trees with hammered gold. In the same way, for the entrance to the main hall he made door frames out of olive wood that were one fourth of the width of the hall. He also made two doors out of juniper wood, each having two leaves that turned in sockets. He carved cherubim, palm trees and open flowers on them and overlaid them with gold hammered evenly over the carvings.
>
> 1 Kings 6:31

The doors may equally have been separated one from another for some cultic purpose. If so, this would explain the symbolism of having two palaces that are both attributed with the letter *daleth*; this letter is related to the pictogram of a door.

Door opening rituals are known to have been practiced in other ancient Near East Temples, and the first Temple was opened and closed every morning and evening with golden tools that were probably a type of key. It may be that when one door was opened in the morning the other was closed, and with the advent of the evening the morning door was closed and the evening door was opened. Again, from the literature there is nothing to suggest that the House of God was shut up for the night, or that cultic worship was strictly a day time affair—although this seems to be a common assumption. On the Wheel of the Chariot the entire left hand side appears to be associated with the daylight hours while the whole of the right hand side would correspond with the night time.

Once we have entered into the Temple, we find ourselves in a long room twice as long as wide known as the outer sanctum (*Heykhal*). The floor was laid with cypress wood and the walls and ceiling were paneled with fragrant Cederwood. The room is decorated and engraved with gourds and calyxes, continuing on with Garden of Eden motifs. Two side buildings flanked the *Heykhal*, again corresponding to the circumference, and these may have functioned as scriptoria and as storage areas for scrolls.

It was possible to walk about on the roof of the temple, and some Freemasons have suggested that the tabernacle may have been erected on the roof once a year in order to make the temple visually resemble a mountain.

At the far end of the *Heykhal* was the most important place in the Temple, the divine residence—Holy of holies—or *D'bir* which is an ornately decorated room with calyxes, palmettes, and cherubs. Outside in the *Heykhal* the sidewalls are lit with ten golden lamp stands containing golden oil lamps that illuminate the rest of the cultic furniture present, such as a table with an offering of bread and drinking vessels for the divine victuals. In front of the doors leading to the *D'bir* was an incense altar made of Cedarwood and plated with gold.

When entering the inner chamber to the divine residence you would pass within a short corridor surrounded by five interlocking frames. The walls were made of Cedarwood and covered with pure gold, although the room featured no illumination of any kind. In the center of the Holy of Holies there were two giant golden Cherubs with wings that filled the chamber.

According to Hurowitz these cherubs represented God's divine throne, and were the basis of the epithet "he who sits upon the Cherubs" (1 Sam. 44), and "Rider of the cherubs" (Ps. 18.11) and we are told that according to the Book of Chronicles, this cherub throne is a model of the Merkabah. The throne represented the seventh palace of the Merkabah wheel which is a place where, according to the *Zohar*, the "Ancient of Days" dwelt—a place where humans could not enter. Under the wings of the cherubs was the golden Ark that housed the tablets of the covenant containing the Ten Mitzvoth given by God to the Jewish people to obey.

> The gradual increase in the value of the materials and the sophistication of design parallels an increase in sanctity and limitations on those who may enter. The outer court would have been visited by the public at large, where the inner court was restricted to priests, and the inside of the Temple was open only to the high priest.
>
> Hurowitz

And all this was built in harmony to the Name, and the essentially organized nature of this harmony expressed in the Name has resounded down through the ages, influencing rationalists and mystics alike.

> Though G-d's incomprehensibility is an essential tenet of Judaism, harmony was seen as an integral quality of the Divine. This quality was apparent, too, in G-d's Ineffable Name. According to Maimonides, as well as the kabbalists, the Ineffable Name denoted G-d's essence, and described His 'absolute existence' and His causing existence. Medieval commentaries saw the Tetragrammaton as deriving from the words 'He was, Is, Will be' (יהיה הוה היה.) In the liturgical poem, Adon Olom (אדון עולם'), Master of the World', this description of G-d's transcendence was described with the adjective tif'oroh (תפארה') (beauty' or 'harmony'), implying that G-d's beauty and harmony becomes apparent through the unfolding of world history. Furthermore, as creation was seen as structured and beautiful, G-d's Name, responsible for its constant manifestation, expressed cosmic harmonic unity.
>
> Rabbi David Rubin[39]

f. The Holy Names

To the modern person, one of the most curious and surprising things about the story of the first Temple was that it was built for God's name.

> Now it was in the heart of my father David to build a house for the
> Name of the LORD, the God of Israel. But the LORD said to my
> father David, 'Since it was in your heart to build a house for My
> Name, you have done well to have this in your heart. Nevertheless,
> you are not the one to build it; but your son, your own offspring,
> will build the house for My Name.
>
> 1 Kings 8:17–19

One of the epithets for God is השם, Hashem, which means "the Name".
In the ancient Levant, names were secret and magical. Names were
gates to the soul of a being, and were bound to them. If a higher being
knew your name, all was well and good and you had a measure of protection; however, if a lower being knew it, chaos and destruction could
ensue. To pronounce a name is to bring something out of the realm of
the mind and down into the physical world.

The members of many primitive tribes have two names, one for public use, the other jealously concealed, known only to the man who bears
it. Even the immediate members of the family never learn what it is. If an
enemy should discover it, its bearer's life is forfeit. In highest antiquity
peoples, the occult power that inheres in the name is recognized, and
the name itself is known to be a mighty and awesome force in the hands
of the magician.[40]

The more such names a magician has garnered, the greater the number of spirits that are subject to his call and command. In Genesis 2, Adam
is given the ability to name all the animals of the earth, and thus Adam
gains the power to control the fate of each animal. In Exodus when Moses
asks the name of God, YHVH replies cagily אהיה אשר אהיה, which translates
as "I am that I am". He is not willing to reveal his name to Moses at first.

In Judaism the pronunciation of the name of God has always been
guarded with great care. It is preferable to say Adonai when in prayer
rather than say the name of God out loud. However it is fair to ask, how
secret can a name that is written in the Torah over 6,000 times be? The
answer to that is, very secret … even if the given name of YHVH is a
notariqon for the real ineffable name.

How the Name was originally vocalized is no longer certain. Its pronunciation was in time restricted to the Temple service, then to the High
Priest intoning it on the Day of Atonement, and after the destruction of
the Temple it received a substitute pronunciation both for the reading of
scripture and for its use at prayer.[41]

This leads to the obvious question—how is it that a name can be unutterable? And why, if the name was really unpronounceable, is it believed that the high priest of the Temple pronounced it once a year on Yom Kippur?

To answer this question we have to take another look at the Seven Palaces and appreciate it in four sections under the domain of the name YHVH:

Yod (220), heh (217), vav (480), heh (93).

The name YHVH is a notariqon for all the alephbet and each path and palace. However, because the letters *gimel* and *shin*, and *daleth* and *tav* share the same value and place order in the alephbet, one would have to have the ability to intone both letters at once in order to say the full name of YHVH. This is, of course, impossible, which is why the name is the ineffable name.

Making the name ineffable is likely the reason for having two letters in the 3rd and 4th positions of the alephbet too. But the point of speaking a name instead of merely thinking it is to open a doorway into the physical world, and the way this was established was through mimicry—essentially, sympathetic magic.

Each part of the First Temple represented a part of the Macrocosm, which meant that when the letter *gimel* was intoned there was a physical representation of the *shin* present, meaning that as long as the order of the letters of the name was known, the name could be said within the Temple to magical effect.

On the Seven Palaces, two of the values for the sections of *yod* and *vav* are referenced by the gematria of Genesis 1:1. 220 is the gematria of בראשית, which means "In the Beginning", and התורה, HaTorah, and also of YHVH when the reverse cipher is applied. 480 is the value of the rest of the gematria from Genesis 1:1: אלהים + השמים + הארץ, meaning "Elohim + the Heavens + the Earth" giving a total value for 1:1 of 700.

The other values are multiplications of 31, which is the value of the word אל for God in Hebrew: 217 = 31 x 7 93 = 31 x 3. The name אל=שדי, El Shaddai, has the gematria of 31 by the Genesis Order.

Hermetic Qabalah also finds these values to hold mystic significance. The magician and occultist Aleister Crowley gave his *Book of the Law* the sub figura number of 220. The first line produces the value Had +

Manifestation + Nuit = 480. The three Egyptian Gods of Nuit + Hadit + Ra Hoor Khuit = 700.

93 is also a number that is synonymous with his philosophy of Thelema, and Thelemites greet each other by uttering this number, and sign it in triplicate at the end of their letters: "93 93/93".

Other names or epithets for God in Judaism are: אל, אלהים, אלוה, אלהי, יהוה. These five names of God are frequently found in the Torah. They are the YHVH, El, Elohim, Eloah, and Elohe. Together, their gematria sums to 231, which is the gate number of the path of *lamed*. Less common names include the name אל ראי, El Rai (Genesis 16:13) which has the reverse cipher gematria of 231.

The *Sefer Yetzirah* speaks of 231 gates through which the world was created, meaning that the gateway of creation is through the combination of letters which represent Divine powers, but it isn't until Gikatilla's *Shaaerei Orah* ("Gates of Light") that we can appreciate how each of the holy names of God are attributed to the Sephiroth and the Palaces, and how meditating upon the names can transport one to a greater resonance with the harmony of God through his creation.

Gikatilla describes the Name as putting on other Names as if they were a suit of clothes or armour, depending upon the requirements of the situation (i.e. if the wicked were saying the name). Gikatilla quotes the Ethics of the Fathers where he says "Those who use the crown will perish", likening the holy names to crowns, and meaning those who use the names of God for their own use will perish.

g. The Shemhamphorash

As I write this, a thunderstorm has moved in and the air is close and anticipatory. It has yet to rain but there is a booming from the heavens that resonates across the land. It takes little effort to anthropomorphize the storm and see consciousness behind its rhythmic rumbles. For the ancients they imagined God riding by on his chariot in the sky, obscured from the view of mortals by the clouds beneath him.

In the minds of the ancients, God was the creator of the heavens and the earth, and his creative power was exercised through the measures of his holy letters, which were also numbers and aspects of creation. Job imagined that God spoke to him from a whirlwind, but beneath the semantic meanings of the book are numerical calculations and significances that are spells to summon the presence and attention of God to specific areas of creation—spells that dealt with everything from the fertility of the rain to the afterlife, to spells for childbirth, sacrifice, and prosperity.

Gematria in the Bible served many purposes for the scribe. It was used to organize compositions, such as the alphabetical arrangement of Genesis 1–2,[42] or the alphabetic acrostic of Proverbs.[43] It was used to explain the seasons and natural cycles.[44] It was used to convey secret, confidential, or slightly impolite information and opinion.[45] It was used to make jokes.[46] It was used to praise God. And it was number magic.

The psychology behind magic and ritual in ancient times are probably broadly similar today. Partly, it would have served to allow individuals the illusion of having some control over circumstances that were beyond their ability to affect through any other means. Rituals provide a sense of stability in life to the regular practitioner. Magic could be a reassurance, as well as an appeal to God.

Once these spells were extracted and spoken it was believed that the power of God would manifest.

According to tradition, Moses was believed to have parted the red sea using a spell within Exodus 14:19–21, commonly called the Shemhamphorash meaning "The Name Explicit".

> And the angel of God, who had gone before the camp of Israel, withdrew and went behind them. The pillar of cloud also moved from before them and stood behind them, so that it came between the camps of Egypt and Israel. The cloud was there in the darkness, but it lit up the night. So all night long neither camp went near the other. Then Moses stretched out his hand over the sea, and all that night the LORD drove back the sea with a strong east wind that turned it into dry land. So the waters were divided.

The act was a metaphor for the birth of Israel out of Egypt. The parting of the waters represented the breaking of the waters of the placenta. The letter tsade (90) represented birth, and thus the birth of a nation required the number of the spell to be 90 magnified by 100.

The Shemhamphorash is also known as the 72-fold name of God. Each line has 72 letters. Using the Reversal Cipher (see pg. 86) these three verses sum to exactly 9000.

ויסע מלאך האלהים ההלך לפני מחנה ישראל וילך מאחריהם ויסע עמות הענן מפניהם ויעמת

מאחריהם ויבא בין מחנה מצרים ובין מחנה ישראל ויהי הענן והחשך ויאר את הלילה ולא קרב

זה אל זה כל הלילה ויט משה את ידו על הים ויולך יהוה את הים ברוח קדים עזה כל הלילה וישם

את הים לחרבה ויבקעו המים = 9000

Rashi[47] suggested a reversal of line 20, and so it was thought by later writers that the Shemhamphorash should be read boustrophedonically to reveal 72 angelic names, although I think Rashi was hinting at the use of the Reversal Cipher. Perhaps inspired by Rashi, the *Sepher Raziel* details these supposed angelic names and corresponding letters of the Shemhamphorash.

Recitation of the 72-fold name supposedly had the power to cast out demons, heal the sick, prevent natural disasters, and bring death to enemies, and it has intrigued and inspired various authors through history, including Roger Bacon, Johann Reuchlin, Heinrich Cornelius Agrippa, Athanasius Kircher, Thomas Rudd, Blaise de Vigenère, and Samuel Liddell MacGregor Mathers.

i. The Trees of Life

There are several main versions of the Tree of Life that belong to different schools. Each one has different letter attributions and different shapes, so it can be difficult for the new Kabbalist to decide which one they should be working with.

We're going to look at the history and development of each one and assess their merits. The Tree of Life is the microcosmic counterpart of the Seven Palaces and shares many of the same letter attributions with it.

Even if we have not seen the Seven Palaces before, with a little bit of detective work it is possible to reconstruct its form and attributions from the Tree. This perhaps explains why early drawings of the Tree of Life do not show the letter attributions to the paths. In 1516 a diagram of the Tree of Life was drawn by Johann Reuchlin and it came to appear

Etz Chaim by Rabbi Chaim Vital (1573).

on the cover of Paolo Riccio's Latin translation of Joseph Gikatilla's Gates of Light.

Though a Christian, Reuchlin could not accept the authority of the Vulgate and was fascinated with Kabbalah. He spent most of his career

The Lurianic Tree.

focused on advancing German knowledge of Greek and Hebrew and he would become a leading figure in the fight against the proposed confiscation of Jewish books.

Johann Reuchlin's depiction of the Tree shows seventeen of the twenty-two paths and lacks the letter attributions. He had visited Rome in 1498 and had returned to Stuttgart laden with Hebrew books. His drawing visually expresses concepts he had likely only heard about through those manuscripts.

In 1573 Rabbi Chaim Vital wrote about the teachings of his master, the Ashkenazi Rabbi Yitschoq Luria (the Ari), and published a literary work on Kabbalah called *Etz Chaim* (עץ חיים). It includes a drawing of the *Sephiroth* but shows no paths between them.

Interestingly, in the original manuscript the sphere of Tiphareth is not included but Da'ath is.

Pardes Rimonim 1592.

However, the usual design that is associated with the Ari includes both Da'ath and Tiphareth; it excludes the paths between Malkuth, Hod, and Netzach and adds two extra paths between Geburah and Chokmah, and Chesed and Binah. Furthermore, there is no natural resonance with the Seven Palaces. Though generally ascribed to the Ari,

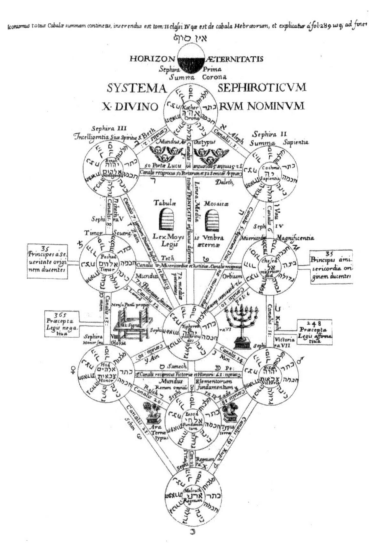

Oedipus Aegyptiacus 1652–1654.

the provenance of this tree is unknown and now Jewish Kabbalists use both trees in their studies.

In 1592 an unknown artist depicted a Tree with twenty-two paths, and a picture of it was printed in the posthumous editions of Moses Cordovero's Pardes Rimonim. The artist drew the same shape as the later Kircher Tree (sans the path of *peh*), but the letter attributions were absent.

Between 1652 and 1654, Athanasius Kircher (German Jesuit scholar and polymath) published a version of the tree in Oedipus Aegyptiacus. Kircher was an interesting man. He was instructed in Hebrew by a Rabbi and he taught mathematics and Hebrew at the University of Würzburg.

Kircher drew a Tree that was of the same shape as the one which appeared in Pardes Rimonum, but it included the letter attributions as well as some astrological features. It was the first time that anyone had published a version of the Tree with letters on it. Though the tree

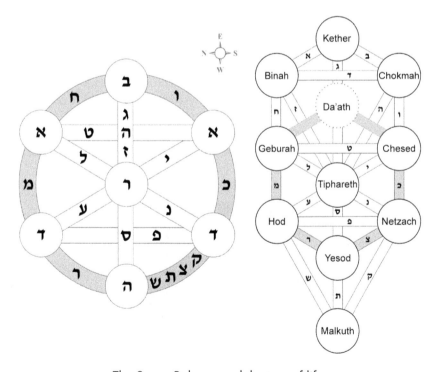

The Seven Palaces and the tree of life.

The image shows a fragment of text in Latin and Hebrew/Aramaic from the Sefer Dtzeniouthia.

§. 11. *Quid autem intelligitur, per illud: Et contemnentes vos silependentur? hic est talis, qui non potest instituere unionem nominis Sancti, nec intilere nexus veritatis; & derivare (superna) in locum requisitum; & honorare nomen Domini sui; Huic melius fuisset, si non offereretur, & multo magis, qui non attente meditatur, cum dicit Amen!*

The Sefer Dtzeniouthia, translated by Knorr von Rosenroth (1677–1678).

was taught in Kabbalistic schools, it was knowledge that was secret to Judaism, and Jewish scholars did not draw the letters' attributions in books that might have fallen into the hands of Gentiles. Kircher probably received the secret teachings about the tree by a Rabbi, because he believed Kabbalah could explain the mysteries of Christian religion.

The Seven Palaces remained hidden and outside Jewish circles few suspected that the Tree had begun its existence as an elaboration of the Seven Palaces.

The Palace of the Beth had been split up into the supernal *sephiroth* of Kether, Chokmah, and Binah. The Palace of the Heh had been divided into Yesod and Malkuth. The letters of the Palaces were redistributed onto the Tree, and paths that had included several letters were distributed evenly into separate paths. However, even with this redistribution there were fourteen paths (out of twenty-two) on the Tree that retained their original letter attributions. There was a clear lineage for the tree and one of Rashbi, Moses de Leon, or possibly his translator Christian Knorr von Rosenroth (it is not certain who), left a little riddle[48] in the

Christian Knorr Von Rosenroth.

annotations of the Zohar that gave cryptic instructions on how one would go about turning the Tree back to the Seven Palaces.

Rabbi Eliezer Tzvi wrote the following about the *Sepher Dtzeniouthia* in his text *Zohar Chai*:

> Sifra diTzni'uta was composed by Rashbi … and he arranged [it] from baraitas that were transmitted to Tannaim from mount Sinai from the days of Moshe.

Although claims such as these tend to be dismissed by modern historians, there is some truth to this because the *Sepher Dtzeniouthia* addresses the ancient knowledge of the Seven Palaces and the riddle shows an insider's perspective. However, I don't think the translator—Rosenroth himself—was such an insider, although his efforts to delineate the Hebrew Kabbalistic system would have a profound effect upon the type of Qabalistic system that was developed by the Hermetic Order of the Golden Dawn.

Δικτυον + γην + ιχθυων + μεγαλων + 153 = 777

Jesus told them, 'Bring some of the fish you have just caught.'

So Simon Peter went aboard and dragged
the net [161] to land [61].

It was full of large [193] fish [209], one hundred fifty-three [153].
And although there were so many, the net was not torn. = 777

John 21:10–11

CHAPTER 9

Gematria and the New Testament

C an you imagine what would happen to all the living beings on the earth if the sun never set and the night never came? According to the ancient way of seeing these things, the sun died every evening and was born anew each morning. In the Gospels, Jesus personifies the Solar journey as God's visible image of worship. Thus the gematria of "IHSOU Christou" represents the amount of time in a twelve-hour day. In the biblical story, Jesus has to die to save us all for the same reason that the sun has to die. Its a part of the solar narrative.

It should not be a surprise to modern Christians to discover gematria in the New Testament, since it is well known that the books of the New Testament were nearly all written by Jewish Christians.

Although it is not the tradition of the surviving Christian churches in the modern day to interpret their scripture using gematria, in the early years of Christianity the Church Fathers regarded the numbers of Holy Writ as full of mystical meaning and as an important branch of exegesis:

For the scripture saith; And Abraham circumcised of his household eighteen males and three hundred. What then was the knowledge given unto him? Understand ye that He saith the eighteen first, and then after an interval three hundred In the eighteen 'I' stands for ten, 'H' for eight. Here thou hast JESUS (IHSOYS). And because the cross in the 'T' was to have grace, He saith also three hundred. So He revealeth Jesus in the two letters, and in the remaining one the cross.

Barnabas 9:7

Gnostic Christianity drew their hermeneutics from both Jewish and Pythagorean sources, but the Church Fathers were quick to reject the suggestion that their own number mysticism was founded on the work of the philosophers. In a letter to Horontianus, St. Ambrose made this clear as he spoke of the Sabbath, saying:

> The number seven is good, but we do not explain it after the doctrine of Pythagoras and the other philosophers, but rather according to the manifestation and division of the grace of the Spirit; for the prophet Isaias has enumerated the principal gifts of the Holy Spirit as seven.

Yet after the Gnostic churches were persecuted into extinction, Christian teachers didn't want charges of heresy aimed at them and the practice of teaching any numerical component to Christian hermeneutics fell into disuse. The numerical teachings of the Church Fathers were largely forgotten, and the Isopsephy values used with the New Testament were lost to history with the most appalling consequences for Christian churches. With no hermeneutical element being taught to offer the requisite insight into the mysterious texts of the New Testament, Christian teachers and theologians began to make up their own interpretations of the text, which often wandered far from the original intent of their authors.

Churchmen interpreted scripture for political and financial gain and to reinforce oppressive Roman patriarchal attitudes towards women, reversing the relatively liberal attitudes that had pervaded the first century. There was a chance during the Reformation that a course correction could have been made. Johann Reuchlin made a strong case to Luther that only through Kabbalah could the Christian Scripture be truly understood, but Luther rejected the argument.

We can only imagine what the effect upon history may have been if Luther had embraced the notion of holistic exegesis that included the hermeneutical methods of the scribes themselves. One thing we might have predicted is a greater closeness between Christian and Jewish people which was based on their understanding of the worldview and spiritual conceptions held by ancient scribes. That is the goal of many scholars in theory, but in practice, cross cultural understanding of the hermeneutical devices of ancient scribes tends to be limited and superficial due to the secrecy that surrounded them.

The gematria of the New Testament has some quirky differences in comparison to Biblical Gematria. There are some words, such as the names of God, that appear in Greek only as placeholders for the Hebrew names and their corresponding number value. This is a particular feature of the Book of Revelation, so watch out for it! For example, in Revelation 1:8 we have the following sum: εγω ειμι + אלהים יהוה + α α α α + παντοκρατωρ = 777. The original text reading KURIOS DEOS ("Lord God") should be valued as YHVH ALHIM.

In general, the Gospels pay great attention to the time of day or night at which some events occur, and that should be taken special note of. The time element is important to the Gospels, so converting sums to base 60 can be an element of biblical wordplay.

The number of the name of Jesus Christ in Greek (Ιησου Χριστου) is 719, and every twelve hours the hour hand and second hand of an analog clock align exactly 719 times. Why is this significant? Because in John 11:9 it says: "Jesus answered, 'Are there not twelve hours of daylight? If anyone walks in the daytime, he will not stumble, because he sees by the light of this world.'" 719 minutes is 11:59; just one minute shy of twelve hours. What might this one minute have signified to Gospel writers?

The answer is: love. אהב. It is a mnemonic and it carries the value of 1. Jesus is a full twelve hours of day if you give him your love. Likewise, if you receive his "teaching"—which is also a mnemonic with the value of 1—your 1 would be added to the day.

There are many elements of a ritualized Merkabah ascent narrative that run through the gospels. In particular, those initiatory episodes where Jesus and the disciples ascend mountains and Jesus is anointed, so in general it is a good idea to check results from the text against the gates of the Seven Palaces. The scribes of the gospels try quite hard to be cryptic. When the text of the New Testament refers back to the Tanakh then it's best to check both texts for cross-matching gematria.

Some particular verses to pay attention to in the study of Revelation are those with the word Ἰδοὺ which is the Greek version of הנה ("behold!").

In Christianity, the motifs of the man, lion, ox, and eagle were used as symbols for the four gospel-writers, Matthew, Mark, Luke, and John, and thus they are frequently found in church decorations and architectural features. They are called the Zoë, and surround the throne of God in Heaven along with twenty-four elders and seven spirits of God (according to Revelation 4:1–11). These figures are originally found in Ezekiel 1:10:

ודמות פניהם פני אדם ופני אריה אל־הימין לארבעתם ופני־שור מהשמאול לארבעתן ופני־נשר לארבעתן

And the likeness of their faces, the face of a man and the face of a lion on the right side [of the word] to them four and had the face of an ox to the left [of the word] to them four and had the face of an eagle to them four.

As you can see immediately, there is some cryptic word-play in this calculation. What you don't see immediately is that, like the calculations in Genesis 1:1–2, there are multiple layers of calculations that involve different ciphers. This is what marks Ezekiel as a master gematrist.[49]

Taking the calculation as straight Biblical Gematria to begin with, we replace the words meaning "to them four" with the value of 4. To do this in the gematria calculator I replace the words for a *daleth* or *tav*. We then remove the words "on the right side" and "on the left side"

because these are flagwords that tell us to split each word and remove
the letter on the opposite side. Thus אריה ("Lion") becomes ארי, and שור
("Ox") becomes ור, and the calculation is:

ודמות פניהם פני אדם ופני ארי ת ופני ור ת ופני נשר ת = 1550.

1550 is precisely half of 3100 (God (אל) * 100).
By the Genesis Order this calculation gives us 400 (half of 800).
But there's more. Consider the 4 values that we now have for the
Man, Lion, Ox, and Eagle:
Man = אדם = 45.
Lion = ארי = 211.
Ox = ור = 206.
Eagle = נשר = 253.
These numbers are all gate values (pg. 159) on the Seven Places.
Man = Gate of Mem 45.
Lion = Gate of Yod 211.
Ox = Fourfold (*shin, tav, tsade, qoph*) Gate 206.
Eagles = Palace of Aleph 253.
Now let's add together all the letters from these Gates.
Mem (40) *yod* (10) *shin* (3) *tav* (4) *tsade* (90) *qoph* (100) *aleph* (1) = 248.
To the Jews this number was synonymous with the Patriarch
Abraham. It is as Rabbi Shimon ben Lakish said:

The patriarchs they themselves were the Divine Chariot!

The patriarchs were thought to be three legs or supports to the Holy
Throne of God which was set upon the Chariot.
To the Christians, 248 was similarly synonymous with the name
Ἐμμανουήλ ("Immanuel"), which is a curious construction in Hebrew:
עמנו אל. The last two letters (אל) spell out the word for "God", but the first
word appears to be a construction of the *ayin* (O, the eye, meaning "to
see") and the word מנו, *MNV*, which means "his number" so we might
come to a rough translation of Immanuel as "See his number God" or
perhaps "See God's number".
Christians believe that Isaiah was prophesizing the coming of Jesus
Christ as the messiah when he wrote:

לכן יתן אדני הוא לכם אות הנה העלמה הרה וילדת בן וקראת שמו עמנו אל

> Therefore will adoni [65] himself [12] to you a sign [a letter]—
> Behold! the virgin [150] will become pregnant [*2] and bear [*2] a
> son and call his name OMNV [166] AL [31].

When you have a "behold!" thrown into the middle of a line like this, it's a good bet that there's gematria both before and after it, but a "behold!" can show where one calculation stops and another begins. As far as the semantic meaning of the sentence goes, we should be able to find out what letter Isaiah was referring to.

Adoni himself = 77.

Virgin × 2 × 2 = 600 (Vav = 6).

OMNVAL = 197.

Adoni himself OMNVAL = 274 (gate value for the *ayin*).

But let's see what happens when we take the child from the virgin:

Adoni himself + (Virgin × 2 × 2) – OMNVAL = 480

… which is the gate value of the Vav in the Holy Name. Aha!

In the early days of Christianity, saying that you were "the Christ" could get you into hot water, but did anyone say they were "a Christ" perhaps?

εγω ειμι α χριστος = 777: meaning "I am a Christ".

I imagine in my mind's eye, an ancient long forgotten Christian ceremony at the Holy See or among the Cathar Christians of Languedoc—the billowing incense, the singing echoes, the murmur of prayers in front of the idol of Christ, and then a man or a woman steps forward to receive … *something* that would show they were now one of the perfecti,[50] and they take it up, lift their arms to the heavens and declare in resonant, passionate tones to the host and all their brethren in the congregation:

εγω ειμι α χριστος!

I don't know whether it actually happened or not, but Ritualists build their ceremonies around such potent gematria, with the intent of exciting the spirit and causing a spiritual change to the psyche, which is probably why the Greeks called Jesus a Magician.

The Catholic Church employs similar numerical devices in its rituals, most notably in the ritual of the Eucharist in drinking the wine and eating the wafer, which is a symbolic recreation of the last supper (the Passover meal). The gematria of the ritual can be traced to the gematria of the Gospels directly.

Ἐσθιόντων δὲ αὐτῶν λαβὼν ὁ Ἰησοῦς ἄρτον καὶ εὐλογήσας ἔκλασεν καὶ δοὺς τοῖς μαθηταῖς εἶπεν Λάβετε φάγετε· τοῦτό ἐστιν τὸ σῶμά μου.

They were eating now of them having taken O Jesus bread and having blessed broke and having given to the disciples He said "Take, eat, this is the body of me."

Matthew 26:26

If we recall, "to bless" has the conventional meaning of "to double" in gematria, which is why we "double" the bread, and "to break" or "divide" or "get between" means "to divide by 2". The first gematria is found by the blessing:

ο ιησους αρτον αρτον = 1010

1010 being the sum total of the letters of the holy Name on the Seven Palaces, but the full calculation is:

ο ιησους αρτον αρτον/b + μαθηταις = 777.

Over the next couple of verses, the gematria involves the cup, thanksgiving, the blood of the covenant and the forgiveness of sins for a total that is 777 + 888:

ποτηριον ποτηριον αιμα διαθηκης αφεσιν αμαρτιων = 1665 = 777 + 888.

Corresponding to the names of the four Gospel writers, Matthew + Mark + Luke + John:

Μαθθατ + Μαρκου + Λουκας + Ιωαννου = 888.

Goodness only knows what Jewish Christian writers would have thought of the idols of Christ in Christian Churches, but we know what the Sages thought about it. The idolatry in Christian Churches meant that Jews were forbidden to *daven* (pray) in Christian Churches.[51]

If there is bitterness in the writings of John of Patmos it may be because he was suffering three exiles at once—a physical exile on the Island of Patmos; an exile from his Christian flock; and a third, self-imposed exile from his tribe, but I don't think John (et al) ever lost the sense of his Jewish identity. Rather, the act of writing and composing gematria upon such lofty topics as the chariot of God and the creation seems to have been an affirmation to him. Whatever else was happening in the world, whatever sorrows he'd endured, John saw himself as a servant to God, with duties given to him by God, and by such graces his life possessed meaning and purpose, and lent an inspired quality to his writing and gematria.

From Revelation 1:8: "I am the alpha and the omega [the beginning and the end], says Lord God, one being, and one was, and one coming, one almighty."

Εγω ειμι יהוה אלהים α α α α Παντοκρατωρ = 777.

The first and last letters of the Hebrew alphabet spell out *ath* which is a preposition that means to add. This is probably a clue to use Hebrew for the Holy Name instead of the Greek. John often used the Hebrew values for the names of God even while writing their equivalents in Greek, so it's nice of him to spell that out for us at the beginning of the Book. Κύριος Θεός ("Lord God") is replaced with YHVH ALHIM. To give you a second example, turn to Rev. 7:3:

δουλους + אל יהוה + μετωπων = 777:
"Servants" + "God YHVH" + "Foreheads" = 777.

John of Patmos wasn't the only New Testament writer to whom it was the convention to make the Greek words of God hold the value of their Hebrew counterparts. For a third example take John 1:1 with the reversal cipher. In this calculation, we see that John has replaced the value of the Greek word for God, *Dios*, with the Hebrew One, αλ.

Ἐν ἀρχῇ ἦν ὁ Λόγος, καὶ ὁ Λόγος ἦν πρὸς τὸν Θεόν, καὶ Θεὸς ἦν ὁ Λόγος.

In the Beginning was the Word, and the Word was with God, and God was the Word.

εν αρχη λογος λογος αλ αλ λογος = 777.

χαος + ΒΑΒΑΛΩΝ + BAFOMITh + θελημα = 777
Chaos + Babalon + Baphomet + Thelema

CHAPTER 10

Gematria and the Occult

It is true that some of the so-called secrets are significant, but as a rule they are so only to those who already know what the secret is.

Aleister Crowley

Though there are naturally factions that are in deep denial about it, Crowley's "Class A" texts owe much to the Temple religion of ancient Israel. The magical architecture of Solomon was appropriated in a straight-forward manner in the WMT before matters of "cultural appropriation" were ever a thing.

Aleister Crowley corresponded the tarot to the Merkabah, and Astrology, the Runes, Ritual and Numerology, until it became Thelemic Qabalah, but even so, the ancient Hebrew architecture still stands behind it all because it is as useful now as a macrocosmic system of classification as it was back in 1440 BCE.[52]

Modern Occultism is a descendant of the Western mystery tradition which itself refers to a wide range of loosely related ideas and movements which have developed within Western society during the Middle Ages. They are united—at least upon surface inspection—by their dissimilarity to the orthodox Judeo-Christian religion and the rationalism of the Enlightenment, and are qualified by having a hidden, inner tradition only known to initiated members.

The earliest traditions that lead to these movements emerged in the Eastern Mediterranean during Late Antiquity, where Hermeticism, Gnosticism, and Neo-Platonism developed as schools of thought that were distinct from mainstream Christianity.

By the seventeenth century, initiatory societies such as Rosicrucianism and Freemasonry flourished, and by the eighteenth century this had led to the development of new forms of esoteric thought that by the nineteenth century and continuing into the twentieth century had come to be known as "occultism". Prominent groups included the Fraternitas Rosae Crucis, the Sanctum Regnum, the Theosophical Society, the Ordo Aurum Solis, the Hermetic Order of the Golden Dawn (GD), the Quest Society, the A∴ A∴, the Ordo Templi Orientis (OTO), the Fraternity of the Inner Light, the Ancient Mystical Order Rosae Crucis (AMORC), the Association of Hebrew Theosophists, the Order of the Cubic Stone, and the Builders of the Adytum (BOTA), among a great spawning of others.

Each of these organizations entertained mystical speculations surrounding the practice of gematria, either as a type of symbolic presentation of universal ideas, or as keys to understand the secret content of scriptural or inspired writings. Some of the later organizations like the Golden Dawn and the A.'.A.'. employ the Seven Palaces in their system, but it's partly repurposed there from its role in the original ancient Hebrew system or in Jewish Kabbalah.

a. Rosicrucians

The Rosicrucians may have known Biblical Gematria. The principle texts of Rosicrucianism are three anonymous manuscripts called the *Fama Fraternitatis* (1617), the *Confessio Rosae Crucis* (1615) and the *Chymical Wedding of Christian Rosenkruetz* (1618).

The *Fama* tells the story of the Father C.R. and his ill-fated pilgrimage to Jerusalem; his subsequent tutelage by the sages of Dhamar in Arabia, from whom he learned various aspects of ancient esoteric knowledge; his return through Egypt and Fes, and his presence among the Alumbrados in Spain. According to historian Tobias Churton, the *Fama* was written by a group of Lutheran scholars at Tubingen in 1612. The manuscript was intended to be circulated privately but soon escaped the control of the authors and subsequently set off a movement which took on a life of its own.

Sir Francis Bacon.

Some authors raise the possibility that the *Confessio* was written by Sir Francis Bacon. It is a brief document that discusses the true Philosophy, and it answers criticisms and accusations made about the mysterious Brothers of the Rose Cross. It was published in the same volume as the *Fama* in 1617 and was wildly popular. The *Chymical Wedding* is an allegoric romance divided into Seven Days, or Seven Journeys, parallel to Genesis 1–2. It recounts how Christian Rosenkruetz was invited to go to a wonderful castle full of miracles, in order to assist the Chymical Wedding of its King and Queen. American occultist and author Paul Foster Case made a special study of the manuscripts and concluded:

> … every member of the special class of persons to whom the Fama and the Confessio were addressed was familiar with Gematria. Furthermore, they were fully persuaded of the value of biblical interpretations based on this ancient system of combining numbers and letters. They employed it in their endeavors to understand the scriptures, so as to apply the principles laid down in the sacred oracles to the better direction of their lives. This was true of men who had no particular interest in alchemy and other occult arts. It was even truer for the inner circle that was devoted to such esoteric doctrines. Thus, the principle key to the cryptic writings of the seventeenth century occultists is Gematria.[53]

I understand that there is currently a study going on to see whether the Biblical Gematria ciphers might provide the keys to the Rosicrucian Texts, which is an interesting avenue of exploration, but I cannot speak to whether Paul Foster Case was right or not at the moment. However both James Eshelman[54] and Paul Foster Case point out that 220 (the value of Brashith[55], and YHVH with the Reversal Cipher) is one of the key numbers of Rosicrucianism:

> The Fama is the tale of an aspirant identified only as C.R. or C.R.C Some interpret this to mean Christian Rosy Cross (or Rosencreutz). More important to out present topic, though, are the initials. He founded a fraternity with the initials R.C. One of their very few rules was that 'The word C.R. should be their Seal, Mark and Character.' To this day, the Inner College of the A.'.A.'. is called, simply, R.C., despite Golden Dawn precedents to the contrary. The Fama is a Qabalistic work. The German letters C.R. or R.C., are equivalent to the Hebrew : ר: כ:, Kaph Resh. These enumerate to 220.
>
> James Eshelman

Paul Foster Case's comment is puzzling, because by Standard Gematria the word "pure" as he has spelt it is 611, and by Biblical Gematria it is 215, but the proper spelling of "pure" is טהור (a *teth*, not a *tav*) which does sum to 220.

> The Mode of intelligence attributed to Yesod is "Pure Intelligence." In Hebrew, "pure" is spelt ThHVR (tah-hore), and the numeration of the word, 220, is also the number of C.R. or KR, "car" the "Lamb", and of R.C. or RK, "rok" meaning "tenderness". In discussing the Rosicrucian allegory it has been said that 220 represents Hebrew letters and the 10 powers corresponding to the Sephiroth. Qabalists say of Pure Intelligence that "it purifies the emanations, proves and corrects the designing of their representations; it disposes their unity with which they are combined without diminuation or division[56]."

b. WMT Traditions

Ceremonial magic in the Western Mystery Tradition usually combines several related systems into a tapestry of ceremonial practice that is designed to bring about balance and homeostasis in the psyche.

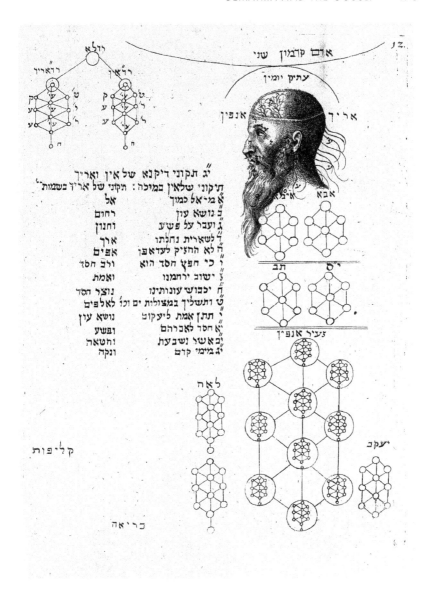

The Name of God, YHVH, is corresponded to the four classical elements of fire, water, air and earth, and thus to the magical or elemental weapons used in ritual invocations or evocations. The Golden Dawn (and most similar organizations) use Kabbalah as a basis for their system, but often change the way the Kabbalistic worlds are used or conceptualized.

Among Jewish Kabbalists there was a split in the general curriculum. There were people engaged in the study of Creation (Ma'aseh Bereshith) and others engaged in the study of the Merkabah (Ma'aseh Merkabah). There was quite a lot of superstition about the Merkabah. In the Pardes story, Ben Azzai dies, Ben Zoma goes mad, and Elisha becomes a heretic. Only Rabbi Akiva emerges unharmed. There is also the story of a boy who recognized the meaning of Ezek. i. 4 and experienced spontaneous human combustion (Ḥag. 13b), and the perils connected with the discussion of these subjects are often described (Ḥag. ii. 1, Shab. 80b). Thus those Kabbalists who didn't use the Seven Palaces (those engaged in Ma'aseh Bereshith), used the Tree across the four worlds because that was safer. At the same time, the Ari (Rabbi Yitzchak Luria) founded a whole new Kabbalistic system that involved adding an extra component to the four worlds which was called "the world of shells".

For Christian Kabbalists this created a confusing picture. Kabbalah was naively thought of as one tradition with one system, not three. Rosenroth decorated his partial translation of the *Zohar* with drawings of a slightly wrong Tree of Life and an attempted depiction of the four worlds which included a depiction of the Seven Palaces without paths.

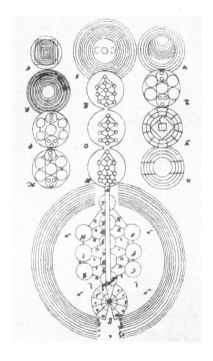

Most likely, he borrowed the shape of the Tree from one of the works of Ma'aseh Bereshith and tried to combined it with what he'd read about the Merkabah and the Palaces. I don't believe he did this to deliberately misrepresent Kabbalah, but I think he was missing the Jewish perspective, and also trying to make sense of the Gnostic component to Christian Kabbalah.

It may be that he copied the "Portae Lucis" diagram by Johann Reuchlin (that has no *daleth*, *teth*, and *peh* paths) and just snipped off the supernals to get the basic seven Palace shape, sans the horizontals. He also suggests by his drawings that the Tree of Life and the Seven Palaces spanned all the four worlds.

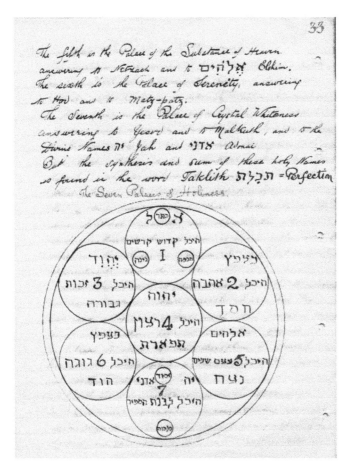

Golden Dawn Student papers.

The Golden Dawn system was heavily influenced by Knorr Von Rosenroth's drawings in the "Kabbalah Denudata" manuscript. For the Golden Dawn, the framework of the Tree/Palaces/Worlds presented in the Rosenroth diagrams were adapted by changing the Tree to include the horizontal paths (of the Kircher diagram) and by adding a world of shells beneath the Sephirah of Malkuth. The Tree of Life diagram and the Seven Palaces were propagated throughout the four worlds but like the Rosenroth illustrations, their Seven Palaces had no paths between them.

'Before the Fall'—MacGregor Mathers,
Hermetic Order of the Golden Dawn.

Although the idea of *qlippoth* was drawn from the Kabbalah of Isaac Luria, in that system the seven *qlippoth* (in the Kingdom of Shells) are replicas of the bottom seven lower *sephiroth* from Chesed to Malkuth, rather than being an averse reflection of the Seven Heavenly Palaces.

In putting forward an averse version of the Seven Palaces, the Golden Dawn introduced a novel variant that is not seen in the Lurianic system, which itself splits off from the traditional Kabbalah/Merkabah in putting forward the idea of the *qlippoth* at all.

> The GD picked the eyes out of the teachings attributed to Lurian thought, and their application was not always conducive to many traditional applications. The issue here is that kabbalism in the GD is one carriage only and not the whole train pulling to the station. Many of the GD applications, such as godforms, would raise the ire of the more traditional kabbalist. However the system works. And for me that is the bottom line.
>
> Pat Zalewski (Golden Dawn Adept/Author)

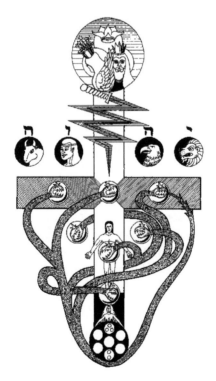

'After the Fall'—MacGregor Mathers.

By passing through the degrees of the order, those who proceed through the system take a mental and spiritual journey ascending the Tree of Life to rectify the "fall".

Inscribed on the wall of the waiting room before initiation would be the sign "V.I.T.R.I.O.L", a notariqon of "Visita Interiora Terrae Rectificando Invenies Occultum Lapidem," meaning "Visit the interior of the earth and rectifying [purifying] you will find the hidden stone."

The Hebrew Seven Palaces has Man inside Creation inside God, but when the seven sleeping "infernal" palaces appear underneath the Tree in the Golden Dawn system it seems to present God inside Creation inside Man, and perhaps that's the point—to begin the work of correcting the mistaken impression of the ego that it is the overall ruler of the psyche.

In a second depiction of the Tree and Qlippoth, "After the fall", the infernal Palaces appear once again beneath the foot of the Tree of Life but this time they have become activated or awakened, and the seven heads and ten horns of the Beast from the St. John's Book of Revelation are shown:

> From the Three Supernals follow the other Sephiroth of THE TREE OF LIFE. Below the TREE, proceeding from MALKUTH is THE TREE OF KNOWLEDGE of GOOD AND of EVIL which is between the Tree of Life and the World or Assiah or Shells, represented by the Coiled Up DRAGON with Seven Heads and Ten Horns—being the Seven Infernal Palaces and the Ten Averse Sephiroth.
>
> The Fourth Knowledge Lecture of the
> Golden Dawn (Practicus Degree)

It takes a degree of mental dexterity to step from the ancient biblical system to Kabbalah (which splits in Ma'aseh Merkabah and Ma'aseh Bereshith) to Christian Kabbalah (which conflates Ma'aseh Bereshith and Merkabah and draws in more Pythagorean elements), to the Golden Dawn, to Crowley. By the time we get to Crowley, although the keys are still the same, the system has undergone a radical change.

But for most people, their systems hadn't changed, and the Standard Gematria cipher for was taken at face value by the occult community. The reasons for Crowley's corrections to the tarot (the *heh/tsade* switch) were not understood by the wider magical community and so were largely not accepted outside of the Thelemic community. In 1912, Allen Bennet and Aleister Crowley published *Sepher Sephiroth*[57] using the Standard cipher and for most folks that was the end of the matter and proof enough that Crowley used it, as if a man was ever condemned to the use of only one cipher. But the truth is that gematrists usually have a favorite cipher that "works for them", because these guys and girls are doing something else with gematria than work out the math of the Bible, Kabbalah and other occult texts. The way the modern day magical community uses Standard Gematria is to daisy-chain associations in a type of guided but free-flowing state of association.

> Like a mountain goat leaping ecstatically from crag to crag, one thought springs into another, and another, ad infinitum. You can continue, almost forever, connecting things that you never thought were connected. Sooner or later something's going to snap and you will overcome the fundamental defect in your powers of perception.
>
> Lon Milo Duquette (2001)

To most sections of the occult community, that essentially is "the whole point" of gematria. You might as well object to someone praying or singing in the park as object to that.

Influenced by the likes of Crowley, Kenneth Grant and Paul Foster Case (all huge gematrists) there are now many gematria dictionaries using the Standard Gematria cipher, and a plethora of pseudo-ciphers, but it doesn't matter. Just because there is an actual cipher for the Bible which is something other than Standard Gematria, it doesn't make the point of these practices invalid—because you can't invalidate your own consciousness (or can you?).

In some senses these practices are similar to those used by conspiracy theorists, but in all the senses that matter they are a million miles away because intent is everything in magick. If you are intent on heaven you will find heaven. And if you are intent on finding out what the heck those biblical scribes of long ago were talking about, you can find that too.

The Golden Dawn didn't really teach gematria beyond giving their initiates the number values for the letters. It was expected that they would get on with learning it for themselves. In modern times the Builders of the Adytum (BOTA) are renowned for having a curriculum that is, in the view of some students, top heavy with Gematria.

Crowley presents a system in *Magick, Book 4* which is basically of Ma'aseh Bereshith (the tree is across the four worlds, etc.), but he also uses the Seven Palaces as a type of "table of contents" for some of his A.'.A.'. papers which are intended for different Grades, from Liber Tau to Liber B vel Magi. I would argue that this is very much in keeping with having it in the world of Yetzirah as the macrocosmic constant to the microcosmic mirror. He writes:

> All these numbers are of course parts of the magician himself considered as the microcosm. The microcosm is an exact image of the Macrocosm; the Great Work is the raising of the whole man in perfect balance to the power of Infinity....
>
> Our magical alphabet of the Sephiroth and the Paths (thirty-two letters as it were) has been expanded into the four worlds corresponding to the four letters of the name Yod-Heh-Vau-Heh; and each Sephirah is supposed to contain a Tree of Life of its own. Thus we obtain four hundred Sephiroth instead of the original ten, and the Paths being capable of similar multiplications, or rather of subdivision, the number is still further extended. Of course this process might be indefinitely continued without destroying the original system.
>
> Magick, Book 4, Chap 0

There's no mention of the Seven Palaces here but there's an acknowledgement by Crowley that we're not working with the original (Hebrew) system but rather an expansion of it. That expansion was needed to pull in astrology (for instance), or the *I Ching*.

c. Elemental Weapons

The practice of ceremonial magick involves crafting one's own elemental ritual weapons, and these correspond to the Name YHVH which corresponds to sections of the Seven Palaces and their gematria.

Magicians usually create their own elemental weapons to ensure that they form the strongest magical link with them, but there's some latitude regarding the sword. It's not always possible or practicable to take up metallurgy and smithing.

י	ה	ו	ה
FIRE	WATER	AIR	EARTH
WAND	CUP	SWORD	DISK
220	217	480	93
YOD, LAMED, NUN, SAMEKH, AYIN	ALEPH, ALEPH, GIMEL, HEH, ZAYIN, RESH	SHIN, TAV, VAV, CHETH, TETH, KAPH, MEM, TSADE QOPH RESH	DALETH, DALETH, HEH, PEH

A magician always has their elemental weapons to hand at all times in any case, whether their images are by your side or not. You can feel the heat in your blood, the spark of the next thought that fires upon your neurons, your creative fire, your wand. Most of the human body is water—your cup. Take a deep breath (air). Clap your hands (earth). Fire, water, air and earth, and your consciousness itself adds spirit. You are the Temple.[58]

It isn't known who originally married the elements and weapons of the Hermetic Tradition with the alphabet, tree, palaces and four worlds of Kabbalah. Frances A. Yates claimed it was Pico Della Mirandola, but other authors suggest the influence of Agrippa. In his *Three Books of Occult Philosophy* he discusses the Tetragrammaton and in almost the same breath he brings up the four elements, though he doesn't assign the elements to the four letters of the Name. My own feeling is that the syncretism arose from out of Gnostic Christianity before it was harshly suppressed by the Roman Catholic Church and any remaining texts went underground.

Magicians use material symbols, weapons, and implements to symbolize ideas and types of consciousness, whereas the Temple environment as a whole represents the soul and creation. By creating or altering a weapon to make it yours, you form mental links between yourself and your weapons and make them better suit your purpose.

The rituals you use can be polished and elaborate ones written by great wordsmiths of their era, and/or they can be compositions of your own that chime with your intent and resonate within the balance of your eternal being. The two are not mutually exclusive.

By crafting the weapon yourself you are there at every step of the process, creating a weft of mental associations and conceptions. It is usually recommended that magicians spend some time carving or getting involved in metallurgy, or that you ensure to cut the wood for your wand from a certain tree at a certain hour of the day and month of the year ... but there are shortcuts.

Each elemental weapon represents the qualities of the letters in the holy name, and thus corresponds to a section of the Seven Palaces, and thus to a letter grouping and a gematria number.

Israel Regardie recommended that you light a candle for fire, fill a glass with water, create a paper fan for air, and offer a rose or other suitable flower for earth. Lon Milo Duquette recommends that a cocktail stick and a beer coaster can, at a pinch, be used for a sword and a disk "very effectively".

There are many types of rituals; in magical orders and fraternities there is usually one or more ritual for each grade and step in the great work. There are also rituals that stand outside of grade work (Liber Resh, for example). A common elemental chant exists in witchcraft, and is adapted to any number of operations goes:

> I call Earth to bind my spell, Air to speed my magic well, bright as
> Fire shall it glow. Deep as tide of water flow. Count the elements,
> fourfold, and in the fifth the spell shall hold ...

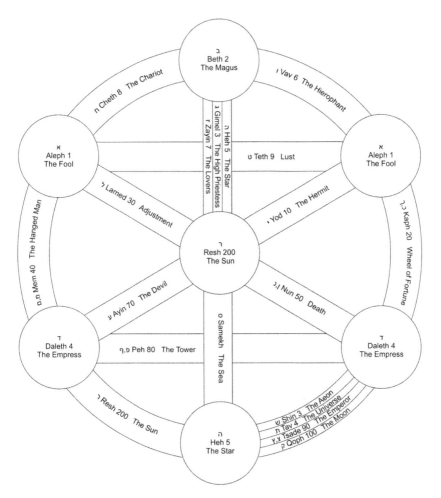

Tarot Correspondences to the Seven Palaces.

d. The Tarot

Each card of the Major Arcana of the tarot has a Hebrew letter, and it exists today as a pictorial representation of the letters of the Holy Name, but the tarot cards started off as game pieces in fifteenth century France and England. They were swiftly turned to the purposes of divination, and to represent core Kabbalistic concepts from Genesis 1–2. The twenty-two cards of the Major Arcana were first numbered (Tarot de Marseille) and then assigned to the twenty-two letters of the Hebrew alphabet by Éliphas Levi.

Eliphas Levi, of the Sanctum Regnum.

Aleister Crowley changed two incorrect letter attributions of the tarot to finalize the syncretization of the Hebrew alphabet and the tarot. He changed the *heh* from the Emperor to the Star, and the *tsade* from the Star to the Emperor.

In the Western mystery tradition, the tarot card of the Emperor is perfectly appropriate to the letter *tsade* because of the legends about the miraculous (at the time) birth of Emperor Caesar by Caesarean Section. Aleister Crowley's comments about the card also suggest that he is commenting on childbirth:

> The power of the Emperor is a generalization of the paternal power; hence such symbols as the Bee and the Fleur-de-lys, which are shown on this card. With regard to the quality of this power, it must be noted that it represents sudden, violent, but impermanent activity. If it persists too long, it burns and destroys.

Obviously, Crowley's take on the *tsade* is a very paternal and masculine one (he's retained the idea of the patriarchy), but "a violent and impermanent activity which destroys if it persists too long" certainly fits a description of childbirth. This may account for his switch of the *heh* and *tsade*'s attributions to the tarot for the Star and the Emperor too, which is especially understandable, as the *heh* governs verses 1:16b–18 of Genesis (the creation of the stars).

Going back to the Egyptian Royal Standard with the image of the placenta upon it, it's quite likely that Crowley connected this with the origin of words such as Tsar and Caesar[59]. But while there may be some truth to this, the irony of this in respect of the letter *tsade* and Crowley's treatment of it is that the power to put a new Pharaoh on the throne of Egypt (thus expressed by the symbolism of the placenta upon the Egyptian standard) was in the hands—or rather "the wombs"—of the royal matriarchy, which is a point that is often neglected in modern treatments of the Emperor.

0. I. Beth: The Magus (2)
1. 0. Aleph: The Fool (1)
2. II. Gimel: The Priestess (3)
3. XX. Shin: The Aeon (3)
4. III. Daleth: The Empress (4)
5. XXI. Tav: The Universe (4)
6. XVI. Heh: The Star (5)
7. V. Vav: The Hierophant (6)
8. VI. Zayin: The Lovers (7)
9. VII. Cheth: The Chariot (8)
10. VIII. Teth: Lust (9)
11. IX. Yod: The Hermit (10)

12. X. Kaph: The Wheel of Fortune (20)
13. XI. Lamed: Adjustment (30)
14. XII. Mem: The Hanged Man (40)
15. XIII. Nun: Death (50)
16. XIV. Samekh: Art (60)
17. XV. Ayin: The Devil (70)
18. XVI. Peh: The Tower (80)
19. IV. Tsade: The Emperor (90)
20. XVIII. Qoph: The Moon (100)
21. XIX. Resh: The Sun (200)

The influence from Aztiluth reaches out to create the twenty-two spirits of the letters in the world of Beriah, which creates the Seven Palaces in the world of Yetzirah (macrocosm) and the ten *sephiroth* of the world of Assiah (microcosm).

To find the location of a card on the Tree of Life we must first consider its location on the Seven Palaces and see how their influence reflects downwards into the world of Action.

The correspondences between the Palaces and the Tree are more complex than a one-to-one relationship, with single elements on the Palaces sometimes affecting a group of correspondences on the Tree of Life.

a. The Magus represents the combined *sephiroth* of Kether, Chokmah, and Binah on the Tree of Life.
b. The Fools correspond to the *sephiroth* of Chesed and Geburah.
c. The Empress corresponds to the *sephiroth* of Netzach and Hod.
d. And the Star corresponds to both Yesod and Malkuth as well as the path between Chokmah and Tiphareth.

Upon holy mysteries of this sort, Aleister Crowley quipped about his initiation to the Golden Dawn:

> At my initiation, ... I had been most solemnly sworn to inviolable secrecy. The slightest breach of my oath meant that I should incur 'a deadly and hostile current of will, set in motion by the Greatly Honoured Chiefs of the Second order, by the which I should fall slain or paralyzed, as if blasted by the lightning flash'. And now I was entrusted with some of these devastating though priceless secrets.

They consisted of the Hebrew alphabet, the names of the planets
with their attribution to the days of the week, and the ten Sephiroth
of the Cabbala.

The Confessions of Aleister Crowley, pg. 177

Most commentators assume this remark is merely making fun of the
Golden Dawn's initiation, inferring that it was a bit of a let down, and
that was what I originally thought too, but now I think he may have
been speaking nothing but the truth, and that's a joke for those who are
in on the secret (like us). You should know by now all the keys to the
Hebrew alphabet.

The days of the week are: ראשון שני שלישי רביעי חמישי שישי
שבת = 777.

ראשון שני שלישי רביעי חמישי שישי שבת
= 777 =
The days of the week

שבת
Shabbat

רביעי
4th

שלישי
3rd

שישי
6th

חמישי
5th

שני
2nd

ראשון
1st

Sunday= 260 = Sun's day
Monday = 63 = Moon's day
Tuesday = 56 = Mars's day
Wednesday = 71 = Mercury's day
Thursday = 292 = Jupiter's day
Friday = 26 = Venus's day
Saturday = 9 = Saturn's day

777

Another matter which many readers have taken lightly is the claim
by Aleister Crowley to have discovered the "lost word", and yet he did
indeed possess the gematria keys to the Bible, New Testament, magick
and Kabbalah, so it was not beyond his ability to know this.

e. Aleister Crowley

It was in 1900 while he was going through a stage with Scottish
Freemasonry that Crowley hit on the right gematria cipher for the Bible
and the Seven Palaces and he got tremendously excited about it all.

The way the matter had been framed for him by Scottish Freemasonry, Aleister Crowley drew the natural (and actually correct by its lights) conclusion that he had discovered the "lost word"[60], and thus he was a master mason indeed, and not just in name. He had the keys to the Hebrew Bible, to the New Testament, to Theosophy, to the tarot and to magick. He recorded the moment in his diary which He recorded the moment in his diary, which resonates with awe and wonder at his discovery of one of the great mysteries of the ancient world:

Aleister Crowley (1875—1947).

As I lay one night sleepless, in meditation, bitter and eager, upon this mystery I was suddenly stabbed to the soul by a suggestion so simple, yet so stupendous, that I was struck into shuddering silence for I know not how long before I could bring myself to switch on the electric light and snatch my notebook. At the first trial the solution sprang like sunlight in my spirit. I remained all that night in an ecstasy of awe and adoration. I had discovered the lost Word!

To understand why he was in such paroxysms of ecstasy, let us review some literature on "the lost word".

The hunt for the lost word is the central mystery of Freemasonry, for the word is believed to hold the key to the architectural design of the First Temple. In order to complete their masonic degrees the brothers search for a substitute word, even while searching for the true fabled lost word that would hold the key to rebuilding the Temple of Hashem, which they hoped would see the dawn of a new day for humanity. It would have been unusual for Aleister Crowley to have not been possession of the following work and no doubt it colored his thoughts on the matter. In *The Symbolism of Freemasonry* (1882) by Albert G. Mackey, the 31st chapter, entitled "The Lost Word", describes it in these terms:

> The mythical history of Freemasonry informs us that there once existed a WORD of surpassing value, and claiming a profound veneration; that this Word was known to but few; that it was at length lost; and that a temporary substitute for it was adopted. But as the very philosophy of Masonry teaches us that there can be no death without a resurrection,—no decay without a subsequent restoration,—on the same principle it follows that the loss of the Word must suppose its eventual recovery.

The document is written in a vague and rather waffling style, but it settles down enough to impart the opinion that;

> It was among the idolatrous multitudes[61] that the Word had been lost[62]. It was among them that the Builder had been smitten, and that the works of the spiritual temple had been suspended; and so, losing at each successive stage of their decline, more and more of the true knowledge of God and of the pure religion which had originally been imparted by Noah, they finally arrived at gross materialism and idolatry, losing all sight of the divine existence. Thus it was that the truth—the Word—was said to have been lost …

After finding the biblical cipher, Crowley pursued the practice of gematria and employed it in the creation of in numerous works, including *Liber AL vel Legis*, *Liber Ararita* and *Liber Arcanorum*—but in secrecy! In his public writings he made it look as if he was using Standard Gematria, just as many of the Rabbis did as the Talmud was being written.

Inevitably though, due to the syncretic nature of magick, he ran into difficulties that the Rabbis had never faced. For instance, the tarot was keyed to the letters by Éliphas Levi but Levi changed the attributions for *heh* and *tsade*. When correcting the attribution, Crowley couldn't merely claim divine inspiration for the swap, so after being badgered for a number of years by his students, he eventually presented them with an explanation concerning astrology and effectively gave them the brush off.

On the whole, Crowley seemed to favor the notion of keeping the keys secret, at least in his own day if not in the future. When he translated *The Key of the Mysteries* by Éliphas Levi he added the footnote:

> This is all deliberately wrong. That Levi knew the correct attributions is evident from a MS, annotated by himself. Levi refused to reveal these attributions, rightly enough, as his grade was not high enough, and the time was not ripe.

In *The Equinox*, vol. 1, no. 5 he tells us that he shall give us examples "showing the falsity and absurdity of the un-initiated path, the pure truth and reasonableness of the hidden way" and then quotes from the Introduction of S.L. Mathers' *Kabbalah Unveiled*:

> ... with regard to Gematria of phrases (Gen xlix. 10), IBA ShILH, Yeba Shiloh, "Shiloh will come" = 358, which is the numeration of the word MshICh, Messiah. Thus also the passage, Gen. xviii. 2, VHNH ShLShH, Vehenna Shalisha, "And lo, three men," equals in numerical value ALV MIKAL GBRIAL VRPAL, Elo Mikhael Gabriel Ve-Raphael, "These are Mikhael, Gabriel and Raphael"; for each phrase = 701.

Let's recalculate all this using the biblical cipher to see "the truth" of the initiated path:

IBA ShILH = 61, MshICh = 61.
VHNH ShLShH = 107, ALV MIKAL GBRIAL VRPAL = 701 (107 backwards).

For Crowley the number 61 was chiefly associated with the word *AIN* ("Nothingness"), which is one of three primordial states that are said by Kabbalists to have preceded the Tree of Life: the Ain, the Ain Soph, and the Ain Soph Ur. And in *The Book of the Law* there is a riddle in four verses where "Nothing is Perfect" is proven with some really incredible gematria, which add context to both the verse and Crowley's commentary to *The Book of the Law*.

> The Perfect and the Perfect are one Perfect and not two; nay, are none.
>
> *AL* 1:45

Perfect + Perfect + 1 + 2 = 777.

Perfect = 220 (via the Reversal Cipher).

In his commentary to the verse he speculated:

"Perhaps means that adding perfection to perfection results in the unity and ultimately the Negativity. But I think there is much more than this."

Note that his comments give the impression that he was not aware of the gematria in the verses. He had previously claimed that the Book was dictated to him by a supra-human being who called himself 'Aiwass', but there's no reason for the reader to depart from common sense and believe him. Indeed, Crowley preferred that his students employ doubt and skepticism in their review of magical and mystical texts and practices.

He considered the number 7 to be "the holiest and most perfect of numbers", so he would consider the 7 in triplicate along these lines. In the next sum (AL 1:46–47) he gives us a total of 1012, which is the sum total of the value of all the letters of the Seven Palaces, representing God and all creation:

> AL 1:46: "Nothing is a secret key of this Law. Sixty One the Jews call it; I call it eight, eighty, four hundred & eighteen."
> AL 1:47: "But they have the half: unite by thine art so that all disappear."
> 8 + 80 + 418 = 506 × 2 = 1012.

To Crowley's thinking, there was no division between everything and nothing. Any perception of division at all was thought to be below the abyss. For that transcendental consciousness above the abyss, all dualities were united, and below the abyss, for the mundane consciousness, all dualities were divided.

In his gematria work, he loved the number 777 quite as much as much as he did his own number of 666.

AL 1:48 "My prophet is a fool with his one, one, one; are not they the Ox, and none by the Book?"

666 + 111 = 777.

"The Ox" is the letter Aleph, and "the Book" is the Tarot. The Fool Trump is card 0 and is corresponded to the letter Aleph.

Crowley wasn't above fooling with the reader. Consider AL 1:24–25, and note Nv is 56:

I am nuit – nv + divide + add + multiply + and understand = 777.

I love this one because it is wonderful example of misdirection. Whenever a scribe is being a little too obvious it's best to get suspicious, especially if that scribe is Aleister Crowley.

Nuit is all created existence (777) but all created existence is not everything. She is perhaps two thirds of everything?

1012 – 777 = 235.

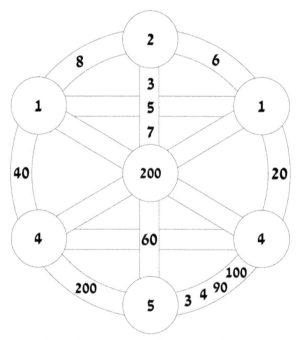

Left Column: 2 + 8 + 1 + 40 + 4 + 200 + 5 = 260.
Middle Column: 2 + 3 + 5 + 7 + 200 + 60 + 5 = 282.
Right Column: 2 + 6 + 1 + 20 + 4 + 100 + 90 + 4 + 3 + 5 = 235.
260 + 282 + 235 = 777.

She is the left, middle, and the right column, q.e.d., but 235 is the value of the column to the right. And note how this 777 value for the three columns is achieved: the *beth* and the *heh* are both used three times, once for each column, thus demonstrating that the sum of the whole is greater than the parts, and the source of all things is given three ways and received in three ways here upon earth. But at the end, it is one diagram, a single unified conception of everything, one idea, and all (61) = Nothing *AIN* (61).

Crowley prided himself on his mathematical skills, and like all the greats, he tried to stretch the reach of gematria beyond simple arithmetic into new and cryptic territories. One great example is an approximation of pi that is right to the first seven places in *AL* 1:3[63].

Every man + Every Woman = 710.

Every = 226.

710 / 226 = 3.14159292035.

He makes frequent use of notariqon and uses the ampersand (&) symbol as a simple "+", although much later in life (1943) he would refer to notariqon as "the accursed art of making words out of initials" and temurah as "almost always frivolous". But he didn't change his mind about the intrinsic value of gematria:

> Gematria methods serve to uncover spiritual truths. Numbers are the network of the structure of the universe, and their relations the form of expression of our Understanding of it.
>
> A.C. Magick without Tears (letter G)

As skilled as he eventually grew in the art, the gematria of *The Book of the Law* strikes me as the sort one might expect from someone who has the keys, but has not yet fully delved into the conventions of the biblical art. For instance, he uses the term "not", *la*, to represent 31 rather than using it in the biblically conventional sense to indicate that one should "not" count the next word, and this is entirely consistent for someone who had had only four short years to study Biblical Gematria before commencing a major work with it. His gematria is, at times, idiosyncratic (more in the vein of Ezekiel or Job than true to the style of Genesis), although he does seem to have taken the indexing of Genesis 1–2 as inspiration to author some of his own works along these same lines. Each verse of *Liber Arcanorum* corresponds to a tarot card, but also to one of the Hebrew letters that represents a palace or a path on the Seven Palaces, rather than to the Tree of Life. With variations in ordering, Crowley took this "key system" approach to a great many of his A∴A∴ texts.

Crowley was not a Hebrew speaker, and his attempts to compose Hebrew gematria with the biblical cipher usually prove perplexing for readers of Hebrew. In *Liber Ararita* 1:1 he gives us:

אחד ראש: אחדותו ראש ייחודותו: תמורתו אחד = 777.

AChD RASh: AChDVThV RASh YYChVDVThV: ThMVRThV AChD

Which is supposed to mean "One is His Beginning; one is His Individuality; His Permutation One!", but you might see some eyebrows raised if you were to show it to a Hebrew-speaker and ask for a translation. Nevertheless, he was such an inventive and creative fellow, intent upon the spiritual significance of the numbers as he contemplated the divine plan. It's a pleasure to do the sums in *The Book of the Law*, to take up the contemplation with him, and perhaps acknowledge that he may, at times, have been brilliant.

(השמים רכב אש וסוסי אש / 2) + (2 * אליהו בסערה) + (2 * אליהו) = 777

After they had crossed over, Elijah said to Elisha, "Tell me, what can I do for you before I am taken away from you?"

'Please, let me inherit a double portion of your spirit,' Elisha replied.

'You have requested a difficult thing,' said Elijah. 'Nevertheless, if you see me as I am taken from you, it will be yours. But if not, then it will not be so.'

As they were walking along and talking together, suddenly a chariot of fire with horses of fire appeared and separated the two of them, and Elijah went up into heaven in a whirlwind.

2 Kings 2:9–11

CHAPTER 11

Exegesis with Gematria

O nce you have sufficiently developed your skill with gematria and you are able to draw the numbers from a hermeneutical text, the next step is the interpretation of those numbers relative to the text.

The four methods of traditional Jewish interpretation (PaRDeS) that need to be considered, and these are;

Peshat ("surface")—"straight", or the literal (direct) meaning.

Remez ("hints")—or the deep (allegoric: hidden or symbolic) meaning beyond just the literal sense.

Derash, from Hebrew *daresh* ("inquire", "seek")—the comparative (*midrashic*) meaning, as given through similar occurrences.

Sod (pronounced with a long O as in "sore")—the "secret" ("mystery") or the esoteric/mystical meaning.

The *Peshat* means the plain or contextual meaning of the text. It does not refer to any traditional interpretations or Mishnah, although these may be invaluable to consult, but only to the actual plain meaning of the text itself. *Remez* is the allegorical meaning. *Derash* includes the metaphorical meaning, and *Sod* represents the hidden meaning.

As a general rule, the *Remez*, *Derash*, and *Sod* never contradict the *Peshat* meaning. What we are aiming for when we come to interpret our verses is a holistic exegesis that incorporates all the different modes of interpretation at once and without contradiction. This does not come quickly. Time must be allowed for a properly considered interpretation to develop, and it may take days, weeks, or even years for a mature exegesis to develop. We may leap at an explanation today that seems satisfying to us, but that a few months later may seem naive or lacking the proper amount of nuance. However this is all just part and parcel of learning. Exegesis has a natural rate of development that we can only impede by stubbornly attaching to our initial views as the right views.

An example of an integrated PaRDeS interpretation would go something like this. The *Peshat* (plain) meaning of Genesis 1:1 couldn't be simpler—Elohim created the heavens and the earth.

A *Remez* "hint" that we can take from the sentence is that the word ברא ("created") is only used for creations of God and never used for creations of man. Another is that the first letter of the first word of the Torah begins with the prefix letter *beth* ("in beginning"), not simply ראשית ("beginning").

The *Derash* shows Elohim as the creator of phenomena that other cultures personified as sky or harvest gods. Elohim created the heavens and the earth so there are no sky or harvest gods, and this is a powerful polemical statement in the ancient world. And in the Talmud (Haggidah 14a) Rabbi Yonatan is reported to have said:

> With each and every word that emerges from the mouth of the Holy One, Blessed be He, an angel is created, as it is stated: "By the word of the Lord the heavens were made, and by the breath of His mouth all their hosts
>
> Psalms 33:6

The hosts of heaven are the angels, who, he claims, are created from the mouth of God, rather than from the River Dinur.

To uncover the *Sod* we have to apply gematria. The verses of the Torah begin (and end) with the value of 700.

בראשית + אלהים + השמים + הארץ = 700.

In the beginning + Elohim + the Heavens + the Earth
Genesis 1:1

The first word, *bereshith*, sums to 220, which is the same value of the name of the creator by the Reversal Cipher—יהוה‎ = 220.

$$220 = (4)\ ת + (10)\ י + (3)\ ש + (1)\ א + (200)\ ר + (2)\ ב = בראשית$$

If we use notariqon on the initials of this sentence it is בבאאהוה‎, and the reverse cipher of this has a value of 800. What do we know about these numbers? 220 divided by 7 divided by 10 yields an ancient approximation of pi (3.142857). It is also the value of התורה‎, the Torah, and קדש וקדש‎ ("Holy of Holies").

700 has a twofold relevance—to the seven days of creation and to the Seven Palaces of the heavens and the earth.

800 may be explained by a little more *Derash*. In the ancient world, Hebrew culture and Ugaritic culture was broadly similar, tending to share the same world view. In Canaanite literature sevens and eights are often mentioned together in a symbolic fashion. In the Ba'al texts it says that El the bull lifted up his voice from the seven chambers, from the eight openings.[64] While sevens denote nature and completion (God rests on the seventh day from his labors), the eights tend to denote the divine source of all things. The gematria of 8 x 31 is as important to scripture as 7 x 31.[65]

Also, consider the Holy Name when multiplied in sequence:

$Y \times H = 50,$

$50 \times V = 300,$

$300 \times H = 1500,$ which is 700 + 800.

Doubtless we could also go and check the Torah to compare other instances where 700 and 800 comes up too, but let's consider the *Peshat* meaning again. The sentence seems simple on the surface, and even a little vague. But by taking the *Remez* and the *Derash* into account we can appreciate it as a powerful polemic statement, and the *Sod* shows us that it isn't vague at all but refers to the Seven Palaces. We gain a detailed idea of the creator within his Holy of Holies, from his Palace of the Beth, whirling the Seven Palaces of the heavens and earth into being using the letters of the primordial Torah, and indeed this is how the creation is imagined in Kabbalistic circles.

This is by no means an exhaustive exegesis. We might go on to ana-lyze the fact that Elohim + the heavens + the earth = 480 and draw com-parisons and conclusions from Kings 6:1 which says:

> In the four hundred and eightieth year after the Israelites came out
> of Egypt, in the fourth year of Solomon's reign over Israel, in the
> month of Ziv, the second month, he began to build the temple of
> Yahweh.

From here we might proceed to check for other correspondences between the story of the building of the Temple and the creation story of Genesis, once again applying *Peshat*, *Remez*, *Derash* and *Sod* in our interpretations, but for the purposes of this guide-book this example shall suffice.

When uncovering the *Sod* we may find exegesis that does not con-tradict the *Peshat* meaning of the text, but changes the way we inter-pret it according to tradition. As an example, there is a strong indication from the *Sod* that Jacob and Esau were personifications of Summer and Winter. In all likelihood their stories were probably inspired recitations of a Sumerian tale—the debate between Summer and Winter. Yet this dimension isn't one that is noted by tradition or the culture which is more focused on the patriarchal lineages of these brothers.

When we consider everything in the round, it makes a lot of sense for God to leave land to be managed by the seasons. No *Peshat* mean-ing is overturned by this interpretation and clarity is brought to the text about his motivations. But how legitimate is this type of interpretation, departing as it does from tradition? That really depends on who you're talking to. An interpretation based on the text like this may be perfectly welcome in academia, but it will probably fall on its face in religious circles. Whether it is right or not is hardly the point. The point of Jewish and Christian traditions is to obey the Will of God and come closer to him, not to argue points of comparative theology or historical context, as interesting as they might be. But on the other hand it can be said that arguing points in debate towards a common consensus that is based on a rational and rigorous testing process is to make use of the talents that we as homo sapiens have to the betterment of all, or the Common-Wheel and thus incidentally, doing one of the mitzvoth. This is basi-cally an argument suggesting we should seek to better ourselves before God. But Aleister Crowley wrote the wonderful line "Yea! deem not of

EXEGESIS WITH GEMATRIA 201

change: ye shall be as ye are, & not other." The words are chosen with
Crowley's usual exactitude.

The following are walk-throughs of three gematria sums I've been
working on recently. Follow the steps with me to get a working idea of
how gematria is done in practice.

a. Biblical Exegesis

We will look up the next two examples on Biblehub. They have an excel-
lent interlinear dictionary, although it's a good idea not to place your
total reliance on their judgment about whether any word is a preposition, noun, verb or adjective.

When considering whether a word is a verb or a noun it is better to
consider how a more literal thinking ancient scribe may have thought
of it. For instance, was time a thing in itself to them, and therefore a
noun? Or did they think of time as a process and therefore a verb? If
we are unsure then the matter must be put to the test and scientifically
deduced from the data.

To demonstrate exegesis with the Tanakh, I've chosen Genesis 18:10
for two reasons. The first being that I haven't worked it out before-hand,
so I'm strongly motivated to decode it.

Genesis 18:10:

We know there is gematria in this verse because it contains the flagword "behold!". However, there are mnemonic elements in the verse,
such as the "door" reference for the letter *daleth* (4), and the word for
"to your woman" (111) that we need to take into account, and I am not
certain that the word האהל ("to the tent") is an innocent noun. We need

חיה	כעת	אליך	אשוב	שוב	ויאמר
of life	in your time	to you	I will return	surely	And he said

שמעת	ושרה	אשתך	לשרה	בן	והנה
was listening	And Sarah	your wife	to Sarah	a son	And Behold

אחריו:	והוא	האהל	פתח
behind him	that was	to the tent	at the entrance

to be sure of what values all of these words represent before we can decode this verse.

To begin work, we strip away any verbs, adjectives and prepositions that are not part of the sum. Let's get rid of the verb *somat*. It might indicate addition, but since we're going to add the value of Sarah to "the door" ("at the entrance") then we don't need to investigate this word at the moment. Let's also strip out *wehu* as that is filler and consider the word אחריו as a potential clue:

בן לשרה אשתך ושרה שמעת פתח האהל והוא אחריו

אחריו is translated as "behind him" in this verse. In other verses it is used to supply the meanings of "after", and "after him". It carries the sense of something being at the end. It comes from the root word אַחַר which means "the hind" or "following part".

If אחריו has a mnemonic value associated with its root word, might אחריו and אַחַר represent the last letter of the alphabet, which is the letter *resh*? Possibly. It's something that we need to put to the test. Let's add it to the calculation speculatively.

בן לשרה אשתך ושרה פתח האהל ר

And let's replace the word פתח ("door") with the mnemonic value of the *daleth* (4), and the word אשתך ("your woman") with it's mnemonic value of 111 (קיא):

בן לשרה איק ושרה ד האהל ר = 860

This is certainly a significant sum. It is the value of the name of God, אלהים, Elohim, multiplied (magnified) by 10. But I am still not happy about האהל. I still think we might be dealing with a mnemonic. But for what?

It is here that I am reminded of something I was told about the extent of female authority in nomadic tribal cultures—that a woman's authority did not extend beyond her own tent, but within that tent it was her absolute domain. Might it be then, that the tent took the number of "woman" (111) because it was a symbol of her authority over her domain? Again, it is an intriguing hypothesis and we shall have to check it out. If it is correct we arrive at the sum:

1 [e]	1961 [e]	1931 [e]		2989 [e]	853 [e]	5711 [e]	3205 [e]
'ā·ḇî	hā·yāh,	hū		yā·ḇāl;	'eṯ-	'ā·ḏāh	wat·tê·leḏ
אֲבִי	הָיָה	הוּא	–	יָבָל ־	אֶת־	עָדָה	וַתֵּלֶד 20
the father	was	He		Jabal	-	Adah	And bore
N-msc	V-Qal-Perf-3ms	Pro-3ms		N-proper-ms	DirObjM	N-proper-fs	Conj-w | V-Qal-ConsecImperf-3fs

		4735 [e]	168 [e]	3427 [e]
Genesis 4:20		ū·miq·neh.	'ō·hel	yō·šêḇ
	.	וּמִקְנֶה:	אֹהֶל	יֹשֵׁב
		and [raise] livestock	in tents	of those who dwell
		Conj-w | N-ms	N-ms	V-Qal-Prtcpl-msc

בן לשרה איק ושרה ד איק ר = 930

This is a wonderful sum because it is the value of אל, El, God x 3 x 10. But we need to check whether our hunches about אחריו and האהל are correct. If they are used in that sense here, then they're going to be used in the same way in other verses and probably in other books.

Let's start with "the tents" האהל. Select "Hebrew" from the dropdown menu at Biblehub, then enter האהל into the search bar to see how many cases we have to choose from. It's from the word אֹהֶל, ohel ("tent") which is Strong's number 168. There are 345 occurrences of the word in the Tanakh, many of them in Genesis, and it first appears in Genesis 4:20:

ותלד עדה את יבל הוא היה אבי ישב אהל ומקנה:
    And bore Adah + Jebel he was father of dwellers tent and livestock.

The verbs are ותלד ("and bore"), הָיָה ("was"), and יֹשֵׁב ("dwellers"), although I believe this last one would have been judged to be a noun by an ancient scribe, so we will leave it and add a note against it and check the matter later. I also disagree that "and livestock" was a noun rather than a verb, i.e. I believe the word expresses the sense of a job; it was something you did—a doing word—thus a "verb". את is a calculating word that means "add". The preposition הוא is just filler, so remove it too. We are testing אהל for 111, which we write as איק, AIQ, and we are left with: Adah + Jebel + father of + dwellers + 111.

עדה יבל אבי ישב איק = 260 with Biblical Gematria.

This is the gate value of the left hand column of the Seven Palaces: בחאמדרה = 260. All three columns sum to a total of 777. It may be that people thought of themselves and others as having originated from that column, and given that the left side of the Palaces is the side of daylight from the Palace of the Aleph, it suggests a mythology descending from or influenced by the Egyptian concept of the solar journey, and the marriage of the sun and moon.

260 = YHVH (26) × 10.

I count this find to be significant so it's one point to the hypothesis that "tents" should be איק (111). Let's go again. This time we shall look for the presence of "behold" to signal there is gematria in the verse. Genesis 18:9 satisfies this requirement:

ויאמרו אליו איה שרה אשתך ויאמר הנה באהל:
> And they said to him Where is Sarah your woman? And he said Behold! In the tent!

אשתך ("your woman") has a value of 111, as does באהל ("in the tent"). I don't believe this is a calculation or sum as much as is it a simple joke or play on words, because the gematria value of אשתך ("your woman", 111) is the same as "in the tent". The flagword of "behold!" (here translated as merely "here") only flags the last word, באהל, and so is supportive of this view.

The hypothesis that אהל ("tents") should be איק (111) now has three points in support of it. Because this line includes the gematria value in the narrative structure of the text itself then it earns 2 points.

We should go again because it still might be a coincidence. If we get 3 for 3 I'll start getting excited. 5 out of 5 would provide enough surety to warrant putting it on the list of known mnemonics.

If we pursue the matter, we are looking for the word אהל ("tents") in the same verse as הנה ("behold!") and this time we're looking outside of the Book of Genesis too so that we can establish whether the mnemonic was a strongly established convention, bearing in mind that not all books of the Bible are embedded with gematria. However, the point of giving you a walk-through here is to show you how it's done, not establish whether אהל is a mnemonic for 111, so we shall stop here.

802 [e]	8283 [e]	346 [e]	413 [e]	559 [e]
'iš·te·ḵā;	śā·rāh	'ay·yêh	'ê·lāw,	way·yō·me·rū
אִשְׁתֶּ֑ךָ	שָׂרָ֣ה	אַיֵּ֖ה ،	אֵלָ֔יו	9 וַיֹּאמְר֣וּ
your wife	Sarah	where [is]	to him	And they said
N-fsc | 2ms	N-proper-fs	Interrog	Prep | 3ms	Conj-w | V-Qal-ConsecImperf-3mp

		168 [e]	2009 [e]	559 [e]
		ḇā·'ō·hel.	hin·nêh	way·yō·mer
٠		בָאֹֽהֶל: ،	הִנֵּ֥ה ،	וַיֹּ֖אמֶר
		in the tent	Here	so he said
		Prep-b, Art | N-ms	Interjection	Conj-w | V-Qal-ConsecImperf-3ms

Our takeaways? When you are choosing verses of the Tanakh to test potential mnemonics or calculating words, then remember to check whether the words are in books that are embedded with gematria in the first place, and if possible locate those instances where the presence of gematria is specially flagged with a הנה ("behold!").

The next walk-through is in Greek, from the Book of Revelation, and it's everyone's favorite—the infamous line about the beast numbering to 666.

b. Christian Exegesis

Words often come by their meanings differently in different cultures and thus every language has its own cultural inheritance that must be respected before any exegete is made of a foreign text. A language inherits wordless expressions, ways of thinking, worldviews, perspectives, habits, and shared cultural values and norms. It's built into the words themselves.

The majority of writers in the Christian canon were Jewish and used Greek. They used words that had undergone some degree of Hebraism,[66] and so Jewish cultural norms underpin the New Testament and undermine the pagan normative patina of the Greek language. I'll demonstrate this with the word "Atonement". In Hebrew it is כפר, *KPR* (transliterated) with a value of 300. It comes from a primitive root word meaning "to cover", as you might cover over a fire, or as you might "cover over" a difficult situation by paying reparation. One of the meanings of this word is a bribe or ransom. Looking a bit deeper into it we find that פַּר, PR, means a bullock, calf or ox (i.e. a sacrifice). This informs us about how the ancient Hebrews thought of atonement as an offering made to God in order to win back his favor.

There is also an abstract and hermeneutic dimension to the gematria of the Christian canon. The letter *aleph* has the gematria value of 1, and it began its existence as a pictogram of the head of an ox. Its name is אלף, with the gematria value of 111. There are words in the Hebrew gematria system that carry a set value of 1, such as "love", and "teach". These meanings carry over from Hebrew to Greek, so to give 1 by love or teachings to the name of Jesus Christ when written in Greek was to make a whole 12 hour day (719 + 1 = 720 = minutes in twelve hours).

Another way that New Testament writers used to place a stamp of Judaic culture upon their works is to use translated Greek words for hermeneutical conventions. A mnemonic word like "fire" (for instance) always has the value of 3, whether the word is written in Hebrew or Greek. Hebrew flagwords have Greek counterpart words. For instance, הנה ("behold!") is ἰδού and there are examples of calculating words too.

A specific and unique feature of the Gospels of Ματθατ Μαρκου Λουκας Ιωαννου (888) ("Matthew, Mark, Luke, and John") is their obsessive attention to the passage of time according to the hours of the day. It can be important to be able to convert your decimal result into base 60. Luckily for us this can be done on modern online time calculators such as Unitarium.

The following exegete illustrates how steeped in Jewish literature and hermeneutical methodology the writers of the New Testament were.

It's become the fashion of late for professors to adopt a position on Revelation 13:18, often to suggest the Emperor Nero as the identity of the beast, 666. I have a different explanation:

ανθρωπου εστιν
A Man's it is!

What we can tell of John was that he was a scholar of the Tanakh and knew of its true cipher and the conventions that ride with the practice of gematria, and thus in all likelihood he had been born and raised a Jew in a Jewish household and received a Jewish education before becoming caught up in the Christian movement. He may have been exiled to Patmos at one point (because "prophesy" was classed as "sorcery" or "magic", and was outlawed). But as a Jewish scholar he would have known Hebrew and the gematria of Genesis 1–2. He would definitely have spent a great deal of time working out its calculations, and therefore he would have known that the first time we see the calculation of 666 is in Genesis 1:26. This verse concerns the creation of man:

בדגת הים ובעוף השמים ובבהמה ובכל ויאמר אלהים נעשה אדם בצלמנו כדמותנו וירדו
הארץ ובכל הרמש הרמש על הארץ:

> And said Elohim 'let us make Adam in our image according to
> our likeness and let them rule over fish of the sea and over birds of
> the air and over livestock and all the earth and all moving things
> that move on the earth.

The words צלמנו and כדמותנו are calculating words and they indicate multiplication by 2, while על ("on" or "upon") indicates subtraction.

I'll break down the resulting calculation for you:

אדם = 2 * 2 * 180

בדגת הים ובעוף השמים ובבהמה הארץ = 686

הרמש הרמש - הארץ = 200

180 + 686 – 200 = 666.

John would have known this and he writes ανθρωπου εστιν! ("A man it is!") to identify the Adam. John even manages to write the 666 number in gematria in Rev 13:18:

> One having understanding

Take the "One" as 1 and know "understanding" has the mnemonic value of 3

ανθρωπου εστιν = 662

Thus: 4 + 662 = 666.

Some people find John's book to be intimidatingly loaded with symbols and fantastic visions, and John himself wrote, "Confused and complicated will be those who pick up this book and read it" (Rev 1:3).

Of course this tends to be the case about most biblical books, even those with more down-to-earth stories, because their writers hid key pieces of information in their gematria that would make holistic good sense out of the open text.

Although some people moan about this and argue that God would not hide anything from them, the fact of the matter is that God didn't write the Bible; scribes did. Several of those scribes appear to have been inspired by God, and their gematria compositions are a type of work that I think they thought brought them closer to God.

Ultimately, these scribes were writing for themselves first, and secondly for an audience that would have understood them. In their own time period, gematria and "the work of the Chariot" (*Ma'aseh Merkabah*) had been practiced since the time of the first temple, across hundreds of years, and the New Testament is essentially a product of that culture, of their worldviews and their beliefs. It was never about people two thousand years in the future trying to read the book and throwing their pacifier out of the pram when they found out it wasn't a matter of simply "reading it".

If you take a Biblical Studies degree in America today, especially if you attend a private Christian college, then you will be liable to emerge from your matriculation with a very strange picture of ancient Israel. You will be see Israel, alone amongst the civilizations of the ancient Near East, not to develop their own traditions of mathematics and science. As a consequence of your "advanced studies" you might end up believing that the people of ancient Israel thought pi was just 3, or that any gematria practiced was "a very simple affair".[67] You may hear your professors opine that the subject isn't taken seriously by scholars of antiquity because it isn't interesting or compelling, and they may suggest that there isn't enough evidence to support an argument for the existence of any substantial gematria in the Tanakh at all. These attitudes and responses are all in line with the type of Christian scholarship that is promoted by the Presbyterian Church in America. In one of their web articles, Pastor David Murrey writes on "10 problems with the Old Testament":

No Christian scholar should abandon the presuppositions of biblical inspiration and infallibility when studying the Word of God.
Nor should he attempt to approach the Word of God with an
"open" mind and so-called "neutral" presuppositions, in order to
interact with unbelieving scholarship.

When academics take their cues from private religious sponsors
and employers who espouse these narrow-minded and restrictive
approaches to Biblical Studies, then you may find that they trash the
very idea of scribal hermeneutics, and be entirely unaware that there is
any other reasonable or logical position to take.

Their students are often not aware of how shallow the studies of these
towering figures of academic authority frequently are in this particular
area of Biblical Studies. I suspect that those who opine upon gematria
(usually the 666 of Revelation 13:18) tend to do so in order to raise their
profile ahead of some book release of other. It's a safe bet that the tab-
loids will pick up on such obvious press fodder. But the reality of the
matter is that the last significant paper about gematria and notariqon
that was published in any reputable journal was in 1986 (Lieberman),
thirty-five years ago. In it, the author notes the rule that "the best exegesis of a text flows from methods actually used by its writer", but this is
often paid lip service to by many of these types of seminary scholars
today.

So what's with this attitude from this section of Professors in the
USA? Why can't they just "get with the times" and enjoy having a
new and extremely valuable tool for biblical exegesis at their disposal?
When leading academics ignore more cutting-edge but reputational,
costly positions, in favor of the safer old-school position, the hostage in
all this is the field of Biblical Studies itself.

It is said that an absence of evidence is not evidence of absence. When
the biblical cipher was unpublished and still unknown to the academic
community, the reasonable position to take was that expressed by Professor Stephen J. Lieberman:

> ... we must admit that its possible such techniques [as gematria
> and notariqon] were employed in biblical texts. The means were
> available, and if the desire was present, it was certainly possible for
> hidden messages to be put into the Bible.

There is virtue in such caution, but it's more usual in these times to see Christian academics in an almost casual state of denial about the existence of ancient Hebrew rhetoric math, even when they are supplied with the correct cipher, a list of the scribal conventions of the time, and an extensive database of examples of actual gematria calculations drawn from the Bible itself. It is at such times that I find myself reflecting upon the words of Aleister Crowley when he wrote:

> The sin which is unpardonable is knowingly and willfully to reject truth, to fear knowledge lest that knowledge pander not to thy prejudices.

Those who reject the notion of gematria in the Bible based on the simple rationale that "God would not hide 'his word' from mankind", appear to suffer from some degree of cognitive dissonance when they are shown convincing evidence of it. They are people who are not able to distinguish between an inspired text and one that has been channeled directly but, unfortunately, they hold the academic purse-strings of American academia.

Some scholars try and argue that the Tanakh has enough scribal interpolation in it to make reading the math impossible, but this is self-defeating, because gematria is actually a valuable tool with which to spot scribal interpolation and determine the original spelling of the text.

So is there any hope for Biblical Studies? Well, the story isn't one that is completely doom and gloom. There are voices within Biblical Studies that are calling for scholars to pay more respect to the methodology of ancient scribes in order to form the best exegesis. A principle is a principle, and this is a welcome one.

c. Occult Exegesis

While there are many tidbits of interesting gematria in rituals and texts that were not composed or adapted by Aleister Crowley, his work is of immediate interest to the gematraist because we know for a fact that he possessed the keys of Biblical Gematria, so we shall demonstrate an example of Occult Exegesis using *The Book of the Law*, with the following caveat:

The Tunis comment[68] contains this line: "All questions of the Law are to be decided only by appeal to my writings, each for himself." Thus, while I, you, and the fishmonger's wife can learn to use the hermeneutics that Crowley himself used and thus seek the best exegesis that is possible, according to Crowley there can never be an exegesis of *The Book of the Law* that is ever so correct as to become doctrinal to Thelema, unless it is made by the Beast 666 himself. Thus we are challenged by the scribe to parse the meaning of *The Book of the Law* for ourselves. The curious phrase "as centers of pestilence" turns out to have a reverse gematria value of 666, and I'm going to let you come to your own conclusions as to whether that is simply a coincidence (or if it's not), and what he meant by that in the context of the full line: "Those who discuss the contents of this Book are to be shunned by all, as centers of pestilence."

Most likely, Crowley intended that anyone reading, studying, or discussing the book had gone through a type of initiation upon reading it. Should one follow some arbitrary rule laid down by Crowley? Or should one "do thy will?" Those who do the latter are capable of questioning external authorities, even that of a prophet, and are following their own God-given destiny.

Although most of Crowley's gematria is written in English, it has some notable features that bear some comment upon. Crowley counts the value of the word "not" as the Hebrew לא, *LA* (31) instead of using it as a flagword that discounts the next word, as is the convention in Biblical Gematria. He uses this alternate convention in *Liber AL vel Legis*, but this doesn't preclude him having knowledge of the biblical convention. He may have known about it but decided to do something different. In any case, it is a convention in his writings.

By my estimation, if the 1904 date of the writing of *The Book of the Law* is correct, then Crowley would have known the biblical key for four years, but how many biblical conventions he discovered in that time is difficult to estimate. I am sure that he knew of the biblical practice of using mnemonics, for he used them frequently himself, but his knowledge of calculating words is far less certain.

There are a fair amount of puzzles in *The Book of the Law* that either don't involve gematria or reference it in an oblique way. For instance, *AL* II:16:

I am The Empress & the Hierophant. Thus eleven, as my bride is eleven.

The Empress is attributed to the *daleth* and the Hierophant is attributed to the *vav* which gives us the total of 10, not 11, so what can he mean by this?

Due to the fact that every Major Arcana card of the tarot has a Hebrew letter, they may be ordered according to the order found in Genesis 1–2 as follows;

0 The Magus,
I The Fool,
II The Priestess,
III The Aeon,
IV The Empress,
V The Universe,
VI The Star,
VII The Hierophant,
VIII The Lovers,
IX The Chariot,
X Lust,
XI The Hermit,
XII The Wheel,
XIII Adjustment,
XIV The Hanged Man,
XV Death,
XVI ART,
XVII The Devil,
XVIII The Tower,
XIX The Emperor,
XX The Moon,
XXI The Sun

Thus the solution to the riddle is:

IV (The Empress) + VII (The Hierophant) = XI (The Hermit).

In *AL* 1:57 there is also another tarot mystery—the changing of the attributions of the *tsade* to the Emperor and the *heh* to the Star:

All these old letters of my Book are aright; but צ {Tsade} is not the
Star. This also is secret: my prophet shall reveal it to the wise.

Crowley neglects to directly explain why this is so, except according to
an explanation via astrology, but if we consider the qualities of the letters according to their ancient correspondences in the Book of Genesis's
creation story, we discover that the verses for the *heh* describe the making of the Stars and the verses for *tsade* describe the creation of Eve as
the first "birth".

The card of the Emperor is named after the most famous Roman
Emperor of all time—Caesar—because there was a legend that Caesar
was born by the (then) miraculous procedure now called the Caesarean
section. Thus the Star and the Emperor are a natural fit for *heh* and *tsade*.

Let us try a verse with gematria:

Change not as much as the style of a letter; for behold! thou, o
prophet, shalt not behold all these mysteries hidden therein.

AL 1:54

To get at the gematria of the verse we start by stripping away all the
elements that don't belong in the sum—those elements that are "code
filler" from a cryptographer's perspective. We begin after the first
"behold!" and strip away all the verbs, adjectives and prepositions to
leave only the nouns:

O + Prophet + Mysteries = 913.

O(70) + P(80) r(200) o(70) ph(80) e(5) t(9) + M(40) y(10) s(60) t(9) e(5)
r(200) i(10) e(5) s(60) = 913.

But this number is chiefly of known relevance to the first word of
Genesis (בראשית) when calculated with the Standard Gematria cipher,
so what can it mean here? It's also rather low-hanging fruit in terms
of gematria. This "mystery" is one that anyone with a knowledge of
Standard Gematria could solve because there are no words involved
with the digraphs of Sh or Th, and so the sum is the same regardless of
whether it is checked in Biblical Gematria or Standard Gematria.

One of the most startling ways that Aleister Crowley used gematria
was to replicate the gematria of the first line of the Book of Genesis in
the first line of *The Book of the Law*:

Genesis 1:1:
BraShiTh = 220
Alhim + Hshmim + HarTs = 480
BraShiTh + Alhim + Hshmim + HarTs = 700.
The Book of the Law 1:1:
The Book of the Law Sub-figura number: 220.
Had + Manifestation + Nuit = 480
220 + 480 = 700.

As we might expect from Crowley's preoccupation with the solar mysteries, he liberally embedded his share of 666's in the text of *Liber AL vel Legis.*

For example:
Sun + winged secret flame + hadit = 666
Moon + stooping starlight + nuit = 666 (Reversal Cipher)
As centers of pestilence = 666 (Reversal Cipher)

The last one is part of the Tunis comment which is attached to the end of the book, rather than in the original manuscript:

> Do what thou wilt shall be the whole of the Law. The study of this Book is forbidden. It is wise to destroy this copy after the first read-ing. Whosoever disregards this does so at his own risk and peril. These are most dire. Those who discuss the contents of this Book are to be shunned by all, as centers of pestilence. All questions of the Law are to be decided only by appeal to my writings, each for himself. There is no law beyond Do what thou wilt. Love is the law, love under will.

With notariqon, the entire comment sums to 719, which is the number of Ιησου Χριστου (Jesus Christ).

> d w th w sh b th w o th l. th s o th b i f. i i w t d th c a th f r. w d th d s a h o r a p. th a m d. th w d th c o th b a t b sh b a, a c o p. a q o th l a t b d o b a t m w, e f h. th i n l b d w th w. l i th l, l u w. = 719 (with the Genesis Order).

Having lost the key to their own books, the Christians (with the excep-tions of the Cathars) were made dependent upon professional clergy for a dogmatic interpretation of the holy texts rather than coming to their own doctrinal conclusions. The peril for Thelema was that, because the keys were not made public by Crowley, *The Book of the Law* could become yet another bible for people to interpret according to their biases.

Crowley was being anything but anti-intellectual by his practice of gematria. He leaves clear breadcrumbs for the seeker to find if they have a will to do the job. Do what thou wilt and make up your own mind.

Rituals of the OTO are also crafted with Biblical Gematria. For example, the body, the blood, the seed, and the cup are all symbolic components of the Gnostic Mass, and have masculine (positive) and feminine (negative) qualities, which when translated to signs for addition and subtraction yield:

$$+ \ \sigma\omega\mu\alpha - \alpha\iota\mu\alpha\tau\circ\varsigma + \sigma\pi\varepsilon\rho\mu\alpha - \pi\circ\tau\eta\rho\iota\circ\nu = 31$$

One of the fun things about Crowley's gematria is that he uses all the main writing scripts and several languages to elevate the art of gematria to new horizons.

tmontuotcohemaewiaseniitindhmowlotimubtcombthmscmhmtbiir
batmohpktkiitkntkitkwttkabmlsoylmsbfstsrtmtktaftmabtgtmafcfoc
utstyfoliaayaiymeiiymjitsyjatgaitnsonsbietktsaohtwgtsbamoaankn
yskttcpaoisitpptbaihwctswiapgtsgmcitftsbtgotsithomfhieasasambt
hitwsfathtssbyanscbutbossoalwbuttkotriitswwihguhwtgtaiantdnsm
taauteiahatinogtmamlhntiaktybmnnathbasnwiwghwalhkmsiaisatist
dyatbnltbndmaybaotaotfttchbwaitlhbtcoaianamwisafdamautstpaso
tbowaiawsbtsssahbdalfobataphlhutbehlbaflahsfnhtlftkatssbmetcot
coetoombttpasutqoskhlbatdohlbhwbiassposoncoohlibettmsnotaoba
naltsnotaastacnbtlffotsatfiadflsftcoutitcotwttpodianatjodaftfomat
wcntaatflwiibbwjbyamcoompfotoomksmottjomlwryfaptisisibtvomb
bmshatbaicgbaidoyattpfiadtossutqohwuutowuutrwuutlbsstoiwntrs
bhkahctlifatttwittbolmsaanktpotpsniolctbbltbfhsctbtworhkatmast
oatwtwotwatwotsthslathmtbhmmstotwotliθwcutwdnwihlbcitwftatt
gthatlatmoedwtwsbtwotltwosiromrntwiswolitwdtinbtcutdblaeiaca
abittahlibtsombalswtathnrbtdtwdtanossnfpwuopdftloriewptpatpa
opantnanniaskotlsotjciicieefhebththubtastadmpiafwhoooanttoanbt
baaaraoawasrhkhthsiteateotgalabwiwaaobtanomlabtaitshihsnasitl
itiawtsathtbtatoioaimbgitwtgmptfltfbtiiatlcoithtyhsssslnokwtotaf
gtoptfotpiosaglljataarsjrateodlheitoaotfglhsotfotpwhnsahwitssbta
mambgtdyaifaerfadswawtfatyfawolaywwwawwywbaumitbnaiyctsm
staoostamitrbneumtetdjorhktsrtwtlwmsmhmtuwistkaosapttbotpisn
atnatbebtajoeetmtmcnamatsoalfbtopsnbatmhttcotbhsbtehnftenftwf
fnehctcaawasaaptsottualstfhoteltsubthaitclastnaitdimumslitlluwn
ltfmlftalaltitdatitscywhmphcktlotfatgmothogatolombaabȝintstais
mpsrittwigujoecnfwiludpurendidaismiiorwgatinbtbomhttoemniaat
nwaoutfpswacitmtcirmcibttbbtbgasotsaihagfttlmbtlmibtatiutnsitd
tpbmibmimwaphatsfttscaltlimbfokwttbwtgabwgopodslaithysggaso
wasyswrjysetnoteispbaitlomassyctmjicyetcbmiasracwarhilyiytypo
pvoviwaapapadotisdypotwaatcswycumaammwystpsahesbwdassbar
imsttmtmcftfothoaihlcstrlsumbtmpwtmjdtmfilyilyiatbldosiatnbotv
nstmtmtmoniaae = 50,000.

This is the Notariqon of Chapter 1 of the Book of the Law, minus the first word: Had. Multiplication of the first words of Chapter 1 & 2:

$H \times A \times D \times N \times U = 6000$.

$50,000 + 6000 = 56,000$.

"I am Nuit and my word is six and fifty" – AL 1:24.

CHAPTER 12

Gematria research

Practicing gematria will naturally lead to you running into words you think might be operational (a calculating word) or mnemonic but are not listed in this guide, and you should have fairly strict criteria about what you accept as operational or mnemonic.

Building your own research log is pretty essential in keeping track of your discoveries. If you have a word of interest (WOI), and there are multiple instances of your WOI in the text you are researching, you can check the gematria of each instance and discover whether your suspicions are correct. To do this you will need to consult a Concordance.

Biblehub.com and various other online Bibles have an Englishman's Concordance that shows you every instance of any word used in the Bible, as well as its variations. Once you've discovered how many instances of the WOI there are you can explore the gematria of each instance and determine whether the WOI is behaving as you think it does. Depending on the results you will arrive at a baseline of probability from 100% to 0%. If you have ten instances of a WOI and in every case they signal (for example) a multiplication by 2, then you have established a 100% probability across ten instances. Your research should record each WOI so that you can cross check it. Ideally you should try for at least five levels of verification, although that is not possible with some rarely used words and in that case you should note the number of instances the word appears so that the probability is seen in context. You should also take care to note whether an operator references the previous word or whether it references the word in front of it. A secondary consideration arrives if the WOI is a unique part of the stylistic repertoire of the scribal author. As an example, John of Patmos never writes the name of God in Hebrew but he expects you to calculate with the value of the Hebrew names, either יהוה or אלהים. This type of WOI can be checked and verified as being peculiar to the style of St. John, but it also applies to other authors of the New Testament. So enter a note into your research log so that you can determine how far the convention was spread.

a. Textual corruption

As far as academic studies go, gematria is a valuable research tool for solving textual corruptions. To demonstrate:

> Not will depart the scepter from Judah and from the staff from between his feet till it comes Shiloh and to him the obedience of the people.

George Lamba suggested a possible corruption of the word Shiloh in Genesis 49:10, but he couldn't prove it. The word seen there is שילה, but in the books of Joshua, Judges, and Samuel the word doesn't have a *yod*—שלה. However because the scribe embedded gematria in that verse, we can find out which word is correct and original to the text. Let's look at the verse and then the sum:

לא יסור שבט מיהודה ומחקק מבין רגליו עד כי יבא שילה ולו יקהת עמים

We have the לא ("not") to tell us to ignore the next word, יסור. We also have the word מבין ("between") to tell us to divide ומחקק ("and the staff") by 2. Thus we have the sums:

שבט מיהודה + (ומחקק/2) + רגליו שילה יקהת עמים = 787 (with the *yod*)
שבט מיהודה + (ומחקק/2) + רגליו שלה יקהת עמים = 777 (without the *yod*)

So obviously, George Lamba was right and the text of Genesis 49:10 has been subject to textual corruption. The word written should be שלה.

The full worth of gematria to academics is multivalent. It is of intrinsic value to our understanding of biblical and occult texts, and it has its own history. It is an art that acts as a lens into otherwise hidden facets of the cultures of antiquity.

b. Programming code

For Python coders, and for people who just love exploring ciphers, the following link will take you to the Python code for a basic gematria calculator for Hebrew and English. It will function on your PC at home as long as you have Python 3.6 or higher installed. Please visit the repository at github.com and download from the url:

https://github.com/BethshebaAshe/Behold/blob/main/Gematria%20Calculator

— ... ?

2 + 2 = 5

— ... ?

CHAPTER 13

Numerology

Although there is often little distinction made between gematria and numerology in the public awareness, they are two quite distinct and separate practices. Being far easier, numerology is by far the more popular of the two.

Most books that advertise themselves as being about gematria are actually about numerology, and most people that say they are teaching gematria are actually teaching numerology. All online gematria calculators (with the exception of Shematria) are programmed with no working gematria ciphers. This means that most people think of gematria in the same category as astrology or tarot card reading. It is numerology to look up the value of a name or date of birth. It's numerology when you're trying to find the result of a football game by calculating the dates and names of the teams. And it's numerology when you attribute special status to the date and time of real events or the names of the participants.

Magick and mysticism without intellectual preparation tend to go awry. The Great Work of the magician or mystic is to unite the microcosm with the macrocosm, and the divine with the mundane. Kabbalistic charts attempt to plot all the various domains of both macrocosm (the Seven Palaces) and microcosm (ten *sephiroth*). It is an attempt to make the Great Work systematic.

The microcosm unites with each domain of the macrocosm by resonating with it, but there are many factors that may impede innate resonance, various types of unconscious psychological complexes that may turn that resonance off. However, there are various divinatory methods that are useful for free association and these are used to bring unconscious complexes into the conscious awareness where they can be properly analyzed and processed.

Numerology is one of these divinatory methods. Tarot is another. Creative writing and art can do the same thing. People usually find that they feel drawn to some myth or story that exemplifies an archetype within their psyche, or a type of story that is related in some fashion to their own. They'll just wander across it one day while playing with the numbers. And generally there is no difficulty in these practices because most practitioners have at least some background knowledge of psychology to work with. The difficulties arise when people use numerology in a less-than-mindful way—as a simple targeting system for a lot of psychological projection. That's numerology, but gematria is not numerology.

In the 70's and early 80's, I used to hear people mixing up the terms astronomy with astrology. This annoyed quite a few astronomers of the day. There is now an obvious mix up in the minds of a section of the general public about the difference between gematria and numerology. Popular numerology channels and websites that advertise their activities as gematria only deepen the confusion. The lure of numerology in respect of current affairs is that it offers people a novel outlet to discuss their anxiety, or to link together a narrative from the free association of ideas, without doing any fact-checking for causality beyond the value of isolated words. There were many people during the Coronavirus pandemic that were moved to look up various words associated with the outbreak. So much so in fact that it prompted five Rabbis on the staff of JewishPress.com to publish an article that questioned whether it was appropriate to look for gematria related to the pandemic. Rabbi Steven Pruzansky acknowledged that "searching for allusions in the Torah to all events has been a Jewish parlor game since ancient times", but said that:

> If the point is to show that G-d is master of the universe, the endeavor will engender humility in mankind, which is often lacking today.

However, if the subtext is "We have precise knowledge on how G-d runs His world because we have deciphered these references," the endeavor is improper as this subtext is incorrect, troubling, and spiritually self-defeating. It is the antithesis of what we should be learning from this calamity.

He spoke of the necessity for people to realize the limitations of the exercise and its propriety, and pointed out that the data can easily be manipulated to produce a desired result which was of limited value.

Rabbi Dr. Gidon Rothstein pointed out that Kabbalah was only for the initiated, and said that he thought gematriot and Torah codes serve the predetermined purposes of whoever "finds" them and have no more authority than if the person came up with the idea on their own.

Chief Rabbi Shmuel Eliyahu reminded his readers that Rabbi Eliezer ben Chiasma had called gematriot the "compliments of wisdom" (Avot 3:18), which was like a dessert that came at the end of a meal. They were not the principal nutritional part of the meal. Giving an example of non-legitimate practice he said:

> But if we found a clever gematria that says that Jewish life in New York is the essence of the Torah, then we have taken a tasty dessert and transformed it into the main dish of the meal. And this erroneous assertion does not line with the teachings of our Sages.

In his view gematriot were there to add depth and support to the Torah, prophets, and writings, and was only legitimate if it led to deductions from these sources that were already known to be true.

Rabbi Simon Jacobson said, "Generally speaking, this approach is frowned upon. It can also lend itself to sensationalism." He advised listening to the advice of Devarim 18:13: *"Tamim tiyeh im Hashem Elokecha"*—"Be wholehearted with G-d." and to Rashi who explained:

> Conduct yourself with Him with simplicity and depend on Him. Do not inquire of the future; rather, accept whatever happens to you with [unadulterated] simplicity and then you will be with Him and to His portion.

Rabbi Raleigh Resnick told a story about Rabbi Yoel Kahan in order to make his point. He said Rabbi Yoel Kahan (a preeminent thinker and

Chassid of the Lubavitcher Rebbe) was once giving a class describing why one of the names of Hashem, "Elokim", reflects Hashem acting through nature. After a number of minutes, he saw the students didn't understand what he was saying, so he told them "Elokim" has the same gematria (86) as the word for nature in Hebrew (ha'tevah). At that point, one of the boys said, "Ah, I got it!" Reb Yoel chuckled when the boy said that because of the following:

> There are relationships between certain ideas, but gematrias are merely expressions of these relationships. They don't create them. The reason two things are connected is not because they share the same gematria. It's because they are inherently connected, and Hashem embedded that connection in the letters of the Hebrew language. So if there is indeed a relationship between, say, doing teshuvah and plagues, and that happens to express itself in certain words, that's interesting, but the gematria is not what creates the relationship; it's what expresses it. So finding expressions of Torah truths in letters and words is wonderful, but to create new ideas or theories based on numerology is improper.

A thing that people do with a gematria calculator when they first encounter one is to look up the value of their own name. Some proceed to calculate the value of the names of their family and friends, and then famous people, and finally they look up their own name again, having quite forgotten its number. Such practices are not serious, and nor do they tell us anything at all about ourselves, except those conceits and delusions that we invent around them.

There is little guesswork in rhetoric math, but numerology on the other hand is the deliberate cherry picking of words that have a certain value, with no regard for whether they have actually been composed in a gematria sum written anywhere, or according to any formal system. Numerology is a kind of guessing game or a free association practice.

Numerologists are mostly harmless. Numerology for most is like reading the tarot or the I Ching. The problem arises when numerologists insist that numerology can be used as evidence for conspiracy theories. The only thing that numerology proves about conspiracy is that people tend to project their Jungian shadow onto external actors using their magical thinking about numbers as a flim-flam justification.

In the recent year, there has been a visible rise in people who are participating in the ritualized numerology of the QAnon cult—people who were mislead into thinking they were learning gematria when actually they were being lead into an exploration of the subconscious that they probably weren't prepared for, using numerology. Lindsay Beyerstein resurrected the term "Numberwang" for QAnon's numerology.

The basic rule of gematria is that if its not written in a book, scroll, or other document of note, then it's numerology. If you're not using the correct cipher the book was written in, then its numerology too. If someone tells you that gematria is about dates, then its numerology, because numerology is whatever you want it to be. If you're practicing numerology then you're the one imagining connections between random words and sentences and imagining that there's a reason beyond coincidence that these words and phrases sum to certain numbers.

Unlike gematria, numerology is 90% guesswork and a lot of fudge. The popular numerology channels on YouTube make heavy use of Simple Gematria to fuel the popular distrust of government, media, and science, and to spread the belief that the lives of ordinary people are being controlled by shadowy cabals and elites. Most of these conspiracy theories are based on antisemitic tropes that were first coined in Nazi Germany. They aren't any more rational when revisited. What they deliberately overlook is that Simple (ordinal) Gematria has a low value spread, so it couldn't be easier to find anything you wanted by cross-referencing the numbers. By cherry-picking results which appear to share in a certain domain or sphere of interest then numerology like this is simply a manipulation of the massive amount of perfectly ordinary coincidences that will arise for any low value number system and twisting them to support your dominant narrative. In other words, numerology can tell you a lot about the numerologist that is using it but that's about it.

With Biblical Gematria we understand that the art and practice proceeded according to certain well established conventions. It was a formal system. Just like modern mathematics, there is no guessing at an answer with a mathematical sum. You can lay down a calculation and be secure that anyone with basic mathematical schooling will be able to follow it.

What the ancient scribes were doing in their writings was documenting their religious mysteries while leaving key pieces of information concealed by gematria. These mysteries were the inspired, esoteric center of the ancient first Temple cult. The goal of Biblical Gematria is to discover the missing pieces for yourself and discover the full meaning of biblical stories. Take the story of the Garden of Eden. Through gematria we know a few key things about this story. We know that the fruit of the Tree of Knowledge was "light" which God had given a purpose to during creation, "to bring light to the Earth". When Adam and Eve took the light into themselves they also bound themselves to its purpose which meant they had to come to earth.

In this context the speech God gives sounds far less like a proclamation of punishment and something more like a lament, simply detailing the hardships they would both endure upon the Earth. The serpent in the Garden of Eden story is also a more complex character with gematria than he appears to be. The serpent represents the mnemonic value of the letter *nun* (50), and thus he is a spirit of God. When he tells the woman "You shall not die but live!", he was perfectly correct because he was speaking of the spirit of Eve and not of her physical body as it would be on earth.

Working out such mysteries is the main function of Biblical Gematria. Numerology calculators are so that people can find out the number of their name in a variety of different ciphers and see whether any of them were cool. People who want to use numbers to "prove" they are special or chosen generally roll with numerology. Conspiracy theorists with dark suspicions about the way the media portrays reality ironically go on to warp it a bit further with numerology.

People try and find connections with numerology. They take two words or phrases and then they invent a narrative that connects these two things in their imaginations. People may feel this is special thing to do but it's something that artists and writers have always done. It's a method of plumbing the surface of the unconscious mind. You cannot find rational external truths that way but it will tell you about some of the archetypes that are major players in your psyche, and for that reason, numerology can be helpful and informative from a psychoanalytical perspective.

Numerology is as informative as dreams. Many types of divination, like numerology, open up the subconscious. There are powerful actors in the subconscious of every mind. A particularly powerful one is the encounter with the Jungian Shadow.

Conspiracy theorists don't check themselves to see whether they might be projecting their shadow onto external actors just so they can reject them. What makes followers so susceptible to the culture of the cult is the lack of knowledge these people have about the subconscious. They dig around and imagine a bunch of terrible things are connected but they never get to the stage of realizing "aha, but it is only myself that is projecting these things". They never take that next step of investigating the Jungian shadow and the powerful actors that inhabit the territory of the unconscious.

If you play with numerology, then whether you're a beginner or an old hand, a decent grounding in Jungian psychology is very helpful to numerologists in general. And if you're not into that, try gematria instead.

APPENDIX 1

Table of Correspondences for the Hebrew letters to the verses of Genesis 1–2.

Letter	#	Theme	Verses
Beth B ב	2	Creation and the House of God.	1:1–2
Aleph A א	1	The Day and the Night.	1:3–5
Gimel G ג	3	The Sky / The Heavens.	1:6–8
Shin S ש	3	Drying the land and dividing it from the seas.	1:9–10
Daleth D ד	4	First life (plants) come to earth.	1:11–13
Tav Th ת	4	Time and the Calendar.	1:14–16
Heh H ה	5	The light of the stars shining on Earth.	1:16–19
Vav V ו	6	Creation of Birds and other living things.	1:20–22
Zayin Z ז	7	Creation of Beasts and Bugs.	1:24–25
Cheth Ch ח	8	Creation of Adam as God's overseer.	1:26–28
Teth T ט	9	Food and sustenance.	1:29–31
Yod Y י	10	Work and rest from Work.	2:1–3

(*Continued*)

Table of Correspondences for the Hebrew letters to the verses of Genesis 1–2.

Letter	#	Theme	Verses
Kaph K כ	20	Fertility.	2:4–6
Lamed ל	30	Spirit/soul.	2:7
Mem M מ	40	Pregnancy (the gestation of Adam in the Garden of Eden).	2:8
Nun N נ	50	Life and the Afterlife.	2:9
Samekh S ס	60	The Great River from heaven to earth.	2:10–14
Ayin O ע	70	Temptation and Desire.	2:15–17
Peh P פ	80	Courtship and Mating.	2:18–20
Tsade Ts צ	90	Childbirth (the birth of Eve).	2:21–22
Qoph Q ק	100	Woman/Marriage.	2:24
Resh R ר	200	The Solar journey through life.	2:25

APPENDIX 2

And Rav Ḥiyya bar Abba said that Rabbi Yoḥanan said: He expounded the verses: "But the Lord was not in the wind. And after the wind, an earthquake; the Lord was not in the earthquake. And after the earthquake, fire; but the Lord was not in the fire. And after the fire, a still, small voice," and it states in that verse: "And behold, the Lord passed by"

I Kings 19:11–12, Chagigah 16a–4.

Four Entered Paradise (Hekhalot Zutarti)

Rabbi Akiva said: We were four who went into the Paradise.

One looked and died, one looked and was smitten, one looked and cut the shoots, and I went in in peace and came out in peace.

And these are they that went into the Paradise: Ben Azzai and Ben Zoma and Aher and Rabbi Akiva.

Rabbi Akiva said to them: Beware! When you approach the pure marble stones of the sixth heavenly palace [which look like water], do not say, "Water! Water!"—according to that which is written: The speaker of lies shall not endure before my sight (Ps. 101:7).

Ben Azzai looked into the sixth palace and saw brilliance of the air of the marble stones with which the palace was paved, and his body could not bear it, and he opened his mouth and asked them: "These waters—what is the nature of them?" and died. Of him, scripture says: Precious in the eyes of the Lord is the death of his saints (Ps. 116:15).

Ben Zoma looked at the brilliance in the marble stones and thought that they were water, and his body could not bear that he did not ask them, but his mind could not bear it and he was smitten—he went out of his mind. Of him, scripture says: Have you found honey? Eat what is enough for you lest you be overfilled and vomit it up (Prov. 25:16).

Aher looked and cut the shoots. [They say when he went to heaven he saw Metatron to whom permission had been given to sit for one hour in the day and write down the merits of Israel. He said, "The sages have taught: On high there is not sitting" and he entertained the thought that there might perhaps be two Powers in heaven.

Rabbi Akiva went in in peace and come out in peace.

APPENDIX 3

Chapters 6 and 7 of 1 Kings, describing the building of the Temple of Solomon.

1 In the four hundred and eightieth year after the Israelites had come out of the land of Egypt, in the month of Ziv, the second month of the fourth year of Solomon's reign over Israel, he began to build the house of the LORD.

2 The house that King Solomon built for the LORD was sixty cubits long, twenty cubits wide, and thirty cubits high. 3 The portico at the front of the main hall of the temple was twenty cubits long, extending across the width of the temple and projecting out ten cubits in front of the temple.

4 He also had narrow windows framed high in the temple.

5 Against the walls of the temple and the inner sanctuary, Solomon built a chambered structure around the temple, in which he constructed the side rooms. 6 The bottom floor was five cubits wide, the middle floor six cubits, and the third floor seven cubits. He also placed offset ledges around the outside of the temple, so that nothing would be inserted into its walls.

7 The temple was constructed using finished stones cut at the quarry, so that no hammer or chisel or any other iron tool was heard in the temple while it was being built.

8 The entrance to the bottom floor was on the south side of the temple. A stairway led up to the middle level, and from there to the third floor.

9 So Solomon built the temple and finished it, roofing it with beams and planks of cedar. 10 He built chambers all along the temple, each five cubits high and attached to the temple with beams of cedar.

11 Then the word of the LORD came to Solomon, saying: 12 "As for this temple you are building, if you walk in My statutes, carry out My ordinances, and keep all My commandments by walking in them, I will fulfill through you the promise I made to your father David. 13 And I will dwell among the Israelites and will not abandon My people Israel."

14 So Solomon built the temple and finished it. 15 He lined the interior walls with cedar paneling from the floor of the temple to the ceiling, and he covered the floor with cypress boards.

16 He partitioned off the twenty cubits at the rear of the temple with cedar boards from floor to ceiling to form within the temple an inner sanctuary, the Most Holy Place. 17 And the main hall in front of this room was forty cubits long.

18 The cedar paneling inside the temple was carved with gourds and open flowers. Everything was cedar; not a stone could be seen.

19 Solomon also prepared the inner sanctuary within the temple to set the ark of the covenant of the LORD there. 20 The inner sanctuary was twenty cubits long, twenty cubits wide, and twenty cubits high. He overlaid the inside with pure gold, and he also overlaid the altar of cedar.

21 So Solomon overlaid the inside of the temple with pure gold, and he extended gold chains across the front of the inner sanctuary, which was overlaid with gold. 22 So he overlaid with gold the whole interior of the temple, until everything was completely finished. He also overlaid with gold the entire altar that belonged to the inner sanctuary.

23 In the inner sanctuary he made two cherubim, each ten cubits high, out of olive wood. 24 One wing of the first cherub was five cubits long, and the other wing was five cubits long as well. So the full wingspan was ten cubits. 25 The second cherub also measured

ten cubits; both cherubim had the same size and shape, 26 and the height of each cherub was ten cubits.

27 And he placed the cherubim inside the innermost room of the temple. Since their wings were spread out, the wing of the first cherub touched one wall, while the wing of the second cherub touched the other wall, and in the middle of the room their wingtips touched. 28 He also overlaid the cherubim with gold.

29 Then he carved the walls all around the temple, in both the inner and outer sanctuaries, with carved engravings of cherubim, palm trees, and open flowers. 30 And he overlaid the temple floor with gold in both the inner and outer sanctuaries.

31 For the entrance to the inner sanctuary, Solomon constructed doors of olive wood with five-sided doorposts. 32 The double doors were made of olive wood, and he carved into them cherubim, palm trees, and open flowers and overlaid the cherubim and palm trees with hammered gold.

33 In the same way he made four-sided doorposts of olive wood for the sanctuary entrance. 34 The two doors were made of cypress wood, and each had two folding panels. 35 He carved into them cherubim, palm trees, and open flowers; and he overlaid them with gold, hammered evenly over the carvings.

36 Solomon built the inner courtyard with three rows of dressed stone and one row of trimmed cedar beams.

37 The foundation of the house of the LORD was laid in the fourth year of Solomon's reign, in the month of Ziv. 38 In his eleventh year and eighth month, the month of Bul, the temple was finished in every detail and according to every specification. So he built the temple in seven years.

* * *

1 Solomon, however, took thirteen years to complete the construction of his entire palace.

2 He built the House of the Forest of Lebanon a hundred cubits long, fifty cubits wide, and thirty cubits high, with four rows of cedar pillars supporting the cedar beams.

3 The house was roofed with cedar above the beams that rested on the pillars—forty-five beams, fifteen per row. 4 There were three rows of high windows facing one another in three tiers. 5 All the

doorways had rectangular frames, with the openings facing one another in three tiers.

6 Solomon made his colonnade fifty cubits long and thirty cubits wide, with a portico in front of it and a canopy with pillars in front of the portico.

7 In addition, he built a hall for the throne, the Hall of Justice, where he was to judge. It was paneled with cedar from floor to ceiling.

8 And the palace where Solomon would live, set further back, was of similar construction. He also made a palace like this hall for Pharaoh's daughter, whom he had married.

9 All these buildings were constructed with costly stones, cut to size and trimmed with saws inside and out from the foundation to the eaves, and from the outside to the great courtyard. 10 The foundations were laid with large, costly stones, some ten cubits long and some eight cubits long. 11 Above these were high-grade stones, cut to size, and cedar beams.

12 The great courtyard was surrounded by three rows of dressed stone and a row of trimmed cedar beams, as were the inner courtyard and portico of the house of the LORD.

13 Now King Solomon sent to bring Huram from Tyre. 14 He was the son of a widow from the tribe of Naphtali, and his father was a man of Tyre, a craftsman in bronze. Huram had great skill, understanding, and knowledge for every kind of bronze work. So he came to King Solomon and carried out all his work.

15 He cast two pillars of bronze, each eighteen cubits high and twelve cubits in circumference. 16 He also made two capitals of cast bronze to set on top of the pillars, each capital five cubits high. 17 For the capitals on top of the pillars he made a network of lattice, with wreaths of chainwork, seven for each capital.

18 Likewise, he made the pillars with two rows of pomegranates around each grating to cover each capital atop the pillars. 19 And the capitals atop the pillars in the portico were shaped like lilies, four cubits high. 20 On the capitals of both pillars, just above the rounded projection next to the network, were the two hundred pomegranates in rows encircling each capital.

21 Thus he set up the pillars at the portico of the temple. The pillar to the south he named Jachin, and the pillar to the north he named Boaz. 22 And the tops of the pillars were shaped like lilies. So the work of the pillars was completed.

23 He also made the Sea of cast metal. It was circular in shape, measuring ten cubits from rim to rim, five cubits in height, and thirty cubits in circumference. 24 Below the rim, ornamental buds encircled it, ten per cubit all the way around the Sea, cast in two rows as a part of the Sea.

25 The Sea stood on twelve oxen, three facing north, three facing west, three facing south, and three facing east. The Sea rested on them, with all their hindquarters toward the center. 26 It was a handbreadth thick, and its rim was fashioned like the brim of a cup, like a lily blossom. It could hold two thousand baths.

27 In addition, he made ten movable stands of bronze, each four cubits long, four cubits wide, and three cubits high.

28 This was the design of the stands: They had side panels attached to uprights, 29 and on the panels between the uprights were lions, oxen, and cherubim. On the uprights was a pedestal above, and below the lions and oxen were wreaths of beveled work.

30 Each stand had four bronze wheels with bronze axles and a basin resting on four supports, with wreaths at each side. 31 The opening to each stand inside the crown at the top was one cubit deep, with a round opening like the design of a pedestal, a cubit and a half wide. And around its opening were engravings, but the panels of the stands were square, not round.

32 There were four wheels under the panels, and the axles of the wheels were attached to the stand; each wheel was a cubit and a half in diameter. 33 The wheels were made like chariot wheels; their axles, rims, spokes, and hubs were all of cast metal.

34 Each stand had four handles, one for each corner, projecting from the stand. 35 At the top of each stand was a circular band half a cubit high. The supports and panels were cast as a unit with the top of the stand.

36 He engraved cherubim, lions, and palm trees on the surfaces of the supports and panels, wherever each had space, with wreaths all around. 37 In this way he made the ten stands, each with the same casting, dimensions, and shape.

38 He also made ten bronze basins, each holding forty baths and measuring four cubits across, one basin for each of the ten stands.

39 He set five stands on the south side of the temple and five on the north, and he put the Sea on the south side, at the southeast corner of the temple.

40 Additionally, Huram made the pots, shovels, and sprinkling bowls. So Huram finished all the work that he had undertaken for King Solomon in the house of the LORD:

41 the two pillars;
the two bowl-shaped capitals atop the pillars;
the two sets of network covering both bowls of the capitals atop the pillars;

42 the four hundred pomegranates for the two sets of network (two rows of pomegranates for each network covering both the bowl-shaped capitals atop the pillars);

43 the ten stands;
the ten basins on the stands;

44 the Sea;
the twelve oxen underneath the Sea;

45 and the pots, shovels, and sprinkling bowls.
All the articles that Huram made for King Solomon in the house of the LORD were made of burnished bronze. 46 The king had them cast in clay molds in the plain of the Jordan between Succoth and Zarethan. 47 Solomon left all these articles unweighed, because there were so many. The weight of the bronze could not be determined.

48 Solomon also made all the furnishings for the house of the LORD:
the golden altar;
the golden table on which was placed the Bread of the Presence;

49 the lampstands of pure gold in front of the inner sanctuary, five on the right side and five on the left;
the gold flowers, lamps, and tongs;

50 the pure gold basins, wick trimmers, sprinkling bowls, ladles, and censers;
and the gold hinges for the doors of the inner temple (that is, the Most Holy Placex) as well as for the doors of the main hall of the temple.

51 So all the work that King Solomon had performed for the house of the LORD was completed.
Then Solomon brought in the items his father David had dedicated—the silver, the gold, and the furnishings—and he placed them in the treasuries of the house of the LORD.

ABOUT THE AUTHOR

 Bethsheba Ashe is a fifty one year old tea-drinking cryptographer who broke the gematria ciphers to the Bible and the Book of the Law. She is the CEO of Lightwood Studio, creator of the popular 'Shematria' online calculator, and inventor of the Galay writing script. Currently she lives in Pennsylvania and is creating an open-world VR Island adventure game with her boyfriend, two cats and a cockatoo, but she says she owes all her success to Tetley.

NOTES

1. *Kabbala Denudata: The Kabbalah Unveiled*, by Mathers, S.L. Macgregor (1887).
2. The *Zohar*: Pritzker Edition volumes present the first translation ever made from a critical Aramaic text of the *Zohar*, which has been established by Professor Daniel Matt.
3. Translation and commentary by Daniel C. Matt. The *Zohar* = *Sefer Ha-Zohar*. Stanford, Calif.: Stanford University Press, 2004–2017.
4. Professor Overmann's work focuses on the fundamental question of how societies form concepts of numbers, and how those concepts then become more complex (e.g., counting sequence and simple arithmetic, things that are necessary precursors to mathematical systems) through the use of material devices like fingers, tallies, tokens, and notations.
5. Hurowitz, Mazar and others.
6. A set is the mathematical model for a collection of different things. A set contains elements or members, which can be mathematical objects of any kind: numbers, symbols, points in space, lines, other geometrical shapes, variables, or even other sets.
7. Translated by Rabbi David Rubin (author of *Eye to the Infinite: A Guide to Jewish Meditation*.

8. The spellings of Kabbalah, Qabalah and Cabala denote a Jewish, Hermetic and Christian influence respectively.

9. The Book of the Law has the formal title of "Liber Al vel Legis", and has an abbreviated form among Thelemites as "AL".

10. The city was walled around 6000 BCE, and is thought to be older, but it started its heyday around 1800 BCE. I get the impression it was the Ankh Morpork of the Ancient World.

11. Gershon Galil is a Professor of Biblical Studies and Ancient History and former chair of the Department of Jewish History at the University of Haifa.

12. Even an atheist can get on board with this proposition by simply changing the definition to "the Will of the Good", meaning the innate ethical sensibilities we are born with in respect of our true selves—Thelema or, more narrowly, Humanism.

13. As shown by a recently discovered early alphabetic inscription from Tel Lachish (located in the Shephelah region in modern-day Israel) that dates to the fifteenth century BCE.

14. Petrovich, D. (2017). The World's Oldest Alphabet: Hebrew as the Language of the Proto-Consonantal Script. Jerusalem: Carta Jerusalem.

15. The writers of the New Testament were mostly Jews who were used to their word for God having the total of 31. This value was the foundation of the entire system of the Merkabah, so instead of using the Greek values for Greek words that meant God (like Θεόν Theon and Θεὸς Theos) they gave them a set value of 31. This calculation, which means Word + God appears in John 1:1. The full sum is:
αρχη λογος λογος אל אל λογος = 1330 with biblical gematria and 700 with the reversal cipher.

16. Professor Douglas Petrovich (2017). The World's Oldest Alphabet: Hebrew As the Language of the Proto-Consonantal Script: PowerPoint Presentation (ancient-hebrew.org):
https://www.ancient-hebrew.org/alphabet/files/alphabet_chart2.pdf

17. The Bahir II:29:
https://pages.uoregon.edu/sshoemak/102/texts/bahir.htm

18. See Douglas Petrovich's Alphabet Chart from:
https://www.ancient-hebrew.org/alphabet/files/alphabet_chart2.pdf

19. The Ancient Hebrew Alphabet | AHRC (ancient-hebrew.org):
https://www.ancient-hebrew.org/ancient-alphabet/tsade.htm

20. https://www.chabad.org/kabbalah/article_cdo/aid/379810/jewish/Exodus-Birth-of-the-Soul.htm

21. Eve does not have a given name until the end of Genesis 3. Until that point she is simply "the Woman" or "this one".
22. Without adding the 1 at the end, this works out to be 253, which is the gate value of the Palace of the Aleph (1) by night!
23. Barkay, G., Lundberg, M. J., Vaughn, A. G., Zuckerman, B., & Zuckerman, K. (2003). The Challenges of Ketef Hinnom: Using Advanced Technologies to Reclaim the Earliest Biblical Texts and Their Context. Near Eastern Archaeology, 66(4), 162–171. doi: 10.2307/3557916
24. Kapelrud, A. S. (October 1968). The Number Seven in Ugaritic Texts. Vetus Testamentum, 494–499.
25. As Solomon was taught by his mother Bathsheba.
26. Solomon is tested by the Queen of Sheba on his knowledge and evidently passed with flying colors.
27. From an inscription found on a potsherd during an excavation in Kuntillet Ajrud (1975–76).
28. By the rule of Colel, any word can be equal to any other word by plus or minus one.
29. Notariqon is a Greek word deriving from "shorthand writer": νοταρικόν.
30. Elie Assis. The Alphabetic Acrostic in the Book of Lamentations. Bar Ilan University, Israel.
31. Hurowitz, V., 2001. The Seventh Pillar—Reconsidering the Literary Structure and Unity of Proverbs 31. *Zeitschrift für die Alttestamentliche Wissenschaft*, 113(2).
32. a half millennia old milk jar fragment was unearthed at Tel Lachish in Israel, containing a partial inscription that dates to the fifteenth century BCE, which is "currently the oldest securely dated alphabetic inscription from the Southern Levant". See Early alphabetic writing in the ancient Near East: the 'missing link' from Tel Lachish | Antiquity | Cambridge Core
33. Ian L Shanahan (2017). Greek Fire - An Introduction to Gematria and Isopsephia in the New Testament of the Holy Bible (Revised Edition)
34. Baraita at the beginning of Sifra; Ab. R. N.
35. an amplification of those from Hillel
36. Halakha is the collective body of Jewish religious laws derived from the written and oral Torah.
37. Translated to English by Rabbi David Rubin, author of *Eye to the Infinite*.
38. It is also reputedly the place where Adam and Eve entered earth.
39. Rabbi David Rubin. *The Concept of Harmony in Judaism*, (2020).

40. Joshua Trachtenberg. *Jewish Magic and Superstition: A Study in Folk Religion* (New York: Meridian, 1961), 79–80.

41. Plaut, W. Gunther, Leviticus/Bernard J. Bamberger. Essays on ancient Near Eastern literature/commentaries by William W. Hallo (1985). [Torah] = The Torah : a modern commentary (4th ed.). New York: Union of Hebrew Congregations. pp. 424–426. ISBN 0807400556.

42. *The Genesis Wheel*, Bethsheba Ashe (2019).

43. *The Virtuous Wife*, which provides a sum total of 777.

44. For example, Esau and Jacob personifying Winter and Summer.

45. Amalek is *haPachaz* ("the Sin") by the Reversal Cipher, and his mother (the concubine), Timna is *Pachazah* ("wantonness").

46. Genesis 18:9, because the value of the words "wife" and "tent" have the same value (I didn't say they were good jokes).

47. Rabbi Shlomo Yitzchaki (22 February 1040–13 July 1105).

48. Whosoever is found among them, is found strong and robust.
    Annotation: But what is to be understood by that passage—"And they that despise Me shall be lightly esteemed?" Such an one is that man who can neither institute the union of the Holy Name, nor bind together the links of truth, nor derive the supernals into the position required, nor honour the Name of his Lord. Better were it for that man had he never been created, and much more for that man who doth not attentively meditate when he saith Amen!
    The *Sepher Dtzeniouthia*, translated by S. L. Macgregor Mathers (1887).

49. Gematraist. Noun, person who practices the art of gematria. And yes, I totally made up that word but somebody had to do it.

50. Perfecti. Those individuals (the perfect) who gave up sex and material wealth and devoted themselves to prayer, contemplation and service to their Cathar communities, but were eventually all slain or converted by the Catholic Church who called them heretics.

51. But not in Mosques.

52. See my study on the calculations of the Mt. Ebal Tablet on pg. 21–22.

53. Case, P. F. (1989). The true and invisible Rosicrucian Order: an interpretation of the Rosicrucian allegory and an explanation of the ten Rosicrucian grades. Boston: Weiser Books.

54. James A. Eshelman. Visions & Voices: Aleister Crowley's Enochian Visions with Astrological & Qabalistic Commentary. The College of Thelema. pp. 510. 2011.

55. The First word of Genesis 1:1, and thus (by established convention) the number and Hebrew name of the Book of Genesis. In Biblical Gematria *brashith* is 220 but with Standard Gematria it is 913.
56. The True and Invisible Rosicrucian Order. Paul Foster Case. 1927.
57. A numerical dictionary or index of numbers from 1–3321 listing their Hebrew word equivalents.
58. *[Via gematria, the magician might say that Fire and Air = 700, and Water and Earth = 310. All these letters are the name (hashem) of God but God is not hashem.* אל *(217) is apart of the Seven Palaces, set on high, within his 'house' (the letter Beth) which is the Seventh Palace.]*
59. See essays on The Emperor in *The Book of Thoth* by Aleister Crowley.
60. Spoken by the High Priest within the presence of God in the tabernacle, and only once a year.
61. Probably a reference to Christianity, because Jews and Muslims are not allowed to pray or *daven* in a Christian Church because the images and statues of Jesus on the Cross are judged to be idols because of the doctrine of the Trinity that claims to grants divinity to a mortal man such as Jesus.
62. It is true that the cipher to the New Testament and the Tanakh was either lost from—or restricted by—the early church.
63. 710 / 226 = 3.14159292035 which is pi accurate to seven digits. See The Glory of Kings ~ AL 1:3 (pythonanywhere.com):
https://vvheel.pythonanywhere.com/wiki67001003?source=67001003
64. Kapelrud, A. S. (October 1968). The Number Seven in Ugaritic Texts. Vetus Testamentum, 494–499.
65. אברהם (Abraham) = 248.
66. A characteristic feature of Hebrew occurring in another language.
67. Eric M. Vanden Eykel: Associate Professor of Religion, Ferrum College
68. Do what thou wilt shall be the whole of the Law. The study of this Book is forbidden. It is wise to destroy this copy after the first reading. Whosoever disregards this does so at his own risk and peril. These are most dire. Those who discuss the contents of this Book are to be shunned by all, as centers of pestilence. All questions of the Law are to be decided only by appeal to my writings, each for himself. There is no law beyond Do what thou wilt. Love is the law, love under will.

INDEX

Milton Keynes UK
Ingram Content Group UK Ltd.
UKHW020743231123
433120UK00015B/336